United States/Middle East Diplomatic Relations 1784-1978

An Annotated Bibliography

by

Thomas A. Bryson

The Scarecrow Press, Inc.
Metuchen, N.J. & London
1979

dedicated to

HARRY N. HOWARD

Library of Congress Cataloging in Publication Data

Bryson, Thomas A 1931-
United States Middle East diplomatic relations, 1784-1978.

Includes index.
1. Near East--Foreign relations--United States--Bibliography. 2. United States--Foreign relations--Near East--Bibliography. I. Title.
Z3014. R44B79 [DS63. 2. U5] 016. 32756'073 78-26754
ISBN 0-8108-1197-9

Manufactured in the United States of America

TABLE OF CONTENTS

KEY TO DISSERTATION SOURCE SYMBOLS

ADD	American Doctoral Dissertations
DA	Dissertation Abstracts International
DD	see DDAU
DDAU	Doctoral Dissertations Accepted by American Universities
Harvard-B	Harvard University. Graduate School of Arts and Sciences
LC	Library of Congress. A List of American Doctoral Dissertations.
SOO 48	Clark University. Doctoral Dissertations.
SO 175	University of Pennsylvania. Doctors of Philosophy of the Graduate School.
SO 330	University of Chicago, Doctoral Dissertations.
Selim	George D. Selim, American Doctoral Dissertations on the Arab World, 1883-1974. Washington, D.C.: Library of Congress, 1976.

PREFACE

There is a growing need for knowledge about the increasing role of the United States in the Middle East. The harsh winter of 1977, with record-breaking low temperatures in the eastern and southern portions of the United States pointed to the growing American dependence upon oil from the Arab world to heat American homes, drive American machines, fuel American industry, and provide the necessary energy to maintain a high standard of living for American people. But the oil connection with the Arab peoples cannot be considered without giving due regard to the special diplomatic relationship that exists between the United States and Israel. The growing energy crisis and the 1973 Arab-Israeli War, with its resultant oil embargo and confrontation between the United States and the Soviet Union, emphasize the heightened American interdependence with the Middle East. That the United States must balance the necessity of drawing an ever-increasing amount of petroleum from the Arab world against the need to supply Israel with the weapons necessary to maintain that country's territorial integrity and political sovereignty greatly complicates the American role in the Middle East.

This bibliographic guide is designed to provide students, scholars, and librarians with a working checklist of books, articles, documents, and dissertations that relate to the American diplomatic experience in the Middle East. Inasmuch as the United States has been involved in the Middle East for all of its two hundred years, this list must cover scholarship that reaches back into the early years of the country's history. During that period many interest groups, often conflicting, made demands on the American foreign policy-making establishment for diplomatic support. Therefore, this compilation of books and other materials must include not only works on diplomatic history, but it must also give some attention to the plethora of missionaries, educators, philanthropists, technicians, military personnel, naval officers, mariners, archaeologists, oil workers, and others who sought American diplomatic support in the pursuit of their varied objectives.

My interest in this bibliography grew out of the necessity of preparing a list of books, articles, documents, and newspapers relating to the writing of American Diplomatic Relations with the Middle East, 1784-1975: A Survey (Metuchen, N.J.: Scarecrow Press, 1977). Although there were numerous books that covered various phases of the American diplomatic experience in the Middle East, there was no single study that attempted to survey the entire subject. In preparing my study, which was prompted by the suggestion of Professor John A. DeNovo of the Department of History at the University of Wisconsin, I had access to several excellent bibliographic aids. DeNovo had prepared and published "American Relations with the Middle East: Some Unfinished Business," in George L. Anderson, ed., Issues and Conflicts: Studies in Twentieth Century American Diplomacy (Lawrence: University of Kansas Press, 1959), pp. 63-98. In this article, the author surveyed the literature in this field as a preliminary exercise to writing a study on American-Middle Eastern relations. Preparatory to writing a second book on his subject, DeNovo published a second bibliographic essay, "Researching American Relations with the Middle East: The State of the Art, 1970," in Milton O. Gustafson, ed., The National Archives and Foreign Relations Research (Athens: Ohio University Press, 1974), pp. 243-64. This essay continued the search for materials needed in the preparation of his book, but it also pointed out numerous areas of research that scholars might pursue to add to our knowledge of the American role in the Middle East. Indeed, it was Mr. DeNovo's suggestion in the latter essay that led to the writing of my survey of the field of study.

In addition to the above-mentioned bibliographic aids, the student interested in American-Middle Eastern relations will need to refer to bibliographic guides to the Middle East and North Africa. Such a guide for undergraduate libraries has been prepared under the direction of Ward Morehouse and Harry N. Howard, a retired Foreign Service officer who pioneered in the field of American-Middle Eastern relations. This work, Middle East and North Africa: A Bibliography for Undergraduate Libraries (Williamsport, Pa.: Bro-Dart, 1971) goes beyond the scope of the present study, but nevertheless it provides needed assistance to the historian. The Middle East Institute in Washington, D.C. periodically publishes editions of its valuable compilation, The Middle East:

A Selected Bibliography of Recent Works, and the historian will find innumerable suggestions in this topically arranged bibliography. A recent bibliographic effort by Leonard Binder, *The Study of the Middle East: Research and Scholarship in the Humanities and the Social Sciences* (New York: Wiley, 1976), contains a brief, but selective bibliography of works pertaining to the history of the Middle East. There is also Derek Hopwood's *The Emergence of Arab Nationalism*, a multi-volume compilation of works pertaining to Arab nationalism recently published by Scholarly Resources, Inc. Also of value to the student of American foreign relations are bibliographic guides by George N. Atiyeh and David W. Littlefield. Atiyeh's *The Contemporary Middle East, 1948-1973: A Selective and Annotated Bibliography* (Boston: G. K. Hall, 1975), while of greater value to the student of Middle Eastern studies, provides a brief bibliography on the United States role in the Middle East and contains a longer section on the states of the Middle East in world affairs. Littlefield's *The Islamic Near East and North Africa: An Annotated Guide to Books in English for Non-Specialists* (Littleton, Colo.: Libraries Unlimited, 1977) contains a brief section on U.S.-Middle Eastern relations, but is of greater use to the student of Middle East studies. Recently published is *The Middle East and North Africa in Regional and International Politics* (Detroit: Gale Research, 1977), a work edited by Ann T. Schulz.

The student interested in the American role in the Middle East will need to search current periodicals such as the *Middle East Journal*, *Foreign Affairs*, *International Journal of Middle East Studies*, the *American Historical Review*, *Muslim World*, the *Journal of Iranian Studies*, the *Journal of American History*, the *Journal of Modern History*, the *American Jewish Historical Quarterly*, and the *Journal of Palestine Studies*, for recent articles, reviews, and notices of recently published books.

Another invaluable aid is the American diplomatic history text book. Several of these have updated bibliographic essays following each chapter. Particularly useful are Thomas A. Bailey, *A Diplomatic History of the American People* (New York: Appleton-Century-Crofts, 1968), Alexander DeConde, *A History of American Foreign Policy* (New York: Scribner's, 1971), Richard W. Leopold, *The Growth of American Foreign Policy* (New York: Knopf, 1962), and Robert H. Ferrell, *American Diplomacy: A History* (New York: Norton, 1969).

Also useful to the scholar is the service offered by the Historical Office, Bureau of Public Affairs, Department of State. For many years this office has aided the student of American foreign relations by publishing the useful series, *Papers Relating to the Foreign Relations of the United States.* This collection has now been brought up to the year 1949, but the decision has been made to move forward rapidly and to cover the early years of the 1950s as soon as practicable. On request, this office will supply applicants with information relative to State Department documents that are related to their field of study.

There are a few selected books that contain valuable bibliographies. For the 18th and 19th centuries, there is James A. Field, Jr., *America and the Mediterranean World, 1776-1882* (Princeton, N.J.: Princeton University Press, 1969), and for the early 19th century there is David H. Finnie's *Pioneers East: The Early American Experience in the Middle East* (Cambridge, Mass.: Harvard University Press, 1967). Of great importance to the scholar of the 20th-century era of American-Middle Eastern relations is John A. DeNovo's *American Interests and Policies in the Middle East, 1900-1939* (Minneapolis: University of Minnesota Press, 1963). There is an excellent bibliographic essay in Robert W. Stookey's *America and the Arab States: An Uneasy Encounter* (New York: Wiley, 1975). My own study, *American Diplomatic Relations with the Middle East, 1784-1975: A Survey* (Metuchen, N.J.: Scarecrow Press, 1977), also contains a useful bibliography.

The bibliography that I have compiled is sufficiently complete to provide the student with at least a minimal number of sources from which to make a point of departure. The time frame of this bibliography covers the period 1784 through 1977. Of course it will in time become dated, and the researcher will want to consult the various journals already mentioned for new publications in the field. I have attempted to be selective in putting this collection together, and items of marginal or peripheral value are omitted. I have attempted to classify the material by era and to some extent by subject within eras (see Table of Contents). An effort has been made to ensure that each separate section is complete, thus avoiding the reader's having to make frequent cross references. This compilation is limited to English-language books, articles, and documents.

The Department of State collection of documents, both

unpublished and published, supplies a necessary body of data that the historian will wish to examine. Elizabeth H. Buck has compiled Materials in the National Archives Relating to the Middle East (Reference Information Paper no. 44, May 1955, the National Archives), which should prove to be of value. In 1861 the Department began publishing the useful collection, Papers Relating to the Foreign Relations of the United States. The collection is not as useful in the years of the 19th and early 20th centuries. But after the outbreak of World War I, when the United States became more deeply involved in the region, the series proves to be of greater help, and it is particularly helpful to the student whose interest lies in the period from World War I to the year 1949. Mention must be made of Treaties and Other International Acts of the United States of America, edited by David Hunter Miller. This eight-volume collection of American treaties, published in the 1930s, with the accompanying notes and commentary, supplies the historian with much-needed information relative to the negotiation of treaties and other agreements. More recently the National Archives has published the multivolume collection, Public Papers of the Presidents of the United States (36 vols., Washington, D.C.: U.S. Government Printing Office, 1934-). This collection has numerous documents relative to American-Middle Eastern relations. In addition the Department of State has published United States Treaties and Other International Agreements (21 vols., Washington, D.C.: U.S. Government Printing Office, 1952-1970) that will prove of interest to the searcher. A valuable source of information is to be found in the published proceedings of the House Foreign Affairs Committee and the Senate Foreign Relations Committee. Appropriate guides to congressional documents will enable the historian to find material pertinent to his subject. The Historical Offices of both the U.S. Navy and the U.S. Army have also published interesting and valuable bibliographic guides to naval and military history that the historian will find of value in locating appropriate collections of documents. For example, the Naval History Division, Department of the Navy, has recently published A Bibliography, a guide that will prove of great assistance. Another collection of documents that will prove of assistance to the student is J. C. Hurewitz' edited work, The Middle East and North Africa in World Politics: A Documentary Record (3 vols., New Haven, Conn.: Yale University Press, 1975), first published in 1956 under the title Diplomacy in the Near and Middle East: A Documentary Record. Volume I covers the period 1535-1914; volume II, the era 1914-1945; and volume III, 1945-1975.

In addition to published books, articles, and collections of documents, I have found a wealth of information in unpublished doctoral dissertations. A number of good dissertations are cited in John A. DeNovo's two bibliographic essays, and the bibliography of his American Interests and Policies in the Middle East also contains a good list of dissertations. I have also relied on Warren F. Kuehl's very valuable two-volume collection of Dissertations in History: An Index to Dissertations Completed in History Departments of United States and Canadian Universities (Lexington: University of Kentucky Press, 1965). Volume I covers the period 1873-1960; volume II brings the index forward to cover dissertations completed in the period 1961 to June 1970. A third volume will appear around 1980 or 1981. But I have also depended upon the services of University Microfilms at Ann Arbor, Michigan, which offers a unique service to scholars. On request, they will run through its computerized list of dissertations and provide a list of those that relate to the researcher's topic, with additional reference to the appropriate dissertation abstract. Dissertation Abstracts was found to be useful in supplementing Kuehl's guide during the period 1873 to the present. Not only does this series provide a comprehensive index for the years 1873 to 1972, but it also lists dissertations in history by year according to subject. I have also made use of Anne M. Avakian's Armenia and the Armenians in Academic Dissertations (Berkeley: Professional Press, 1974) for a list of dissertations related to Turkey, the United States, and the Armenian question. Perhaps the most valuable guide to American dissertations related to the Arab world is the second edition of George Dimitri Selim's American Doctoral Dissertations on the Arab World, 1883-1974 (Washington, D.C.: Library of Congress, 1976). Well indexed, this guide also provides the scholar with a reference to the dissertation abstract number. The reader will also want to consult Frank Joseph Shulman's American and British Doctoral Dissertations on Israel and Palestine in Modern Times (Ann Arbor, Mich., 1973). Wherever I have referred to a dissertation, an attempt has been made to provide an annotation. This has not always been possible, for not all universities cooperate with the publisher of doctoral Dissertation Abstracts. I realize that the list of dissertations herein might not be all-inclusive; they do give the researcher a point from which to start however.

The region under consideration is variously known as the Middle East or the Near East. During the earlier part of the 20th century, it was more fashionable to refer to the region by the latter title, but as time progressed, the former title came to enjoy greater acceptance. For the purpose of this compilation, I have chosen to follow the course taken by J. C. Hurewitz in his Middle East Dilemmas: The Background of United States Policy (New York: Harper, 1953). Hurewitz asserts that the cultural anthropologists generally include in the Middle East the Muslim belt that stretches from Morocco in North Africa across to Afghanistan. This would include the Arab-speaking states of Morocco, Algeria, Tunisia, Libya, Egypt, the Sudan, Saudi Arabia, the various smaller states making up the remainder of the Arabian peninsula, Iraq, Lebanon, and Syria, and it would also include Turkey, Iran, and Israel.

Before moving on to the bibliography, a few words are necessary on the writing of history of the American diplomatic experience in the Middle East and about the history of that experience. With the exception of the generation of historians following World War II, historians have generally neglected the study of American-Middle Eastern relations, a subject that dates from the early years of the republic. The area of study is not without its early pioneers who realized that the Middle East offered a fertile field of study for the diplomatic historian. To Edward Mead Earle, Harry N. Howard, and Leland James Gordon belong the honor of breaking the ground in American-Middle Eastern relations studies. The post-World War II era has given rise to J. C. Hurewitz, John A. DeNovo, and James A. Field, Jr., who have continued to stimulate interest in this region. Concerning the dearth of literature on this subject prior to the second World War, James A. Field asserts that Frederick Jackson Turner's interest in the westward movement of the American frontier gave the writing of American history an impetus away from the Middle East. Other historians continued the westward trend by investigating the American effort to gain the lucrative China trade across the Pacific. But as the United States leaves its bicentennial period, the American people can reflect on about two hundred years of intercourse with the people of the Middle East. Even during the colonial era, American merchant ships made their way to the Turkish port of Smyrna and also traded with the people of the Barbary Regencies, including Algiers, Tunis, and Tripoli, and the country of Morocco. Although a field of study largely forgotten by scholars, American relations with the Middle East have produced some important episodes in the nation's history. It has long been recognized that the Dey of Algiers played a peripheral role in the events leading to the drafting of the

Constitution of 1789 and to the founding of the United States Navy in the 1790s. The interest of the American people in the outcome of the Greek revolt from the Ottoman Empire was closely related to the Monroe Doctrine in December 1823. The Soviet Russian thrust toward the Mediterranean Sea gave rise to the Truman Doctrine in 1947 and to the Eisenhower Doctrine a decade later. The area has grown in importance to the United States in the period following World War II. The search for new sources of oil, the need to contain the Soviets, and the growing interest in the creation of Israel have led to an outpouring of books on this nation's changing role in the ever-changing Middle East. The present energy crisis and the need for additional imports of oil from the Arab world have also given rise to many monographic studies. Today the United States has assumed the role Great Britain formerly had in maintaining stability in the Middle East. The American Sixth Fleet roams the Mediterranean waters, the Suez, and the Persian Gulf, and is a far more potent force than the American Mediterranean Squadron of fir-built frigates that safeguarded this nation's interests in the Middle East in the days of the Barbary pirates.

The pirates of the Barbary coast proved no menace to Americans during the colonial era when British men-of-war protected the numerous Yankee merchantmen that plied the blue waters of the Mediterranean. But with independence, the Americans no longer enjoyed the protection of the Royal Navy or the trading privileges as an integral member of the far-flung British Empire. Following the American War for Independence, trade with the British West Indies was terminated, and American entrepreneurs sought to expand their commerce in the Mediterranean. During the years between the 1780s and 1816, the United States negotiated treaties with Morocco, Algiers, Tunis, and Tripoli for the purpose of expanding trade into the Mediterranean. To protect this trade during the times when the Barbary pirates broke their treaty obligations, Congress found it expedient to found the United States Navy. Although trade with the nations of the Mediterranean did not grow rapidly, and soon the missionary and educator assumed greater importance in the formulation of an American Middle Eastern policy, American trade with the Arabs in the 19th century included the sale of kerosene processed from Pennsylvania oil. This petroleum product was used to fuel the lamps in many Middle Eastern mosques. American missionaries originally entered the Middle East in the 1830s. Failing to win Muslim converts to Christianity, they turned to the founding of schools. American schools, teachers, and printing presses played no small role in arousing the national consciousness of those Middle Eastern peoples who were subject to the Ottoman Empire. Having founded schools from the primary to the university level, American missionaries and educators by the 20th century could point to graduates of its institutions who were serving the peoples of the Middle East in a multitude of useful pursuits.

While the missionary-educator provided a nucleus for a modern system of education in numerous Middle Eastern lands, the American philanthropist played an important role in the region. During times of revolution and strife, American philanthropists were found at work serving Greeks, Armenians, Jews, and Arabs. Their work was frequently aided by the missionaries, U. S. diplomats, and by the ships of the United States Navy.

Although American missionaries and philanthropists did much to bring modernity and succor to the peoples of the Middle East, American military and naval personnel introduced modern technology to the peoples of the region. American shipbuilders helped to rebuild the Ottoman navy following the disaster at Navarino Bay where the Turks suffered defeat at the hands of the Allied navies. Former Union and Confederate soldiers brought new techniques to the Egyptian Army during the years following the American Civil War.

But the greatest American impact on the Middle East came in the 20th century. President Woodrow Wilson's concept of self-determination of peoples, as presented in his 14 Points in 1918, gave the peoples of the Middle East hope of freedom from the Ottoman Empire. Closely following the end of World War I was the advent of American oil interests, which helped to strike oil in Iraq where an international consortium initially found one of the richest Middle Eastern oil fields. Subsequently, Americans moved in to Saudi Arabia, Bahrain and Kuwait, there to locate some of the world's richest reserves of oil. The revenues from oil have enabled the peoples of the Middle East to realize a higher standard of living and to play a role in the world power figuration out of all proportion to their numbers. Americans played no small role in bringing the Middle Eastern peoples to this enviable status. Realizing the vital importance of oil to its Western allies in Europe, the United States took steps in the period following World War II to ensure continued access to the rich sources of petroleum on the Persian Gulf. The postwar era has found the United States assuming a major role in the international relations of the Middle East, a region troubled by the rise of conflicting nationalisms, aspirations of a higher standard of living, and by the addition of the State of Israel.

The American role in the birth of Israel is without parallel. In many respects American assistance to the Jews in creating a new state was an aberration in the total context of this nation's diplomatic experience in the Middle East. During the 19th century, the United States foreign policy establishment rejected the pleas of the peoples of Greece and Crete for assistance in obtaining freedom from the Ottoman Turks. In the 20th century it rejected the petitions of the Armenians and Arabs to assist in the realization of a national existence. Continued American assistance to Israel in the years following the 1967 Arab-Israeli conflict has resulted in a debate in foreign policy-making circles as to the validity of such a decision. This has caused an increase in the literature relative to the American role in the Middle East, for arguments on both sides of the question have been presented.

Inasmuch as the formulation of American foreign policy has been largely in response to the needs of various interest groups, the annotations of this compilation will attempt to show the relationship between policy formation and interest-group needs. Frequent reference will be made to those basic, guiding principles which governed the making of this nation's foreign policy: the Open Door, non-involvement, freedom of the seas, and expatriation and naturalization. Whenever the term national interest is used, it will be employed to encompass those policies that promote American national security and the economic prosperity of the American people.

In completing this work, I wish to acknowledge the assistance of the library staff at West Georgia College: Jane Hersch made numerous suggestions concerning the format of this bibliography; Susan Smith and Jan Ruskell were most helpful in providing interlibrary loan service; Kathleen Hunt assisted me with reference services. Ann Chowns, Bill Foley, and Jackie Davis gave much time in helping me to locate appropriate periodicals and dissertation abstracts. The Faculty Research Committee of this institution supplied me with a grant that assisted with the assembling of the material of this book. Finally, my wife Anne and my children, Tommy and Olivia, were most understanding while the manuscript was in preparation.

Thomas A. Bryson West Georgia College

A

THE BARBARY PIRATES

1 Allen, Gardner W. _Our Navy and the Barbary Corsairs._ Cambridge, Mass.: _Harvard University Press, 1905._

First account of American diplomacy with the Barbary states. This is a detailed, straightforward narrative, with little interpretation. It describes the debate between Thomas Jefferson and John Adams on the formation of a Barbary policy. The majority of this work deals with naval operations during the War with Tripoli.

2 Barnby, H. G. _The Prisoners of Algiers: An Account of the Forgotten American-Algerian War, 1785-97._ New York: Oxford University Press, 1966.

This is the best account of the war with Algeria, for the author couples his narrative with interpretation that connects domestic with foreign policy. He shows the force of the shipping lobby's influence on policy-making. Gives some attention to the influence of Boston merchants and public opinion on policy formulation. A critical account of the conduct of American diplomacy.

3 Bixler, R. W. _The Open Door on the Old Barbary Coast._ New York: Pageant Press, 1959.

Demonstrates the United States effort to establish treaties with the Barbary States to establish the Open-Door principle for American trade. Of minimal value.

4 Cantor, Milton. "Joel Barlow's Mission to Algiers," _Historian,_ XXV (1963), 172-94.

This essay deals with that part of the dissertation that treats Barlow's diplomatic career in Algiers and his role in treaty-making.

5 ________. "The Life of Joel Barlow." Ph.D. dissertation, Columbia University, 1954. (DA 15, p562)

This is a lengthy biography that devotes much space to subject's business ventures and to his life among prominent Republicans in Washington. But it also treats his tour as American consul in Algiers, where he successfully established peaceful relations with the Barbary states.

6 Carr, James A. "John Adams and the Barbary Problem: The Myth and the Record," American Neptune, 26 (1966), 231-57.

This paper answers critics of Adams who claimed that he was trying to purchase peace with the Barbary States and was opposed to the use of naval force. Suggests that Adams would use naval force against the Barbary pirates on conclusion of problems with Britain and France.

7 Clarfield, Gerard H. "Timothy Pickering and American Foreign Policy, 1795-1800." Ph. D. dissertation, University of California, Berkeley, 1965. (DA 26, p3884)

Although Pickering advocated an aggressive policy vis-à-vis Barbary, this dissertation seems to cover Pickering's efforts to deal with British and French problems arising out of conflict on the high seas.

8 Field, James A., Jr. America and the Mediterranean World, 1776-1882. Princeton, N. J.: Princeton University Press, 1969.

Field's well-written study is a monumental work in the field. He combines intellectual and diplomatic history to demonstrate that a multiplicity of Americans ventured into the Middle East to expand American commerce and the republican concepts of democracy. He treats the role of missionaries, merchants, mariners, naval officers, technicians, military advisers, and philanthropists in the region from the inception of the American republic to the British occupation of Egypt. Concerning the American diplomacy with Barbary, he demonstrates that an effective diplomacy depended on the writing of a new Constitution and the implementation of an economic policy that would permit the building of the U. S. Navy that would sustain a diplomatic policy vis-à-vis Barbary.

9 Gallagher, Charles F. The United States and North Africa: Morocco, Algeria, and Tunisia. Cambridge, Mass.: Harvard University Press, 1963.

This book is in the Harvard series on American foreign policy. Actually it devotes little space to the role of the United States in the Barbary wars. The author presents a broad historical sweep of North Africa, with emphasis on the people, the land, government, and politics.

10 Hall, Luella J. The United States and Morocco, 1776-1959. Metuchen, N.J.: Scarecrow Press, 1971.

This is a lengthy treatment of U.S.-Moroccan relations that gives little space to the American involvement with the Barbary pirates. It demonstrates that Morocco was of little concern to the United States during the late 19th century. It is critical of the low caliber of American foreign service officers who served in Morocco.

11 Irwin, Ray W. The Diplomatic Relations of the United States with the Barbary Powers, 1776-1816. Chapel Hill: University of North Carolina Press, 1931.

This is a detailed narrative account that gives little interpretation. It is critical of American policy toward the Barbary States, and is the first account to make extensive use of diplomatic documents. But it adds little not already known about the subject.

12 McKee, Christopher. Edward Preble: A Naval Biography, 1761-1807. Annapolis, Md.: Naval Institute Press, 1972.

While this book concentrates in the main on the role of the U.S. Navy as it relates to the career of Preble, it does indicate that the Navy is only the right arm of American diplomacy. Suggests that Preble had a fine sense of balance in that he used force only to achieve diplomatic ends when other means proved futile.

13 Nash, Howard P., Jr. The Forgotten Wars: The Role of the U.S. Navy in the Quasi War with France and the Barbary Wars, 1798-1805. New York: A. S. Barnes, 1968.

As the title suggests this book is divided between the two conflicts, with about one-half devoted to the Barbary war. This is primarily a naval history and diplomacy is given little attention.

14 Nichols, Roy F. Advance Agents of American Destiny. Philadelphia: University of Pennsylvania Press, 1956.

This work discusses the role of William Shaler as an early American Consul General at Algiers. Suggests that he was competent and an early agent of the American destiny in the Middle East. The book encompasses much more than Shaler's career in the Middle East.

15 ________. "Diplomacy in Barbary," Pennsylvania Magazine of History and Biography, LXXIV (January 1950),

113-41.

This article is merely an early presentation of that portion of Nichols' book mentioned above, and it deals with Shaler's life at Algiers.

16 Paullin, Charles Oscar. Diplomatic Negotiations of American Naval Officers, 1778-1883. Baltimore: Johns Hopkins Press, 1912.

As the title suggests, this study is more than a history of U. S. involvement with the Barbary states. Three brief chapters of uncritical narrative are devoted to the efforts of American naval and diplomatic personnel to obtain treaties with the Barbary regencies.

17 Savage, Marie M., Sister. "American Diplomacy in North Africa, 1776-1817." Ph. D. dissertation, Georgetown University, 1949. (DD 16, 134). [No abstract available.]

18 Schuyler, Eugene. American Diplomacy and the Furtherance of Trade. New York: Scribner's, 1886.

This early narrative history by one of America's first Ph. D.'s devotes one uncritical chapter to American efforts to obtain treaty relations with the Barbary States. He asserts that shipping and agricultural interests supported an aggressive American policy.

19 Smelser, Marshall. The Congress Founds the Navy, 1787-1798. South Bend, Ind.: University of Notre Dame Press, 1959.

Ironically, the author claims that the Algerian problem and Mediterranean trade were relatively small problems when compared to the concern of the American people for the Indian attacks on the Western frontier.

20 Tucker, Glenn. Dawn Like Thunder: The Barbary Wars and the Birth of the U. S. Navy. Indianapolis: Bobbs-Merrill, 1963.

Based on Naval documents related to the United States Wars with the Barbary Pirates, this work is essentially a military account of early American naval commanders--Samuel Barron, Edward Preble, Stephen Decatur, and others.

21 Wright, L. B., and J. H. MacLeod. The First Americans in North Africa. Princeton, N. J.: Princeton University Press, 1945.

This is a critical study of early American diplomatic efforts that were accompanied by bribery and corruption. Relates American Barbary policy to the New England shipping lobby that favored an aggressive commercial policy in the Mediterranean. Timothy Pickering is portrayed as a staunch advocate of an aggressive policy vis-à-vis Barbary.

B

THE GREEK REVOLUTION

22 Booras, Harris John. Hellenic Independence and America's Contribution to the Cause. Rutland, Vt.: Tuttle, 1934.
A simplistic narrative account of little real value.

23 Bryson, Thomas A. American Diplomatic Relations with the Middle East, 1784-1975: A Survey. Metuchen, N.J.: Scarecrow Press, 1977.
An aroused American public was unable to move the U.S. government to intervene in the Greek revolt because national interest demanded nonintervention. Policy decision was based on basic guiding principles and related to the shipping and commercial lobby that favored a treaty of commerce with the Ottoman Turks.

24 Cline, Myrtle A. American Attitude Toward the Greek War of Independence, 1821-28. Atlanta: private printing, 1930.
This study grew out of a doctoral dissertation and is the best account of the American reaction to the Greek episode. Demonstrates the growth of public and Congressional support of U.S. intervention in the Greek Revolution, and indicates that supporters of the national interest, led by John Quincy Adams, headed off American intervention. Shows how American commercial interests opposed involvement in Greece and suggests that when idealism was confronted with realism that the latter carried the stronger weight in policy-making.

25 Curti, Merle. American Philanthropy Abroad: A History. New Brunswick, N.J.: Rutgers University Press, 1963.
Devotes a few pages to the Greek Revolution and demonstrates that a wide tide of pro-Greek, American sentiment was unable to overcome proponents of the national interest in propelling the U.S. into Greek war.

26 Daniel, Robert L. American Philanthropy in the Near East, 1820-1960. Athens: Ohio University Press, 1970.

As the title suggests, this book deals with the broad question of American philanthropy in the region until recent times. Based on a doctoral dissertation, this work devotes one chapter to the Americans who involved themselves as individuals in the Greek cause. Highlights conflict between mercantile and missionary-philanthropic interests in shaping policy. Concludes that American philanthropy in Greece was the prototype of later American philanthropic undertakings in the Middle East in subsequent years.

27 Downs, Jacques M. "American Merchants and the China Opium Trade." Business History Review, 42 (winter 1968), 418-42.

Not directly related to the Greek Revolution and American reaction, but does indicate that American merchants enjoyed a rich opium trade between Smyrna and China and had good cause to oppose American intervention in the Greek Revolution thereby upsetting the Turks who could interrupt the Smyrna trade.

28 Earle, Edward Mead. "American Interest in the Greek Cause, 1821-1827," American Historical Review, XXXIII (October 1927), 44-63.

Repeats the theme of the essay below (item 29) in a less critical manner, but needs to be seen by the scholar.

29 _______. "Early American Policy Concerning Ottoman Minorities," Political Science Quarterly, XLII (September 1927), 337-67.

This is the best short account of American reaction to the Greek Revolution by one of the pioneers of U.S.-Middle Eastern relations. Demonstrates the conflict between popular sentiment and the national interest, showing that even at this early stage American policy-makers were aware of the need to pursue policies in the national interest that promoted American economic well-being. This precedent of nonintervention set the course for later American reaction to the plea of Ottoman minorities for American support for independence.

30 Field, James A., Jr. America and the Mediterranean World, 1776-1782. Princeton, N.J.: Princeton University Press, 1969.

Author devotes one chapter to the topic, and shows that the conflict was between advocates of the national interest and the missionary-philanthropic lobby. The former favored expansion of trade with Turkey and completion of an American-Turkish treaty of commerce and opposed intervention. American aid to Greece set a pattern for later American ventures in overseas philanthropy.

31 Larrabee, Stephen A. Hellas Observed: The American Experience of Greece, 1776-1865. New York: New York University Press, 1957.

As title suggests, is more than account of the American reaction to the Greek Revolution. A well-written narrative that adds little to the material presented by Cline's earlier work.

32 Morison, S. E. "Forcing the Dardanelles in 1810: With Some Account of the Early Levant Trade of Massachusetts," New England Quarterly, I (1928), 208-25.

An early article by a leading American historian who shows that the Boston-Smyrna trade extended to the Colonial era and that there was much criticism in Boston of the pro-Greek interventionists in Congress who favored American assistance to the Greeks.

33 Seaburg, Carl, and Stanley Paterson. Merchant Prince of Boston: Colonel T. H. Perkins, 1764-1854. Cambridge, Mass.: Harvard University Press, 1971.

An excellent biography of an early American merchant who opposed extending aid to the Greeks because it might interfere with the lucrative trade that involved Boston-Smyrna-China. Shows importance of the commercial lobby in policy-making.

C

19th-CENTURY U. S. -TURKISH RELATIONS

34 Abbott, Freeland K. "American Policy in the Middle East: A Study of the Attitudes of the United States Toward the Middle East, Especially during the Period 1919-1936." Ph. D. dissertation, Fletcher School of Law and Diplomacy, 1952. (W 1952, p208, ADD)

Devotes one chapter to the 19th century. Suggests the United States remained aloof and did not want to disturb the Great Powers of Europe. Commercial interests dominated early American policy, but later the missionaries made a bid to determine U. S. policy.

35 Braden, Jean H. "The Eagle and the Crescent: American Interests in the Ottoman Empire, 1861-1870." Ph. D. dissertation, Ohio State University, 1973. (DA 34, p2505)

Indicates that American diplomacy was aided by the missionaries who maintained a constant flow of information to the United States. The founding of Robert College during this period heralded a new era in Turkish-American relations.

36 Brown, Philip Marshall. Foreigners in Turkey: Their Judicial Status. Princeton, N. J.: Princeton University Press, 1914.

A brief discussion of the operation of the capitulary regime as it affected American citizens is presented.

37 Bryson, Thomas A. American Diplomatic Relations with the Middle East, 1784-1975: A Survey. Metuchen, N. J.: Scarecrow Press, 1977.

Surveys early American relations with Turkey, pointing out the long process to obtain a commercial treaty, the growth of trade, evidence of early American technical assistance to Turkey, and the influence of missionaries in shaping American policy with the Turks.

38 Conn, Gary Corwin. "John Porter Brown, Father of Turkish-American Relations; An Ohioan at the Sublime Porte, 1832-1872." Ph. D. dissertation, Ohio State University, 1973. (DA 35, p2082)

Covers the career of an early American Foreign Service officer at Constantinople, highlighting the efforts of the subject to acquire a knowledge of Oriental languages, diplomatic practice, and customs, and the need for the 19th-century American consular official to have proper political connections to further his career aims in the absence of a professional diplomatic service.

39 Cook, Ralph Elliott. "The United States and the Armenian Question, 1894-1924." Ph. D. dissertation, Fletcher School of Law and Diplomacy, 1957. (X 1957, p154, ADD)

Surveys the role of the Armenian question in American diplomacy during more than a generation when it colored American-Turkish relations. Demonstrates the pressure of American Armenophiles to assist American missionaries and the influence of both groups on American diplomacy.

40 Daniel, Robert L. American Philanthropy in the Near East, 1820-1960. Athens: Ohio University Press, 1970.

Discusses in several chapters the early role of American missionaries in Turkey, the growth of their educational institutions, their efforts to obtain diplomatic support from the U. S. government, their involvement in the growth of nationalism among the Turkish minorities, and their role in the Bulgarian revolution of the 1870s.

41 DeKay, James E. Sketches of Turkey in 1831 and 1832. New York: Harper Bros., 1833.

As the title suggests, this book presents an interesting vignette of Americans in Turkey during the crucial decade when the Turco-American treaty was made and ratifications exchanged.

42 Dennis, Alfred L. P. Adventures in American Diplomacy, 1896-1906. New York: E. P. Dutton, 1928.

Presents some interesting material relative to the American involvement in Armenian question during the closing decade of the 19th century.

43 Downs, Jacques M. "American Merchants and the China Opium Trade," Business History Review, 42 (winter

1968), 418-42.

Discusses the growth of the American opium trade with Turkey and relates American Middle-Eastern policy with American Far-Eastern interests.

44 Earle, Edward Mead. "American Interest in the Greek Cause, 1821-27," American Historical Review, XXXIII (October 1927), 44-63.

Demonstrates that American concern for the Greek cause could have had detrimental effects on the course of U. S. -Turkish relations leading up to the negotiation of the 1830 treaty.

45 _______. "American Missions in the Near East," Foreign Affairs, VII (April 1929), 398-417.

Asserts that the missionary was the most important factor in American Middle-Eastern policy through the 1920s. Suggests that missionaries aroused nationalism among the subject peoples, but often gave these people a bad image in America. For example, they created the "Terrible Turk" image of the Turks.

46 _______. "Early American Policy Concerning Ottoman Minorities," Political Science Quarterly, XLII (September 1927), 337-67.

Shows that American reaction of non-intervention in Greek cause set precedent for later American reaction to pleas of Ottoman minorities for assisting their cause for independence.

47 Edwards, Rosaline D. "Relations Between the United States and Turkey, 1893-1897." Ph. D. dissertation, Fordham University, 1952. (W 1952, p208, DDAU)

This dissertation addresses itself to the role of the United States during the Armenian massacres of the 1890s, the dispute between the United States and Turkey over the rights of Turkish subjects to become naturalized Americans and return to their homeland, and the role of the U. S. Navy as an instrument of U. S. policy implementation in the Middle East.

48 Field, James A., Jr. America and the Mediterranean World, 1776-1882. Princeton, N. J.: Princeton University Press, 1969.

Treats the multiplicity of Americans who ventured to Turkey in the 19th century, including missionaries, mariners, diplomats, and technicians. Covers the growth of the missionary movement and its impact on Turkey. Describes the efforts of Americans to obtain a commercial treaty with Turkey, and demonstrates that the U. S. Navy was a most important instrument of policy. Describes in detail the implementation of the policy of non-intervention in the revolts of the Ottoman minorities: Greeks, Cretans, and Bulgarians. Discusses at length the impact of missionaries on Ottoman minorities.

49 Finnie, David H. Pioneers East: The Early American Experience in the Middle East. Cambridge, Mass.: Harvard University Press, 1967.

Published somewhat earlier than Field's work (item 48), this effort pursues the same approach. It reveals that a number of Americans ventured to the Middle East in the early 19th century. While his study covers Egypt, Mesopotamia, Persia, Palestine, and Syria, Finnie devotes considerable space to those early Americans who resided in Turkey, there to pursue varied goals. Discusses technical missions and missionaries in detail, asserting that they were not official instruments of American policy. Discloses that American diplomats did not always properly represent the missionaries. Shows the power of the missionary lobby. Can be considered as a companion volume to that of Field.

50 Gimelli, Louis B. "Luther Bradish, 1783-1863." Ph. D. dissertation, New York University, 1964. (DA 25, p1865)

This biography treats Bradish's mission to Turkey in 1820 when he acted as an executive agent to negotiate a treaty between the U. S. and Turkey. The mission failed, but Gimelli concludes that Bradish's activities demonstrated the advantage of direct conversations with the Turks in place of the practice of using a European power to mediate.

51 Gordon, Leland James. American Relations with Turkey, 1830-1930: An Economic Interpretation. Philadelphia: University of Pennsylvania Press, 1932.

While the bulk of this work concentrates on American economic ties with Turkey, it demonstrates that the missionaries played a big role in the development of a good will investment in Turkey. He treats important 19th-century issues between the U. S. and Turkey that include the Armenian question, the tariff question, the right of expatriation and naturalization, and the application of the Monroe Doctrine to Turkish diplomacy. One of the pioneer works in the field of U. S. - Mideast relations.

52 Grabill, Joseph L. Protestant Diplomacy and the Near East: Missionary Influence on American Policy, 1810-1927. Minneapolis: University of Minnesota Press, 1971.

The bulk of this work is devoted to missionary influence on 20th-century American diplomacy with Turkey. Devotes some space to early missionary efforts in the Middle East. Suggests real tie between missionary-philanthropic work overseas and the progressive phenomenon in the U. S. Missionaries depicted as a most important lobby in early U. S. relations with the Mideast.

53 Greenwood, Keith Maurice. "Robert College: The American Founders." Ph. D. dissertation, Johns Hopkins University, 1965. (Vol. 26, p2161, DA)

Treats the diplomatic negotiations between the American, Turkish, and British governments necessary to the establishment of this college. Describes its role in training Bulgarian nationalists involved in the atrocities of 1876 and its influence on Turkish culture.

54 Griscom, Lloyd. Diplomatically Speaking: Memoirs of Constantinople and Persia. New York: Literary Guild of America, 1940.

Demonstrates the importance of missionaries in shaping diplomacy by placing pressure on State Department to initiate action to obtain redress for Turkish destruction of missionary property during Armenian massacres.

55 Helseth, William A. "The United States and Turkey: Their Relations from 1784 to 1962." Ph. D. dissertation, Fletcher School of Law and Diplomacy, 1957.

A survey of U. S. -Turkish relations that merely gives a brief sketch of the subject during the 19th century. Devoted mainly to the period 1919-1962.

56 Hinckley, Frank E. American Consular Jurisdiction in the Orient. Washington, D. C.: W. H. Lowdermilk, 1906.

Describes consular practice in Turkey during the 19th century, demonstrating the manner in which the U. S. government represented the interests of Americans with respect to trials, extradition, expulsion, mixed tribunals, and missionary rights.

57 Kearney, Helen McCready. "American Images of the Middle East, 1824-1924: A Century of Antipathy." Ph. D.

dissertation, University of Rochester, 1976. (DA 37, p7250)

Focuses on popular American images of Turks, Armenians, and Arabs in the 19th and early 20th centuries, relying on the church, the press, and the pseudoscience of racism. Reflects the reports made by missionaries and diplomats. The Turk was perceived as a barbarian, the Armenian as a servile, tragic person, and the Arab as somewhat less barbaric and fanatical than the Turk.

58 Long, David F. Nothing Too Daring: A Biography of Commodore David Porter, 1780-1843. Annapolis, Md.: U. S. Naval Institute, 1970.

Much the best biography of the subject, it treats in the final pages the Commodore's role as chargé d'affaires at Constantinople. Discloses the practice of nepotism among early American foreign service officers, revealing that this American left much to be desired as a representative of the U. S. at the Sublime Porte.

59 McDonough, George P. "American Relations with Turkey, 1898-1901." Ph. D. dissertation, Georgetown University, 1951. (W 1951, p205, DDAU)

This very long dissertation is devoted to a detailed study of the Armenian question from the standpoint of European diplomacy and in the context of U. S. -Turkish diplomatic relations. It discusses the Turkish massacres of the 1890s and the U. S. reaction and concludes with the employment of U. S. Naval forces to implement U. S. diplomacy vis-à-vis Turkey.

60 McKee, Irving. "Ben-Hur" Wallace: The Life of General Lew Wallace. Berkeley: University of California Press, 1947.

An interesting biography about the personal relations between an author-diplomat and the Sultan of Turkey. Discusses Wallace's efforts to mediate the dispute between Britain and the Sultan, leading to the British occupation of Egypt in 1882.

61 May, Ernest R. Imperial Democracy: The Emergence of America as a Great Power. New York: Harcourt, Brace & World, 1961.

Discusses American involvement in the Armenian question, showing that Britain hoped to make an Anglo-American rapprochement to effect a naval demonstration in Turkish waters. Reveals that nothing came of this overture, since American concern for Cuba greatly outweighed that for Armenia.

62 Mirak, Robert. "Armenian Emigration to the United States to 1915: Leaving the Old Country," Journal of Armenian Studies, I (autumn 1975), 5-42.

Stemming from his dissertation (item 63), this essay lays the background to the Armenian migration to the United States, thus supplying a wealth of data about an important ethnic group that influenced the course of American-Turkish relations for more than a generation.

63 _______. "The Armenians in the United States, 1890-1915." Ph. D. dissertation, Harvard University, 1965.

Analyzes the make-up of the Armenian population in the United States. Important for describing the profile of an important ethnic pressure group which had such influence on U. S. -Turkish relations between 1894 and 1927.

64 Moore, John H. "America Looks at Turkey, 1876-1909." Ph. D. dissertation, University of Virginia, 1961. (DA 22, p1603)

Examines the development of American attitudes toward Turkey during the years 1876-1909. Author treats the Balkan Wars, the personality of Abdul Hamid II, American Protestant missionary efforts among the Armenians, and the quest for trade expansion. Suggests that American concern for the missionary did much to break Americans out of the isolation that captured the American mind during the 19th century.

65 Morison, S. E. "Forcing the Dardanelles in 1810: With Some Account of the Early Levant Trade of Massachusetts," New England Historical Quarterly, I (1928), 208-25.

Describes importance of the Smyrna trade and its relationship to the American reaction to the Greek Revolution.

66 Morse, Laura L. "Relations Between the United States and the Ottoman Empire." Ph. D. dissertation, Clark University, 1924. [No abstract available.]

67 Nordman, Bernard F. "American Missionary Work among Armenians in Turkey, 1830-1923." Ph. D. dissertation, University of Illinois, 1927.

Discusses the advent of American missionaries in Turkey, their missionary work, their educational accomplishments, and the net results of their work.

68 Paullin, Charles Oscar. Diplomatic Negotiations of

American Naval Officers, 1778-1883. Baltimore: Johns Hopkins Press, 1912.

A narrative history, a portion of which describes efforts of early American naval and diplomatic personnel to write a commercial treaty with Turkey.

69 Phillips, Clifton Jackson. Protestant America and the Pagan World: The First Half Century of the American Board of Commissioners for Foreign Missions, 1810-1860. Cambridge, Mass.: Harvard University Press, 1969.

Scope of book goes beyond work of missionaries in Turkey. Indicates that diplomatic protection of missionaries in Turkey left much to be desired and these Americans sought protection of the British diplomats. Concludes that American missionaries were not agents of imperialism.

70 Porter, David. Constantinople and Its Environs. 2 vols. New York: Harper, 1835.

Provides interesting background information during Commodore Porter's tenure as American diplomatic representative in Constantinople from 1831 to 1843.

71 Porter, David Dixon. Memoir of Commodore David Porter of the United States Navy. Albany, N.Y.: Munsell, 1875.

A much-embellished, inaccurate account of Commodore David Porter's life. Misrepresents the facts concerning his work at Constantinople.

72 Rowden, Paul Dennis. "A Century of American Protestantism in the Middle East: 1820-1920." Ph.D. dissertation, Dropsie University, 1959. [No abstract available.]

73 Seaburg, Carl, and Stanley Paterson. Merchant Prince of Boston: Colonel T. H. Perkins, 1764-1854. Cambridge, Mass.: Harvard University Press, 1971.

Demonstrates the opposition of this Boston merchant to American involvement in the Greek Revolution because it would jeopardize American-Turkish trade.

74 Sousa, Nasim. The Capitulatory Regime of Turkey: Its History, Origins, and Nature. Baltimore: Johns Hopkins Press, 1933.

This work involves American treaty rights in Turkey and considers such problems as commerce, extradition, the tariff, property rights, extraterritoriality, missionary rights, and the naturalization-expatriation question. Discusses the early problems related to the Armenian question and its ramifications for American diplomacy.

75 Straus, Oscar. Under Four Administrations: From Cleveland to Taft. Boston: Houghton Mifflin, 1922.
Indicates that the missionary lobby was powerful in directing course of late-19th-century American-Turkish relations. But during Taft administration, commercial interests took precedence, for "Dollar Diplomacy" was the order of the day.

76 Thomas, Lewis V., and Richard N. Frye. The United States and Turkey and Iran. Cambridge, Mass.: Harvard University Press, 1951.
This work is mistitled, for it is not a diplomatic history, but rather gives the history and culture of Iran and Turkey and discusses the rise of nationalism and westernization of these two countries. One brief chapter is devoted to U. S. -Turkish relations.

77 Turnbull, Archibald D. Commodore David Porter. New York: Century, 1929.
One chapter treats the Commodore's career in Turkey.

78 Wallace, Lewis. Lew Wallace: An Autobiography. 2 vols. London: Harper, 1906.
Volume II contains a number of letters relating Wallace's activities as U. S. Minister to Turkey in the 1880s, but there is nothing related to his effort to intervene in the Anglo-Egyptian controversy that led to the British occupation of Egypt in 1882.

D

19th-CENTURY U. S. -EGYPTIAN RELATIONS

79 Brinton, Jasper Yeates. The American Effort in Egypt: A Chapter in Diplomatic History in the Nineteenth Century. Alexandria, Va.: private printing, 1972.

This is a little-known, but interesting survey of American diplomatic, missionary, and commercial relations with Egypt from 1784 to the end of the 19th century.

80 ________. Mixed Courts of Egypt. New Haven, Conn.: Yale University Press, 1930.

Gives a history of the origins of the Mixed Courts, their function and scope, and provides a brief description of the adherence and participation of the United States.

81 Bryson, Thomas A. American Diplomatic Relations with the Middle East, 1784-1975: A Survey. Metuchen, N.J.: Scarecrow Press, 1977.

Provides a brief overview of early American diplomatic relations with Egypt.

82 ________. William Brown Hodgson, 1801-1871: A Biography of an American Foreign Service Officer in the Middle East. Atlanta: Resurgens Pubs. Inc., 1919.

This is a biographical account of an early American foreign service officer in the Middle East that relates the story of his secret fact-finding mission to Egypt in 1834.

83 ________. "William Brown Hodgson's Mission to Egypt, 1834," West Georgia College: Studies in the Social Sciences, XI (June 1972), 10-17.

Gives details on the initial American diplomatic mission to investigate possible diplomatic and commercial ties with Egypt.

84 Chaillé-Long, Charles. My Life on Four Continents. 2 vols. London: Hutchinson, 1912.

This interesting memoir is the account of an American who ventured to Egypt in the post-Civil War period to advise the Egyptian Khedive who was rebuilding his army.

85 Cox, Frederick J. "American Naval Mission in Egypt," Journal of Modern History, XXVI (June 1954), 173-8.
Describes the work of American military advisers to lay the foundation of the modern Egyptian Navy.

86 Crabites, Pierre. Americans in the Egyptian Army. London: Routledge, 1938.
Describes the work of American military advisers in Egypt following the American Civil War. Indicates that they were not official representatives of the American government and that they led numerous scientific and military expeditions in addition to advising the Khedive's army.

87 DeLeon, Edwin. The Khedive's Egypt. New York: Harper & Brothers, 1878.
A history by an American diplomatic figure who postulates that the American Consul was duty-bound to oppose the implementation of the Mixed Courts because he should look after the interests of American citizens.

88 ______. Thirty Years of My Life on Three Continents. 2 vols. London: Ward, Downey, 1890.
Depicts the life of an early American diplomat in Egypt who had to rely on gunboat diplomacy to defend the rights of American missionaries.

89 Earle, Edward Mead. "Egyptian Cotton and the American Civil War," Political Science Quarterly, 41 (1926), 520-45.
American Civil War led to increased cotton production in Egypt to compensate for decreased Southern cotton exports to Britain during the war. This was one factor in Britain's ultimate occupation of Egypt.

90 Field, James A., Jr. America and the Mediterranean World, 1776-1882. Princeton, N.J.: Princeton University Press, 1969.
Treats a wide spate of American activities in Egypt, including the coming of the missionaries, the beginning of commercial relations, the advent of American technical advisers, and American intervention during the British occupation of Egypt in 1882.

91 Finnie, David H. Pioneers East: The Early American

Experience in the Middle East. Cambridge, Mass.: Harvard University Press, 1967.

Covers the activities of early Americans in Egypt, including travelers, missionaries, diplomats, and tourists. Indicates that Americans were more evident in the Egypt of the period than is normally believed.

92 Harrison, Thomas Skelton. The Homely Diary of a Diplomat in the East, 1897-1899. Boston: Houghton Mifflin, 1917.

This is an intriguing vignette of an American diplomat in Egypt during the height of British supremacy. It is of interest to the student of Middle Eastern diplomatic customs and life.

93 Hesseltine, William, and Hazel C. Wolf. The Blue and the Gray on the Nile. Chicago: University of Chicago Press, 1961.

This is a narrative account of the American soldiers of fortune who went out to Egypt as military advisers in the period following the Civil War. Concludes that they did not represent the American government.

94 Hinckley, Frank E. American Consular Jurisdiction in the Orient. Washington, D.C.: W. H. Lowdermilk, 1906.

Describes American consular practice in Egypt during the 19th century, showing how consuls represented American interests. Also discusses the operation of the Mixed Courts.

95 Loring, William W. A Confederate Soldier in Egypt. New York: Dodd, Mead, 1884.

Presents an account of personal activities as an American adviser to the Egyptian Army during its participation in the Abyssinian expedition.

96 McKee, Irving. "Ben-Hur" Wallace: The Life of General Lew Wallace. Berkeley: University of California Press, 1947.

Describes General Wallace's effort as U.S. Minister at Constantinople to mediate the dispute between Britain and Egypt in 1881 just prior to the British occupation of Egypt.

97 Penfield, Frederic C. Present Day Egypt. New York: Century, 1899.

Brief description of American trade with Egypt at the turn of the 19th century and of American use of the Suez

Canal during the Spanish-American War when many U. S. ships passed through the Canal enroute to the Philippine Islands. Suggests that the Suez Canal was an example to be followed by the U. S. at the Isthmus of Panama.

98 Serpell, David R. "American Consular Activities in Egypt, 1849-1863," Journal of Modern History, X (September 1939), 344-63.

Shows that American consuls exercised influence out of proportion to the little American trade with Egypt, but engaged in corrupt practice of awarding protection to Egyptians in order to compensate for the lack of financial remuneration and the high cost of living.

99 Watson, Andrew. The American Mission in Egypt, 1854-1896. Pittsburgh: United Presbyterian Board of Publications, 1898.

This is a lengthy treatment of American missionary work in Egypt from earliest days to the end of the century, with some treatment of the work of American schools in the life of modern Egypt.

100 Watson, Charles R. Egypt and the Christian Crusade. Philadelphia: United Presbyterian Church, 1907.

A thumbnail sketch of British, American, and German missionary work in Egypt is presented, with particular emphasis on that of the United Presbyterian Church.

101 ________. In the Valley of the Nile: A Survey of the Missionary Movement in Egypt. New York: Revell, 1908.

Author gives a sketch of early missions in Egypt during the 18th century, but concentrates on the so-called American Mission of the United Presbyterian Church of North America. Shows the extent to which American schools played a role in the intellectual awakening in Egypt.

102 Wright, L. C. United States Policy Toward Egypt, 1830-1914. New York: Exposition-University Press, 1969.

This is the best single treatment of American-Egyptian relations in the 19th century. Author covers commercial and diplomatic ties from earliest period. Devotes much attention to the American effect on Egypt during and after the Civil War. Touches on American lack of interest in the Suez Canal.

E

19th-CENTURY
U. S. -SYRIAN RELATIONS

103 Antonius, George. The Arab Awakening: The Story of the Arab National Movement. New York: G. P. Putnam's, 1946.

This is an account of the Arab intellectual awakening which emerged in Beirut in the 1840s as a result of the efforts of American missionaries. It traces the rise of Arab nationalism through the end of World War I.

104 Bashshur, Munir Antonios. "The Role of Two Western Universities in the National Life of Lebanon and the Middle East: A Comparative Study of the American University of Beirut and the University of Saint-Joseph." Ph. D. dissertation, University of Chicago, 1964. (X 1964, p56) [Abstract not available.]

105 Daniel, Robert L. American Philanthropy in the Near East, 1820-1960. Athens: Ohio University Press, 1970.

Discusses the role of American schools and missionaries in providing the yeast for the Arab literary awakening. Indicates that American missionaries in Syria did not always receive the best protection from American diplomatic personnel.

106 Efimenco, N. Marbury. "American Impact Upon Middle East Leadership," Political Science Quarterly, 69 (1954), 202-18.

Demonstrates the role of American schools in bringing on the Arab cultural revival. Said that the schools also contributed political ideas which led to development of national ideals and a desire for independence. Schools also contributed to the spirit of reform.

107 Field, James A., Jr. America and the Mediterranean World, 1776-1882. Princeton, N. J.: Princeton University Press, 1969.

Discusses early American commercial contacts and the role of the missionaries and schoolmen in bringing cultural awakening to Syria.

108 Finnie, David H. Pioneers East: The Early American Experience in the Middle East. Cambridge, Mass.: Harvard University Press, 1967.

Treats early missionary efforts in Syria and offers intriguing sketches of early American visitors to that land.

109 Grabill, Joseph L. Protestant Diplomacy and the Near East: Missionary Influence on American Policy, 1810-1927. Minneapolis: University of Minnesota Press, 1971.

Gives only brief treatment to early American missions in Syria. Is primarily concerned with the period during and after World War I.

110 Hatoor Al-Khalidi, Muyhee A. "A Century of American Contribution to Arab Nationalism, 1820-1920." Ph.D. dissertation, Vanderbilt University, 1959. (DA 20, p1340)

Highlights the American contribution to the Arab intellectual awakening and the rise of Arab nationalism in the 19th century.

111 Kearney, Helen McCready. "American Images of the Middle East, 1824-1924: A Century of Antipathy." Ph.D. dissertation, University of Rochester, 1976. (DA 37, p7250)

Examines the nature of popular American images of several Middle Eastern peoples, including the Arabs. Uses publications by the churches, the press, and other written accounts. Suggests the Americans perceived the Arabs as not quite so barbaric as the Turks.

112 Penrose, Stephen B. L., Jr. That They May Have Life: The Story of the American University of Beirut, 1866-1941. New York: Trustees of the American University of Beirut, 1941.

Presents an interesting history of this most important university in the development of Lebanon, and suggests that its impact on the Middle East was far-reaching because of the work of its graduates.

113 Phillips, Clifton Jackson. Protestant America and the Pagan World: The First Half Century of the American

Board of Commissioners for Foreign Missions, 1810-1860. Cambridge, Mass.: Harvard University Press, 1969.

Devotes one chapter to missionary effort in the Near East. Suggests that American diplomatic support of missionaries in Syria was inadequate, causing them to rely frequently on the British.

114 Raleigh, Edward A. "An Inquiry into the Influences of American Democracy on the Arab Middle East, 1819-1958." Ph.D. dissertation, College of the Pacific, 1960. (Index 1959, 111) [No abstract available.]

115 Rowden, Paul Dennis. "A Century of American Protestantism in the Middle East, 1820-1920." Ph.D. dissertation, Dropsie University, 1959. (X 1959, p152, ADD) [No abstract available.]

116 Sarton, George. The Incubation of Western Culture in the Middle East. Washington, D.C., 1951.

Shows the extent to which American colleges played a role in the Arabic revival in mid-19th century.

117 Taylor, Alan R. "The American Protestant Mission and the Awakening of Modern Syria, 1820-1970." Ph.D. dissertation, Georgetown University, 1958. (X 1958, p91, ADD) [No abstract available.]

118 Tibawi, A. L. American Interests in Syria, 1800-1901: A Study of Educational, Literary and Religious Work. London: Oxford University Press, 1966.

Says there is no evidence that American missionary press was responsible for Arab revival in the 19th century. Suggests missionaries did not encourage cultural nationalism, but encouraged Muslim Arabs to keep their own customs and manners. Critical of U.S. lack of diplomatic support of American missionaries.

F

19th-CENTURY U.S.-PERSIAN RELATIONS

119 Benjamin, Samuel G. W. Persia and the Persians. Boston: Tichnor, 1887.

Written by an American minister to Persia, this is mainly a history that shows how far removed Persia was from American commercial and diplomatic interests in the late 19th century. Has brief comments on American diplomatic and commercial interests in Persia and on the operation of the American legation in Teheran.

120 Finnie, David H. Pioneers East: The Early American Experience in the Middle East. Cambridge, Mass.: Harvard University Press, 1967.

Contains vignettes of early American missionaries in Persia.

121 Griscom, Lloyd. Diplomatically Speaking: Memoirs of Constantinople and Persia. New York: Literary Guild of America, 1940.

Furnishes a few short chapters about an American diplomat in Persia at the turn of the century when the U.S. had no vital interests in the remote land of the shahs.

122 Kazemzadeh, Firuz. Russia and Britain in Persia, 1864-1914: A Study in Imperialism. New Haven, Conn.: Yale University Press, 1968.

Contains only brief references to the United States during the 19th century.

123 Ramazani, Rouhollah K. The Foreign Policy of Iran, 1500-1941. Charlottesville: University Press of Virginia: 1966.

Nothing of value to the student of 19th-century U.S.-Persian relations is contained here.

124 Thomas, Lewis V., and Richard N. Frye. The United States and Turkey and Iran. Cambridge, Mass.:

Harvard University Press, 1951.

This study is not a diplomatic history but rather gives the history and culture of Iran and then describes the development of nationalism and the coming of western ideas. One brief chapter is devoted to American-Persian affairs.

125 Yeselson, Abraham. United States-Persian Diplomatic Relations, 1883-1921. New Brunswick, N. J.: Rutgers University Press, 1950.

Best treatment of the subject in the 19th century. Suggests the paucity of American interests which were controlled by missionaries. Points out that some American diplomats did attempt to expand American commercial interests in Persia in the 19th century. U. S. maintained policy of nonintervention in the Anglo-Russian struggle for hegemony.

G

AMERICAN RELATIONS WITH THE BARBARY STATES, 1817-1900

126 Cruickshank, Earl F. "Morocco at the Parting of the Ways: A Study of an Attempt to Reform the System of Native Protection." Ph. D. dissertation, University of Pennsylvania, 1932. (SO 175, p15) [Abstract not available.]

127 Field, James A., Jr. America and the Mediterranean World, 1776-1882. Princeton, N. J.: Princeton University Press, 1969.

Suggests that American policy-makers considered the acquisition of a base in North Africa in the late 19th century and dispatched an agent to the region on a mission to determine if the U. S. could expand its commerce in the region; and that the U. S. presence at the Madrid conference of 1880 on the Moroccan question indicated greater American interest in the region than is normally realized.

128 ________. "A Scheme in Regard to Cyrenaica," Mississippi Valley Historical Review, 44 (June 1957), 445-68.

Treats the little-known American attempt to secure a base in North Africa in the late 19th century.

129 Gallagher, Charles F. United States and North Africa: Morocco, Algeria, and Tunisia. Cambridge, Mass.: Harvard University Press, 1963.

This work is mainly a political and cultural history of the region, but it does furnish brief treatment of the diplomacy of the Barbary states during the 19th century.

130 Gossett, Edward Freeman. "The American Protestant Missionary Endeavor in North Africa from its Origin to 1939." Ph. D. dissertation, University of California, Los Angeles, 1961. (Index, 1960, p115) [Abstract not available.]

131 Hall, Luella J. The United States and Morocco, 1776-1956. Metuchen, N. J.: Scarecrow Press, 1971.

This is a comprehensive treatment of the subject that deals with the minimal U. S. interests in the area, the sale of protection by American diplomatic agents, and American participation in the Madrid Conference of 1880. Critical of the quality of American diplomatic agents who were of low quality.

132 Harmon, Judd Scott. "Suppress and Protect: The United States Navy, the African Slave Trade, and Maritime Commerce, 1794-1862." Ph. D. dissertation, College of William and Mary, 1977. (DA 38, p5004)

Congress had authorized the building of a navy in 1794 to protect the nation's maritime commerce. This dissertation relates the activities, in part, of the Mediterranean squadron's efforts to suppress the international slave trade.

133 Heggoy, Willy Normann. "Fifty Years of Evangelical Missionary Movement in North Africa, 1881-1931." Ph. D. dissertation, Hartford, 1960. (DA 22, p238)

This dissertation treats the growth and problems of missionaries in North Africa during the difficult time of French occupation and the growth of anticolonial sentiment.

134 Phillips, Dennis Heath. "The American Presence in Morocco, 1880-1904." Ph. D. dissertation, University of Wisconsin, 1972. (DA 33, p3553)

Suggests that American consular officials abused the protêgê system by selling protection certificates to wealthy Moroccans to compensate for low salaries. Concludes that tensions between Americans and Moroccans were high because of the cultural gap between the people.

H

PRE-WORLD WAR I DIPLOMACY, 1900-1914

135 Anderson, Eugene N. "The First Moroccan Crisis, 1904-06." Ph. D. dissertation, University of Chicago, 1928. (SO 330, p139) [Abstract not available.]

136 Askew, William C., and J. Fred Rippy. "The United States and Europe's Strife, 1908-1913," Journal of Politics, 4 (1942), 68-79.

Shows the relationship between the proposed U. S. mediation effort in the Balkan War of 1911-1912 and American desire for the Turks to grant the Chester Concession.

137 Beale, Howard K. Theodore Roosevelt and the Rise of America to World Power. Baltimore: Johns Hopkins Press, 1956.

Asserts that President Theodore Roosevelt acted as he did at the Algeciras Conference in order to prevent a world war that might involve the U. S.

138 Bishop, Joseph Bucklin. Theodore Roosevelt and His Time: Shown in His Own Letters. 2 vols. New York: Scribner's, 1920.

Treats Theodore Roosevelt's handling of the Perdicaris telegram and his influence on the Algeciras Conference, where it is asserted that he acted to avert war between Britain and France and Germany.

139 Bryson, Thomas A. American Diplomatic Relations with the Middle East, 1784-1975: A Survey. Metuchen, N. J.: Scarecrow Press, 1977.

Treats a number of episodes, including proposed U. S. mediation in the Balkan Wars, the Armenian question, the Chester Concession, participation in the Algeciras Conference, W. Morgan Shuster's mission to Persia, and concludes that with the exception of the State Department's support of the Chester Concession and President Roosevelt's participation at Algeciras, the United States continued to adhere to the policy of nonintervention.

140 Collins, George W. "United States-Moroccan Relations, 1904-1912." Ph.D. dissertation, University of Colorado, 1965. (DA 26, p7276)

Asserts that President Roosevelt acted at Algeciras to preserve international peace, but that commercial potential held attraction for the U.S. Shows that missionaries demanded support for their work in Morocco.

141 Cook, Ralph Elliott. "The United States and the Armenian Question, 1894-1924." Ph.D. dissertation, Fletcher School of Law and Diplomacy, 1957. (X 1957, p154)

Shows the extent to which the missionary lobby worked to achieve a policy supportive of the Armenians in the Ottoman Empire, and suggests that this lobby would continue to exert pressure on American-Turkish relations for sometime.

142 Davis, Harold E. "The Citizenship of Jon Perdicaris," Journal of Modern History, XIII (1941), 517-26.

Relates the Perdicaris affair to American support for the French in the Moroccan crisis.

143 Dennett, Tyler. John Hay: From Poetry to Politics. New York: Dodd, Mead, 1934.

Asserts that President Roosevelt knew Perdicaris was not an American citizen and that domestic politics determined Roosevelt's action.

144 Dennis, Alfred L. P. Adventures in American Diplomacy, 1896-1906. New York: E. P. Dutton, 1928.

The U.S. participated in the Algeciras Conference, asserts this writer, to prevent a world war from ensuing.

145 DeNovo, John A. American Interests and Policies in the Middle East, 1900-1939. Minneapolis: University of Minnesota Press, 1963.

A major work in the field, this study covers a multiplicity of American interests, including the work of the missionaries, Dollar Diplomacy, the Chester Concession, and reaction to nationalism. Sets the stage for the expansion of the U.S. role in the Middle East with a brief discussion of the Shuster mission to Persia. Relates the formulation of U.S. policy to a plethora of often-competing interests.

146 ________. "Petroleum and American Diplomacy in the Near East, 1908-1928." Ph.D. dissertation, Yale University, 1948. (W 1948, p104, ADD)

Suggests that Americans were not interested in the Near East as a possible source of petroleum, but that Admiral Chester viewed this as a distinct possibility when he began to seek a concession from the Turks.

147 ________. "Petroleum and the United States Navy before World War I," Mississippi Valley Historical Review, 41 (March 1955), 641-56.

Relates that during the Taft administration the State Department began groping toward an official American oil policy that would eventually include the Middle East.

148 ________. "A Railroad for Turkey: The Chester Project of 1908-1913," Business History Review, (1959), 300-29.

Discusses U.S. government involvement in the quest for the Chester Concession.

149 Einstein, Lewis. A Diplomat Looks Back. Edited by Lawrence E. Gelfand. New Haven, Conn.: Yale University Press, 1968.

This diplomat records that President Roosevelt took a pro-French position at Algeciras because he sympathized with French ambitions.

150 Feinstein, Marnin. "The First Twenty-Five Years of Zionism in the United States, 1882-1906." Ph.D. dissertation, Columbia University, 1963. (DA 24, p4647)

Discusses early exponents of Zionism in the United States, concluding that it provoked intense argument among the country's Jews. The movement began to progress shortly after 1898.

151 Gordon, Leland James. American Relations with Turkey, 1830-1930: An Economic Interpretation. Philadelphia: University of Pennsylvania Press, 1932.

Briefly discusses the origins of the Chester Concession. Treats American commercial and missionary role in Turkey in prewar era.

152 Grabill, Joseph L. Protestant Diplomacy and the Near East: Missionary Influence on American Policy, 1810-1927. Minneapolis: University of Minnesota Press, 1927.

Discusses the missionary influence on policy-making during the Theodore Roosevelt administration, and concludes that the Armenian question was looming larger in U.S.-Turkish relations.

153 Hall, Luella J. _The United States and Morocco, 1776-1956._ Metuchen, N.J.: Scarecrow Press, 1971.
Concludes that Roosevelt was motivated by political considerations in the Perdicaris episode and by the desire to support the Anglo-French Entente at Algeciras.

154 Hourihan, William James. "Roosevelt and the Sultans: The United States Navy in the Mediterranean, 1904." Ph.D. dissertation, University of Massachusetts, 1975. (DA 36, p1045)
Discusses President Theodore Roosevelt's employment of the U.S. Navy in Mediterranean waters during the year 1904 to impress the Sultans of Morocco and Turkey, thereby establishing America's right to be treated as an equal by the European Powers.

155 Huntington-Wilson, F. M. _Memoirs of an Ex-Diplomat._ Boston: Bruce, Humphries, 1945.
Indicates author's influence on policy-making vis-à-vis Turkey during the Italo-Turkish War and during the negotiations on the Chester Concession.

156 Kazemzadeh, Firuz. _Russia and Britain in Persia, 1864-1914: A Study in Imperialism._ New Haven, Conn.: Yale University Press, 1968.
Gives generous treatment to Morgan Shuster's mission to Persia. Concludes that corrupt politicians were responsible for the termination of the economic mission.

157 Lewis, Tom Tandy. "Franco-American Diplomatic Relations, 1898-1907." Ph.D. dissertation, University of Oklahoma, 1970. (DA 31, p3475)
Covers all aspects of Franco-American relations during the period, but presents the same conclusion as item 158 on the Moroccan crisis.

158 ________. "Franco-American Relations During the First Moroccan Crisis," _Mid-America,_ LV (January 1973), 21-36.
Roosevelt's support of France at Algeciras was only limited and motivated by the desire to prevent war and to promote the Open-Door policy.

159 McDaniel, Robert A. The Shuster Mission and the Persian Constitutional Revolution. Minneapolis: Biblioteca Islamica, 1974.

Gives much treatment to Persian internal politics and demonstrates that internal opposition to the Shuster mission and Russian resistance to it led to its termination. But is critical of Shuster's inability to maintain lines of communication with British and Russian diplomats.

160 Phillips, Dennis Heath. "The American Presence in Morocco, 1880-1904." Ph. D. dissertation, University of Wisconsin, 1972. (DA 33, p3553)

Discusses background to Perdicaris affair.

161 Ramazani, Rouhollah K. The Foreign Policy of Iran, 1500-1941. Charlottesville: University Press of Virginia, 1966.

Brief treatment is given the Shuster mission.

162 Shuster, William M. The Strangling of Persia. New York: Century, 1912.

An interesting memoir of an early American economic mission to Persia that concludes the Persians wanted financial reform to offset the actions of Britain and Russia that aimed to cripple Persia.

163 Straus, Oscar S. Under Four Administrations: From Cleveland to Taft. Boston: Houghton Mifflin, 1922.

Demonstrates that missionary influence on U. S. -Turkish relations was paramount except during the Taft administration's flirtation with Dollar Diplomacy when primacy was given to commercial interests.

164 Varg, Paul. Open Door Diplomat: The Life of W. W. Rockhill. Urbana: University of Illinois Press, 1952.

Author quotes subject who attributed the defeat of the Chester Concession to German diplomacy.

165 Wright, L. C. United States Policy Toward Egypt, 1830-1914. New York: Exposition-University Press, 1969.

Slim treatment of prewar U. S. -Egyptian relations.

166 Yeselson, Abraham. United States-Persian Diplomatic Relations, 1883-1921. New Brunswick, N. J.: Rutgers University Press, 1950.

Good explanation of the Shuster mission, which is related to Taft's Dollar Diplomacy.

I

WORLD WAR I AND THE ERA OF THE PARIS PEACE CONFERENCE

167 Abbott, Freeland K. "American Policy in the Middle East: A Study of the Attitudes of the United States Towards the Middle East, Especially during the Period 1919-1936." Ph.D. dissertation, Fletcher School of Law and Diplomacy, 1952. (W1952, p208, ADD)

Treats American involvement at the Versailles, including the Armenian issue and the matter of mandates, the operation of the Open-Door policy in the oil fields, the Chester Concession, and American participation at the Lausanne Conference.

168 Adler, Selig. "The Palestine Question in the Wilson Era," Journal of Jewish Social Studies, X (1948), 303-34.

Asserts that Justice Brandeis influenced Wilson to support the Balfour Declaration and that it is doubtful Wilson ever read the King-Crane Commission report.

169 Antonius, George. The Arab Awakening: The Story of the Arab National Movement. New York: G. P. Putnam's, 1946.

Shows Arab disappointment at the secret wartime treaties which undermined the fruition of Arab nationalism in the formation of a Greater Syrian state.

170 Barton, James L. The Story of Near East Relief, 1915-1930: An Interpretation. New York: Macmillan, 1930.

Discusses the inception of Near East Relief, its aims and scope, its history, and claims that the organization was non-political in nature.

171 Brown, Philip Marshall. "The Mandate over Armenia," American Journal of International Law, XIV (1920), 396-397.

Asserts that Senate opposition to American mandate

for Armenia was based on the idea that acceptance was tantamount to adherence to the League of Nations Covenant.

172 Bryson, Thomas A. "Admiral Mark Lambert Bristol: An Open Door Diplomat in Turkey," International Journal of Middle East Studies, 5 (1974), 450-67.
Covers Bristol's role in American-Turkish relations, including his opposition to the Armenian mandate and his espousal of the Open Door to achieve American trading parity with the British and French in Turkey.

173 ________. American Diplomatic Relations with the Middle East, 1784-1975: A Survey. Metuchen, N.J.: Scarecrow Press, 1977.
Encompasses American problems with Turkey during the War, including the Armenian question, the Zionist problem, and the preservation of American neutrality. Discusses the Peace Conference and such allied problems as those pertaining to the Armenians, the Greeks, and the subject peoples of the Ottoman Empire.

174 ________. "An American Mandate for Armenia: A Link in British Near Eastern Policy," Armenian Review, XXI (summer 1968), 23-41.
Discusses British imperial motives for suggesting that the U.S. accept a mandate for Armenia.

175 ________. "John Sharp Williams: An Advocate for the Armenian Mandate, 1919-1920," Armenian Review, XXVI (1973), 23-42.
A discussion of his role on behalf of Armenians.

176 ________. "Mark Lambert Bristol, U.S. Navy, Admiral-Diplomat: His Influence on the Armenian Mandate Question," Armenian Review, XXI (winter 1968), 3-22.
Summarizes his influence on the Senate's decision to reject Wilson's request to accept the mandate for Armenia.

177 ________. "A Note on Near East Relief: Walter George Smith, Cardinal Gibbons and the Question of Discrimination Against Catholics," Muslim World, LXI (1971), 202-9.
Absolves Near East Relief of blame for discrimination.

178 ________. Walter George Smith. Washington, D.C.:

Catholic University Press, 1977.

Biography of an American Armenophile who worked to achieve a mandate for Armenia, relief for the displaced Armenians, and financial aid for them.

179 _______. "Walter George Smith and the Armenian Question at the Paris Peace Conference, 1919," Records of the American Catholic Historical Society, LXXXI (March 1970), 3-26.

An example of how a little-known, lower-echelon figure took part in the decision-making process at the Paris Peace Conference in the case of the Armenian problem.

180 _______. "Walter George Smith and the International Philarmenian League: A Note on the Armenian Question before the League of Nations, 1920," in Robert W. Thomson, ed., Recent Studies in Modern Armenian History. Cambridge, Mass.: Armenian Heritage Press, 1972.

An analysis and description of events leading to introduction of the Armenian issue to the League of Nations in 1920.

181 _______. "Woodrow Wilson and the Armenian Mandate: A Reassessment," Armenian Review, XXI (autumn 1968), 10-28.

An assessment of Wilson's handling of the Armenian question.

182 _______. "Woodrow Wilson, the Senate, Public Opinion, and the Armenian Mandate, 1919-1920." Ph.D. dissertation, University of Georgia, 1965. (DA 26, p2706)

Discusses Wilson's espousal of the Armenian cause at Paris, the growth of Senate opposition to the mandate, and the background of public opinion supportive of Senate action.

183 Buzanski, Peter Michael. "Admiral Mark L. Bristol and Turkish-American Relations, 1919-1922." Ph.D. dissertation, University of California, Berkeley, 1960. (X 1961, p115, ADD)

An analytical treatment of Bristol's service as U.S. High Commissioner to Turkey in the immediate postwar era.

184 _______. "The Interallied Investigation of the Greek Invasion of Smyrna, 1919," Historian, XXV (May 1963),

325-43.
An American diplomat acts with an Allied commission to investigate the Greek landing at Smyrna.

185 Cook, Ralph Elliott. "The United States and the Armenian Question, 1894-1924." Ph.D. dissertation, Fletcher School of Law and Diplomacy, 1957. (X 1957, p154, ADD)
Continues treatment of American reaction to the Armenian issue through the war years and American rejection of the mandate in 1920.

186 Curti, Merle. American Philanthropy Abroad: A History. New Brunswick, N.J.: Rutgers University Press, 1963.
Describes the development of American good works in the overseas region, including the Middle East.

187 ________, and Kendall Birr. Prelude to Point Four: American Technical Missions Overseas, 1838-1938. Madison: University of Wisconsin Press, 1954.
Traces American missions designed to export useful knowledge to other countries.

188 Daniel, Robert L. American Philanthropy in the Near East, 1820-1960. Athens: Ohio University Press, 1970.
Describes and assesses the work of Near East Relief as a prelude to later American assistance programs.

189 ________. "The Armenian Question and American-Turkish Relations, 1914-1927," Mississippi Valley Historical Review, XLVI (September 1959), 252-75.
Demonstrates the influence of the Armenian question on U.S.-Turkish relations.

190 ________. "The Friendship of Woodrow Wilson and Cleveland Dodge," Mid-America, 43 (July 1961), 182-96.
Describes the relationship between two men whose interest in the Armenian question developed on the basis of Dodge's thoughts on the subject.

191 DeNovo, John A. American Interests and Policies in the Middle East, 1900-1939. Minneapolis: University of Minnesota Press, 1963.
Treats American-Middle East relations during the

war years and the growing American involvement in the region at the Paris Peace Conference.

192 Evans, Laurence B. United States Policy and the Partition of Turkey, 1914-1924. Baltimore: Johns Hopkins Press, 1965.
This study considers U. S. -Turkish relations during the war years, demonstrates the American role at the Paris Peace Conference, and traces American participation in the events leading to the Lausanne Conference.

193 ________. "The United States Policy in the Syrian Mandate, 1917-1922." Ph. D. dissertation, Johns Hopkins University, 1957. (X1957, p154, ADD) [No abstract available.]

194 Fisher, Sydney Nettleton. The Middle East: A History. New York: Knopf, 1960.
Demonstrates briefly the impact of World War I on the Middle East and sketches the complexities that ensued at the Paris Peace Conference.

195 Gates, Caleb Frank. Not to Me Only. Princeton, N. J.: Princeton University Press, 1940.
This memoir covers the period of the war and the peace conference.

196 Gelfand, Lawrence E. The Inquiry: American Preparations for Peace, 1917-1919. New Haven, Conn.: Yale University Press, 1963.
Analyzes American preparations for handling the problems associated with the demise of the Ottoman Empire.

197 Gidney, James B. A Mandate for Armenia. Kent, Ohio: Kent State University Press, 1967.
Considers the American involvement in the Armenian mandate issue at the Paris Peace Conference and thereafter.

198 Gordon, Leland James. American Relations with Turkey, 1830-1930: An Economic Interpretation. Philadelphia: University of Pennsylvania Press, 1932.
This study is mainly concerned with American-Turkish economic relations. Deals with the question of the Open Door at time when Powers tried to make secret agreements.

199 Grabill, Joseph L. "Missionary Influence on American

Relations with the Near East, 1914-1923," Muslim World, LVIII (April 1968), 141-54.

Traces the rise of missionary influence on President Wilson during time when debate over the Armenians was prominent.

200 ______. Protestant Diplomacy and the Near East: Missionary Influence on American Policy, 1810-1927. Minneapolis: University of Minneapolis Press, 1971.

Concentrates on the Armenian question at Paris and the missionary influence on President Wilson.

201 Helmreich, Paul C. From Paris to Sèvres: The Partition of the Ottoman Empire at the Peace Conference, 1919-20. Columbus: Ohio State University Press, 1974.

A well-written study on the break up of the Ottoman Empire at the Conference of Paris and the American role in the process.

202 Helseth, William Arthur. "The United States and Turkey: Their Relations from 1784 to 1962." Ph. D. dissertation, Fletcher School of Law and Diplomacy, 1962.

Treats missionary and relief activity in the war years and the partition of the Ottoman Empire at the close of the conflict.

203 Hovannisian, Richard G. Armenia on the Road to Independence, 1918. Berkeley: University of California Press, 1969.

Author analyzes the rise of the Armenian Republic which played a role in U. S. -Mideast relations.

204 ______. The Republic of Armenia: The First Year, 1918-1919. Berkeley: University of California Press, 1971.

A continuation of item 203.

205 Howard, Harry N. "An American Experiment in Peace-Making: The King-Crane Commission," Muslim World, XXXII (April 1942), 122-46.

A brief treatment of the entire subject which was treated in a subsequent book. See item 206.

206 ______. The King Crane Commission: An American Inquiry in the Middle East. Beirut: Khayats, 1963.

An in-depth study of an American commission's efforts to make an equitable peace in the Mideast.

207 ________. The Partition of Turkey: A Diplomatic History, 1913-1923. Norman: University of Oklahoma Press, 1931.
The author discusses at length the partition of Turkey in this early study, but does not give too much treatment to the U. S. role.

208 Kearney, Helen McCready. "American Images of the Middle East, 1824-1924: A Century of Antipathy." Ph. D. dissertation, University of Rochester, 1976.
Discusses the American perception of the Armenians.

209 Knee, Stuart E. "The King-Crane Commission of 1919: The Articulation of Political Anti-Zionism," American Jewish Archives, XXIX (April 1977), 22-52.
The Commission was anti-Zionist in its make-up and its report opposed Zionist goals in Palestine.

210 Latourette, Kenneth Scott. "Colonialism and Missions: Progressive Separation," Journal of Church and State, 7 (autumn 1965), 330-49.
A brief discussion of the missionary influence on diplomacy.

211 Lewbow, Richard Ned. "Woodrow Wilson and the Balfour Declaration," Journal of Modern History, 40 (December 1968) 500-23.
The author asserts that President Wilson delayed endorsement on Balfour Declaration so as not to arouse Turkish ire against American missionary interests.

212 Lenczowski, George. Middle East in World Affairs. Ithaca, N. Y.: Cornell University Press, 1956.
Suggests that Zionist influence on Wilson was pervasive and gained his support of Balfour Declaration. Missionary influence on King-Crane Commission was important.

213 ________. Russia and the West in Iran, 1918-1948. Ithaca, N. Y.: Cornell University Press, 1949.
Book is more concerned with the U. S. role in Iranian-Russian-British relations during World War II and the aftermath than with its role in the earlier period.

214 Lipstadt, Deborah E. "The Zionist Cause of Louis

Lipsky, 1900-1921." Ph. D. dissertation, Brandeis University, 1977. (DA 37, p7921)

Treats career of an early American Zionist whose influence on American Zionism was overshadowed by Justice Brandeis.

215 Lloyd George, David. Memoirs of the Peace Conference. 2 vols. New Haven, Conn.: Yale University Press, 1939.

Superb account of the dialogue at the Peace Conference. Necessary to an understanding of British motives for American participation in the postwar Middle-East settlement.

216 Logan, Rayford W. The Senate and the Versailles Mandate System. Washington, D. C.: Minorities Publishers, 1945.

A concise study of the Armenian mandate as debated in U. S. Senate.

217 Manuel, Frank E. The Realities of American-Palestine Relations. Washington, D. C.: Public Affairs Press, 1949.

Discusses American official reaction to the Jewish issue during World War I.

218 Mirak, Robert. "The Armenians in the United States, 1890-1915." Ph. D. dissertation, Harvard University, 1965. (X 1965, p141, ADD)

Discusses the profile of this important American ethnic group.

219 Morgenthau, Henry. All in a Lifetime. Garden City, N. Y.: Doubleday, Page, 1922.

Treats his representation on behalf of Armenians with Turks. Discusses his feeling on Zionism.

220 ________. Ambassador Morgenthau's Story. Garden City, N. Y.: Doubleday, Page, 1919.

Discusses his intervention with Turks on behalf of the Armenians during the war.

221 Morse, Laura L. "Relations Between the United States and the Ottoman Empire." Ph. D. dissertation, Clark University, 1924. (SOO 48, p91) [No abstract available.]

222 Nevakivi, Jukka. Britain, France and the Arab Middle

East, 1914-1920. London: University of London, 1969.
Treats American consideration of the Armenian issue in the context of the evolving Middle East.

223 Nevins, Allan. Henry White: Thirty Years of American Diplomacy. New York: Harper & Bros., 1930.
Is valuable to an understanding of U.S. reaction to Armenian question because presents the valuable correspondence between Henry White and Senator Henry Cabot Lodge.

224 Nicolson, Harold. Curzon: The Last Phase, 1919-1925: A Study in Postwar Diplomacy. New York: Harcourt, Brace, 1939.
Treats briefly Curzon's views of Wilson's handling of the Armenian issue.

225 Noble, George Bernard. Policies and Opinions at Paris, 1919. New York: Macmillan, 1935.
Author describes the climate of the press at Paris Peace Conference where Big Four made decisions on the Middle East.

226 Nordman, Bernard F. "American Missionary Work Among Armenians in Turkey, 1830-1923." Ph.D. dissertation, University of Illinois, 1927. (L.C. 1929, p99)
Briefly considers American reaction to the Armenian issue and to Allied intent to partition Turkey.

227 O'Brien, Dennis Jay. "The Oil Crisis and the Foreign Policy of the Wilson Administration, 1917-1921." Ph.D. dissertation, University of Missouri, 1974. (DA 36, p489)
Discusses the Wilsonian's perception of an oil crisis in the United States in the closing days of the war. Shows the working relationship between industry and government.

228 Parzen, Herbert. "Brandeis and the Balfour Declaration," Herzl Yearbook, V (1963), 309-50.
Discusses Wilson's consideration of the Balfour Declaration in the context of growing pro-Zionist sentiment among his advisers.

229 Patrick, Mary Mills. A Bosporus Adventure: Istanbul (Constantinople) Women's College, 1871-1924. Stanford, Calif.: Stanford University Press, 1934.
This memoir sheds interesting light on decision-making by some Americans at the Paris Peace Conference.

230 Plesur, Milton. "The Relations Between the United States and Palestine," Judaism: A Quarterly Journal of Jewish Life, III (1954), 469-79.
Considers Woodrow Wilson's reaction to pleas that he endorse the Balfour Declaration. Also treats Franklin Roosevelt's handling of the Palestine issue.

231 Raleigh, Edward A. "An Inquiry into the Influences of American Democracy on the Arab Middle East, 1819-1958." Ph.D. dissertation, Pacific University, 1960. (X 1960, p111, ADD) [Abstract not available.]

232 Ramazani, Rouhollah K. The Foreign Policy of Iran, 1500-1941. Charlottesville: University Press of Virginia, 1966.
Author points out that Iran desired U.S. support during the period when Iran resisted British political influence.

233 Ross, Frank A.; C. Luther Fry; and Elbridge Sibley. The Near East and American Philanthropy. New York: Columbia University Press, 1929.
Treats American philanthropy in Middle East.

234 Rowden, Paul Dennis. "A Century of American Protestantism in the Middle East, 1820-1920." Ph.D. dissertation, Dropsie University, 1959. (X 1959, p152, ADD) [Abstract not available.]

235 Sachar, Howard M. The Emergence of the Middle East, 1914-1924. New York: Knopf, 1969.
Treats the complexities of the Middle East during this crucial period when American interests were minimal and bound up chiefly with missionaries and philanthropists.

236 _______. "The United States and Turkey, 1914-1927: The Origins of Near Eastern Policy." Ph.D. dissertation, Harvard University, 1953. (W 1953, p236, ADD) [Abstract not available.]

237 Stein, Leonard. The Balfour Declaration. New York: Simon & Schuster, 1961.
A definitive, well-researched study of this important pronouncement, which received President Wilson's endorsement.

238 Stookey, Robert W. America and the Arab States: An

Uneasy Encounter. New York: Wiley, 1975.

Touches briefly on Arab reaction to Wilson's policy of self-determination, the King-Crane Commission, and the Arab demands at Paris.

239 Tashjian, James H. "The American Military Mission to Armenia," Armenian Review, V-XVII (1949-1952).

A lengthy discussion of the origins of the Harbord mission, its fact-finding task in Armenia, and its report.

240 Tillman, Seth. Anglo-American Relations at the Paris Peace Conference of 1919. Princeton, N.J.: Princeton University Press, 1961.

Well-documented study of American interaction with Big Powers at the Paris Conference. Discusses proposed American role in the postwar Middle East, with emphasis on the mandate for Armenia.

241 Westermann, William Linn. "The Armenian Problem and the Disruption of Turkey," in Edward Mandell House and Charles Seymour, What Really Happened at Paris: The Story of the Peace Conference, 1918-1919. New York: Scribner's, 1921.

The author discusses Woodrow Wilson's qualified acceptance of the Armenian mandate at the Paris Peace Conference.

242 Yale, William. "Ambassador Henry Morgenthau's Special Mission of 1917," World Politics, I (1949), 308-20.

Prominent American Zionists intervene to prevent the U.S. from initiating a move to make a separate peace with the Turks.

243 ________. The Near East: A Modern History. Ann Arbor: University of Michigan Press, 1958.

This survey touches on the King-Crane Commission's investigation and on the American reaction to Zionist goals as expressed in Balfour Declaration.

244 Yeselson, Abraham. United States-Persian Diplomatic Relations, 1883-1921. New Brunswick, N.J.: Rutgers University Press, 1950.

The U.S. government, prompted in large measure by American oil interests, prevents the ratification of an Anglo-Persian treaty that would have made Persia a virtual British client. This was a victory for the Open Door.

J

THE INTERWAR YEARS AND THE QUEST FOR OIL, 1920-1939

245 Abbass, Abdul Majid. "Oil Diplomacy in the Near East." Ph. D. dissertation, University of Chicago, 1940. [No abstract available.]

246 Abbott, Freeland K. "American Policy in the Middle East: A Study of the Attitudes of the United States toward the Middle East, Especially during the Period 1919-1936." Ph. D. dissertation, Fletcher School of Law and Diplomacy, 1952. (W 1952, p208, ADD)

Discusses the American employment of the Open Door in the case of the Chester Concession, the expansion of American business in Turkey, American participation at the Lausanne Conference, the U. S. interest in the Montreux Convention, and the American unwillingness to make a commitment on the Palestine question.

247 Anbari, Abdul-Amir Ali. "The Law of Petroleum Concession Agreements in the Middle East." Ph. D. dissertation, Harvard University, 1968. (1968, 234, ADD) [No abstract available.]

248 Banani, Amin. "Impact of the West on Iran, 1921-1941: A Study in Modernization of Social Institutions." Ph. D. dissertation, Stanford University, 1959. (DA 20, p3703)

Concentrates on the impact of European influence on Iran during this period.

249 Barton, James L. <u>The Story of Near East Relief, 1915-1930: An Interpretation.</u> New York: Macmillan, 1930.

Discusses the philanthropic work of Near East Relief and carries it through the period when technical education became the chief aim.

250 Beard, Charles A. <u>The Idea of National Interest: An</u>

Analytical Study in American Foreign Policy. New York: Macmillan, 1934.
The author analyzes the U.S. employment of the Open-Door policy in Turkey during the interwar period.

251 Bierstadt, Edward Hale. The Great Betrayal. New York: R. M. McBride, 1924.
Author concludes that the U.S. compromised efforts to achieve goals for the Armenians in deference to American commercial interests.

252 Bryson, Thomas A. "Admiral Mark Lambert Bristol: An Open Door Diplomat in Turkey," International Journal of Middle East Studies, 5 (1974), 450-67.
Demonstrates American employment of the Open-Door policy in postwar Turkey to pave the way for American commercial expansion.

253 _______. American Diplomatic Relations with the Middle East, 1784-1975: A Survey. Metuchen, N.J.: Scarecrow Press, 1977.
Discusses a broad scope of U.S. interests that includes the negotiation of a treaty with Turkey, protection of American rights in the mandates, the expansion of trade, and concern over the Straits.

254 _______. "The Armenia-America Society: A Factor in American-Turkish Relations, 1919-1924," Records of the American Catholic Historical Society, 82 (June 1971), 83-105.
Shows how an ethnic lobby affected U.S.-Turkish relations.

255 _______. Walter George Smith. Washington, D.C.: Catholic University Press, 1977.
The subject of this biography was a leading member of a vocal group of Americans who represented the interests of Armenians during the postwar era.

256 Buzanski, Peter Michael. "Admiral Mark L. Bristol and Turkish-American Relations, 1919-1922." Ph.D. dissertation, University of California, Berkeley, 1960. (X 1961, p115, ADD)
A well-written account of the U.S. High Commissioner's efforts to represent American interests in Turkey in the immediate postwar era. Analyzes Bristol's effort to reconcile commercial and philanthropic aims.

257 Child, Richard Washburn. A Diplomat Looks at Europe. New York: Duffield, 1925.
This diplomat recorded in his memoirs the complex forces affecting American participation at the Lausanne Conference.

258 Cook, Ralph Elliott. "The United States and the Armenian Question, 1894-1924." Ph. D. dissertation, Fletcher School of Law and Diplomacy, 1957. (X 1957, p154, ADD)
Discusses the effort of American Armenophiles to influence the course of U. S. -Turkish relations.

259 Daniel, Robert L. American Philanthropy in the Near East, 1820-1960. Athens: Ohio University Press, 1970.
The author describes the efforts of Near East Relief to meet the needs of suffering Armenians. Suggests that relief efforts which gave way to technical assistance provided the example later employed by the Point Four program.

260 ________. "The Armenian Question and American-Turkish Relations, 1914-1927," Mississippi Valley Historical Review, XLVI (September 1959), 252-75.
An excellent essay that encapsulates the role of the Armenian issue in U. S. -Turkish relations.

261 ________. "The United States and the Turkish Republic before World War II: The Cultural Dimension," Middle East Journal, 21 (winter 1967), 52-63.
Demonstrates how the missionary lobby created the "Terrible Turk" image in the U. S. Shows that numerous Americans joined together to correct this view.

262 Darvich-Kodjouri, D. "Images and Perception in International Relations: A Case Study of Relationships between Iran and the Great Powers, 1919-1953." Ph. D. dissertation, Miami University, 1976. (DA 37, p4600)
This study examines the image held by the Great Powers of Iran.

263 DeNovo, John A. American Interests and Policies in the Middle East, 1900-1939. Minneapolis: University of Minnesota Press, 1963.
Addresses a wide range of problems that includes U. S. -Turkish negotiations over commercial and missionary

disagreements; the quest for oil in Iraq, Saudi Arabia, Persia, and Bahrein; assertion of the rights of Americans in the mandates; trade expansion; and the rights of philanthropists.

264 ________. "The Movement for an Aggressive American Oil Policy, 1918-1920," American Historical Review, 61 (July 1956), 854-76.

Considers the postwar oil shortage and the efforts of government officials and oil interests to put together a comprehensive policy to find new sources of oil.

265 ________. "Petroleum and American Diplomacy in the Near East, 1908-1928." Ph.D. dissertation, Yale University, 1948. (W 1948, p104, DDAU)

Treats the Anglo-American rivalry over commerce and oil and the State Department's support of the Open Door principle. This support extended to the Chester Concession and to the quest for new sources of oil.

266 Earle, Edward Mead. "The Turkish Petroleum Company--A Study in Oleaginous Diplomacy," Political Science Quarterly, 39 (1924), 265-77.

Questions the State Department's effort to assist American oil companies in their bid for new sources of petroleum in the Middle East. Suggests that State Department officials thereby violated the Monroe Doctrine.

267 Evans, Laurence Boyd. United States Policy and the Partition of Turkey, 1914-1924. Baltimore: Johns Hopkins University Press, 1965.

Author addresses the wide range of problems that complicated U.S.-Turkish relations and the effort to reconcile them at Lausanne Conference.

268 ________. "The United States Policy in the Syrian Mandate, 1917-1922." Ph.D. dissertation, Johns Hopkins University Press, 1957. (X 1957, p154, ADD) [Abstract not available.]

269 Finnie, David H. Desert Enterprise: Middle East Oil Industry in its Local Environment. Cambridge, Mass.: Harvard University Press, 1958.

Discusses the advent of American oil companies in the Middle East.

270 Fisher, Sydney Nettleton. The Middle East: A His-

tory. New York: Knopf, 1960.
Gives slim background to interwar period.

271 Gates, Caleb Frank. Not to Me Only. Princeton, N.J.: Princeton University Press, 1940.
Provides a corrective to the "Terrible Turk" image that prevailed in the United States in the 1920s.

272 Gibb, George Sweet, and Evelyn H. Knowlton. The Resurgent Years, 1911-1927: History of Standard Oil Company (New Jersey). New York: Harper Bros., 1956.
An excellent treatment of the State Department's use of the Open-Door principle to back American businesses in their quest for oil in the 1920s. Shows pressure put on government by oil officials and the reaction of government officials.

273 Gidney, James B. A Mandate for Armenia. Kent, Ohio: Kent State University Press, 1967.
Indicates the extent of the church lobby's influence on U.S.-Turkish relations during the 1920s.

274 Gordon, Leland James. American Relations with Turkey, 1830-1930: An Economic Interpretation. Philadelphia: University of Pennsylvania Press, 1932.
Devoted to American-Turkish economic relations in the main. Discusses trade, the use of the Open Door, as well as missionary problems, and the Armenian issue.

275 Grabill, Joseph L. "Missionary Influence on American Relations with the Near East, 1914-1923," Muslim World, LVIII (April 1968), 141-54.
The author discusses missionary influence over the course of U.S.-Turkish relations as concerning the Armenian question.

276 ________. Protestant Diplomacy and the Near East: Missionary Influence on American Policy, 1810-1927. Minneapolis: University of Minnesota Press, 1971.
The author expands the content of item 275.

277 Grand, Samuel. "A History of Zionist Youth Organizations in the United States from Their Inception to 1940." Ph.D. dissertation, Columbia University, 1958. (DA 18, p1777)
This study traces the origin and development of the various Zionist youth organizations in the United States.

278 Gray, Gertrude M. "Oil in Anglo-American Diplomatic Relations." Ph. D. dissertation, University of California, Berkeley, 1950. (W 1950, p178, DDAU)

This dissertation addresses the petroleum rivalry between the United States and Great Britain during the 1920s.

279 Grew, Joseph C. Turbulent Era: A Diplomatic Record of Forty Years, 1904-1945. 2 vols. London: Hammond, Hammond, 1953.

This American diplomat's memoirs cover U. S. participation at the Lausanne Conference and Turkish-American relations during his tenure as U. S. Ambassador. It covers protection of American rights in Turkey, commercial interests, and missionary interests.

280 Hammad, Mohamed Burham. "Middle Eastern Oil Concessions: Some Legal and Policy Aspects of Relations Between Grantors and Grantees." Ph. D. dissertation, Yale University, 1963. (Index, 1962, p130, ADD) [Abstract not available.]

281 Helseth, William Arthur. "The United States and Turkey: Their Relations from 1784 to 1962." Ph. D. dissertation, Fletcher School of Law and Diplomacy, 1962.

This lengthy dissertation treats the re-establishment of U. S. -Turkish relations, the effort to maintain commercial intercourse, and U. S. interests in the Straits.

282 Horton, George. The Blight of Asia. New York: Bobbs-Merrill, 1926.

The thesis of this former consular official is that the U. S. government did not help the American missionaries in the post-World War I era and compromised their interests in favor of commercial men.

283 Housepian, Marjorie. The Smyrna Affair. New York: Harcourt Brace Jovanovich, 1971.

The thesis of this book agrees essentially with that of Horton, item 282, and Bierstadt, item 251.

284 Issa, Mahmoud K. "Trade Between Egypt and the United States." Ph. D. dissertation, University of Minnesota, 1953. (DA 13, p690)

This work addresses itself in the main to commercial relations between the two countries during the interwar period.

285 al-Jazairi, Mohamed Zayyan. "Saudi Arabia: A Diplomatic History, 1924-1964." Ph. D. dissertation, University of Utah, 1971. (DA 32, p868)

Author presents a detailed account of Saudi diplomatic history from 1924 to 1964, coupled with a historical sketch of the establishment and rise of the Saudi dynasty.

286 Johnson, Hugh S. "The American Schools in the Republic of Turkey, 1923-1933: A Case Study of Missionary Problems in International Relations." Ph. D. dissertation, American University, 1975. (DA 36, p3107)

Treats the decline of the missionary schools during the era of extreme Turkish nationalism.

287 Kazdal, Mustafa N. "Trade Relations between the United States and Turkey, 1919-1944." Ph. D. dissertation, Indiana University, 1946. (W 1946, p40, DDAU) [Abstract not available.]

288 Kearney, Helen McCready. "American Images of the Middle East, 1824-1924: A Century of Antipathy." Ph. D. dissertation, University of Rochester, 1976. (DA 37, p7250)

Studies the images projected by Arabs, Turks, and Armenians in the United States, and suggests that all were perceived as lacking in good traits.

289 Klebanoff, Shoshana. Middle East Oil and U. S. Foreign Policy with Special Reference to the U. S. Energy Crisis. New York: Praeger Publishers, 1974.

The initial chapter of this study deals with the interwar period during which the U. S. government is depicted as supporting American oil companies in their quest for new sources of petroleum in the Middle East.

290 Lenczowski, George. The Middle East in World Affairs. Ithaca, N. Y.: Cornell University Press, 1956.

Gives slim treatment to diplomacy in the interwar years.

291 ________. Oil and State in the Middle East. Ithaca, N. Y.: Cornell University Press, 1960.

This study addresses itself to the relations between American oil companies and the host states in the Middle East, with special emphasis on the national aspirations of the latter and the legal rights of the former.

292 ________. Russia and the West in Iran, 1918-1948. Ithaca, N.Y.: Cornell University Press, 1949.
Gives little treatment to U.S.-Iranian relations during interwar years.

293 Lloyd George, David. Memoirs of the Peace Conference. 2 vols. New Haven, Conn.: Yale University Press, 1939.
Gives space to Anglo-American complications regarding the Middle East during the interwar era.

294 Longrigg, Stephen Hemsley. Oil in the Middle East: Its Discovery and Development. London: Oxford University Press, 1968.
Devoted in the main to the technology of oil production in the Middle East.

295 Mansour, Hussein Omar. "The Discovery of Oil and Its Impact on the Industrialization of Saudi Arabia." Ph.D. dissertation, Arizona University, 1973. (DA 34, p2522)
Discusses the discovery of oil in commercial amounts by Americans and the impact of this discovery upon Saudi Arabia.

296 Manuel, Frank E. The Realities of American-Palestine Relations. Washington, D.C.: Public Affairs Press, 1949.
Demonstrates that during the interwar years the U.S. remained committed to the premise that the Jewish quest for a national home in Palestine was a British problem.

297 Mikesell, Raymond F., and Hollis B. Chenery. Arabian Oil: America's Stake in the Middle East. Chapel Hill: University of North Carolina Press, 1949.
Gives brief treatment to the subject during the interwar era.

298 Millspaugh, Arthur C. The American Task in Persia. New York: Century, 1925.
This American businessman discusses the efforts of his first mission to Iran in the 1920s to update the Iranian government that it might modernize the country's economic infrastructure.

299 Mojdehi, Hassan. "Arthur C. Millspaugh's Two Missions to Iran and Their Impact on American-Iranian Relations." Ph. D. dissertation, Ball State University, 1975. (DA 36, p5472)

The purpose of this study is to examine Millspaugh's role in Iranian affairs during his two missions there, from 1922 to 1927 and from 1943 to 1945, and the United State's position regarding these missions.

300 El-Molla, Yehia Mohamed Saber Salem. "Major Aspects of American-Egyptian Economic Relationship: The Interwar Period." Ph. D. dissertation, Harvard University, 1951. (Selim, 82) [Abstract not available.]

301 Morse, Laura L. "Relations between the United States and the Ottoman Empire." Ph. D. dissertation, Clark University, 1924. (SOO 48, p91) [Abstract not available.]

302 Mosley, Leonard. Power Play: Oil in the Middle East. New York: Random House, 1973.

A readable account of U. S. support for American oil companies during the interwar period. Focuses on efforts in Iraq, Bahrein, and Saudi Arabia.

303 Nash, Gerald D. United States Oil Policy, 1890-1964. Pittsburgh: University of Pittsburgh Press, 1968.

Focuses on the relationship between government and business in the latter's quest for overseas oil concessions. The tie was made by Woodrow Wilson and government aid continued to support Americans in Iraq, Bahrein, and Saudi Arabia.

304 Nuseibeh, Hazem Zaki. "The Ideas of Arab Nationalism." Ph. D. dissertation, Princeton University, 1954. (DA 14, p1787)

This study explores the various facets of Arab nationalism and considers the rise of westernization.

305 O'Brien, Dennis Jay. "The Oil Crisis and the Foreign Policy of the Wilson Administration, 1917-1921." Ph. D. dissertation, University of Missouri, 1974. (DA 36, p489)

Describes how American leaders during the war perceived an oil crisis and in conjunction with oil companies sought to alleviate that crisis by an overseas quest for new sources of petroleum.

306 Oder, Irwin. "The United States and the Palestine Mandate, 1920-1948: A Study of the Impact of Interest Groups on Foreign Policy." Ph. D. dissertation, Columbia University, 1956. (DA 16, p2507)

Although American Zionists placed pressure on Congress to pass a resolution in 1922, endorsing the concept of a Jewish home in Palestine, the U. S. government had no desire to be drawn into an Arab-Jewish-British controversy.

307 Raleigh, Edward A. "An Inquiry into the Influences of American Democracy on the Arab Middle East, 1819-1958." Ph. D. dissertation, Pacific University, 1960. (X 1960, p111, ADD) [Abstract not available.]

308 Ramazani, Rouhollah K. The Foreign Policy of Iran, 1500-1941. Charlottesville: University Press of Virginia, 1966.

Concentrates on Dr. Arthur C. Millspaugh's mission to Iran during the 1920s when Iran sought to assert her nationalistic aspirations in the face of British and Russian opposition.

309 Ross, Frank A.; C. Luther Fry; and Elbridge Sibley. The Near East and American Philanthropy. New York: Columbia University Press, 1929.

Relates efforts of Americans to alleviate distress in the Middle East. Does not relate problem to government assistance.

310 Sabri, Marie Aziz. "Beirut College for Women and Ten of Its Distinguished Pioneering Alumnae." Ph. D. dissertation, Columbia University, 1965. (DA 26, p6454)

Shows the influence of the College on the changing status of women in years 1926-1963 by examining the careers of ten distinguished alumnae.

311 Sachar, Howard M. The Emergence of the Middle East, 1914-1924. New York: Knopf, 1969.

Asserts that U. S. had no political interests in the Middle East during the interwar period, few commercial interests, and that the missionaries had the most far-reaching influence on the shaping of policy.

312 ________. Europe Leaves the Middle East, 1936-1954. New York: Knopf, 1972.

Concentrates on U.S. reaction to the Zionist question in Palestine during this period.

313 _______. "The United States and Turkey, 1914-1927: The Origins of Near Eastern Policy." Ph.D. dissertation, Harvard University, 1951. (W 1953, p236, DDAU) [Abstract not available.]

314 Shwadran, Benjamin. The Middle East, Oil, and the Great Powers. New York: Praeger, 1955.
Demonstrates the ease with which government and industry worked during the interwar era to obtain concessions in the Middle East that would alleviate a projected oil shortage in the period following World War I.

315 Sousa, Nasim. The Capitulatory Regime of Turkey: Its History, Origins, and Nature. Baltimore: Johns Hopkins University Press, 1933.
Asserts that the Chester Concession was a factor in U.S. participation at the Lausanne Conference.

316 Stocking, George W. Middle East Oil: A Study in Political and Economic Controversy. Nashville: Vanderbilt University Press, 1970.
Claims that the State Department initiated an aggressive Middle-Eastern oil policy by use of the Open-Door policy.

317 Stookey, Robert W. America and the Arab States: An Uneasy Encounter. New York: Wiley, 1975.
Treats the American oil effort in the Middle East during the interwar years when Americans entered the race for oil in Iraq, Bahrein, Saudi Arabia, and Kuwait.

318 Trask, Roger R. "The Terrible Turk and Turkish-American Relations in the Interwar Period," Historian, XXXIII (November 1970), 40-53.
Missionaries raised the Terrible Turk image in the U.S. in 1920s. American Friends of Turkey sought to correct this, thus laying the foundation for better relations.

319 _______. "Turco-American Rapprochement, 1927-32," in Sidney D. Brown, ed., Studies on Asia. Lincoln: University of Nebraska Press, 1967.
American diplomats in the interwar era were able to persuade the nation's various interests to accommodate to Turkish nationalism, thus laying in a fund of Turkish good will toward the U.S.

320 ________. "The United States and Turkish Nationalism: Investments and Technical Aid During the Ataturk Era," Business History Review, 38 (spring 1964), 58-77.
Author relates American commercial expansion and rendering of technical assistance during a crucial period of Turkish development.

321 ________. United States Response to Turkish Nationalism and Reform, 1914-1939. Minneapolis: University of Minnesota Press, 1971.
Demonstrates that American interests in Turkey in the interwar era accommodated to the rise of Turkish nationalism. Even so, Americans continued to pursue economic and philanthropic interests and laid foundation for good U.S.-Turkish relations during the period of World War II and thereafter.

322 ________. "Unnamed Christianity in Turkey during the Ataturk Era," Muslim World, 55 (1965), 66-76; and 55 (1965), 101-111.
American missionaries curtailed the teaching of Christianity in Turkey, thus gaining Turkish good will.

323 Turner, Michael Allan. "The International Politics of Narcotics: Turkey and the United States." Ph.D. dissertation, Kent State University, 1975. (DA 36, p6295)
Gives some background to a problem that later exercised Turkish-American relations.

324 Twitchell, K.S. Saudi Arabia: With an Account of the Development of Its Natural Resources. Princeton, N.J.: Princeton University Press, 1958.
Treats Twitchell's early efforts to find oil in Saudi Arabia and his success in locating an interested American oil company to explore.

325 Wall, Bennett H., and George S. Gibb. Teagle of Jersey Standard. New Orleans: Tulane University Press, 1974.
A very readable biography that includes Teagle's efforts to secure Jersey Standard's entry into the international oil consortium in Iraq in the 1920s.

326 Walt, Joseph William. "Saudi Arabia and the Americans, 1928-1951." Ph.D. dissertation, Northwestern

University, 1960. (DA 21, p1548)

Encompasses American quest for oil in Saudi Arabia during the 1930s, the efforts to retain the concession during World War II, and continued commercial and diplomatic problems in the postwar era.

327 Yale, William. The Near East: A Modern History. Ann Arbor: University of Michigan Press, 1958.

Provides background to the interwar era and concentrates more on the quest for oil, the Zionist question in Palestine, and the rise of Turkish nationalism.

328 Yeselson, Abraham. United States-Persian Diplomatic Relations, 1883-1921. New Brunswick, N.J.: Rutgers University Press, 1950.

Briefly treats Anglo-American rivalry in Persia in the period following World War I.

K

WORLD WAR II

329 Abu Salih, Abbas Said. "History of the Foreign Policy of Lebanon, 1943-1958." Ph.D. dissertation, University of Texas, 1971. (DA 32, p6325)

This dissertation covers Lebanese diplomacy from the time of independence--which goal the United States took an interest in, pursuant to the goal of self-determination--to 1958.

330 Agwani, Mohammed Shafi. The United States and the Arab World, 1945-1952. Aligarh, India: Institute of Islamic Studies, 1955.

Asserts that the United States adhered to an aggressive policy independent of Britain in order to achieve economic goals that encompassed access to oil fields and markets.

331 Bailey, John A., Jr. "Lion, Eagle, and Crescent: The Western Allies and Turkey in 1943: A Study of British and American Diplomacy in a Critical Year of the War." Ph.D. dissertation, Georgetown University, 1969. (DA 31, p1168)

This study examines Anglo-American relations with Turkey in 1943. Although British leaders worked for Turkish entry into the war, the Americans were opposed, for neither President Roosevelt nor the American military chiefs favored this plan of action.

332 Blair, Leon Borden. "Amateurs in Diplomacy: The American Vice Consuls in North Africa, 1941-43," Historian, XXXV (August 1973), 607-20.

Concludes that the American consuls in Morocco, Algiers, and Tunisia were hurriedly recruited men who had little guidance in performing their tasks. Further, that Roosevelt had no interest in Moroccan independence.

333 ________. Western Window in the Arab World. Austin: University of Texas Press, 1970.

Examines the role of the United States in the Moroccan effort to achieve independence, and concludes that President Roosevelt did not encourage the Moroccans to expect U.S. assistance in winning self-determination after the war.

334 Brown, L. Carl. "The United States and the Maghrib," Middle East Journal, 30 (summer 1976), 273-90.
Asserts that Operation Torch marked a new beginning for American relations with the Maghrib. Claims that Roosevelt's meeting with the Moroccan Sultan was viewed by the French as the "beginning of their troubles." Process of decolonization began here.

335 Bryson, Thomas A. American Diplomatic Relations with the Middle East, 1784-1975: A Survey. Metuchen, N.J.: Scarecrow Press, 1977.
This study covers a broad range of topics, including American extension of Lend-Lease aid to Saudi Arabia, the wartime role in Iran, the reaction to the Palestine issue, participation in the Middle East Supply Center, problems with Turkey, Syria and Lebanon, and Anglo-American differences of opinion.

336 Buhite, Russell. Patrick J. Hurley and American Foreign Policy. Ithaca, N.Y.: Cornell University Press, 1973.
Suggests that General Hurley was little more than a gadfly who had little influence of any kind on President Roosevelt's thinking about the Middle East.

337 Burns, James MacGregor. Roosevelt: The Soldier of Freedom, 1940-1945. New York: Harcourt Brace Jovanovich, 1970.
Treats Anglo-American differences of opinion on overall wartime strategy that included the Middle East.

338 Campbell, John C. Defense of the Middle East: Problems of American Policy. New York: Harper, 1960.
Asserts that the United States had no comprehensive Middle Eastern policy during World War II and deferred to the British in this area.

339 Churchill, Winston S. The Hinge of Fate. Boston: Houghton Mifflin, 1950.
Highlights Churchill's strong favor of Turkish entry into World War II and his support for a Balkan strategy.

340 Clark, Mark W. Calculated Risk. New York: Harper, 1950.
This memoir records General Clark's effort to make an agreement with the Vichy French in North Africa, prior to the Allied landings, as well as the events leading to the Clark-Darlan accord which achieved French cooperation.

341 Craven, Wesley Frank, and James Lea Cate. The Army Air Forces in World War II: Europe: Torch to Pointblank. Chicago: University of Chicago Press, 1949.
A good description of American air power in the North African campaign.

342 Darvich-Kodjouri, Djamchid. "Images and Perception in International Relations: A Case Study of Relationships between Iran and the Great Powers, 1919-1953." Ph.D. dissertation, Miami University, 1976.
Focuses on the image of Iran held by Great Britain, the United States, and the Soviet Union.

343 DeNovo, John A. "The Culbertson Economic Mission and Anglo-American Tensions in the Middle East, 1944-1945," Journal of American History, LXIII (March 1977), 913-36.
Highlights the tension between the U.S. and Britain over Middle-Eastern trade and demonstrates that American concepts of free trade clashed violently with Britain's adherence to state control over trade.

344 Dohse, Michael A. "American Periodicals and the Palestine Triangle, 1936-1947." Ph.D. dissertation, Mississippi State University, 1966. (DA 27, p3395)
Concludes that American journals had numerous shortcomings in their presentations on the issue.

345 Eddy, William A. FDR Meets Ibn Saud. New York: American Friends of the Middle East, 1954.
This work contains the only authentic note of the conversations between President Roosevelt and King Ibn Saud relative to the creation of a Jewish national home in Palestine.

346 Eisenhower, Dwight D. Crusade in Europe. New York: Doubleday, 1948.
This memoirist treats in detail the political problems stemming from the Allied effort to win French support

of the war in North Africa. Indicates that U.S. considered Middle East as subsidiary to future operations in Europe.

347 Engler, Robert. *The Politics of Oil: A Study of Private Power and Democratic Directions.* New York: Macmillan, 1961.

Claims that private American oil companies brought pressure to bear upon the U.S. government during the war to achieve an aggressive Middle-Eastern oil policy.

348 Feis, Herbert. *Petroleum and American Foreign Policy.* Stanford, Calif.: Stanford University Press, 1944.

This paper highlights government concern over an anticipated shortage of oil in the postwar era and argues that the U.S. must seek foreign reserves in the Middle East to make up for the wartime drain on domestic reserves.

349 ________. *Roosevelt, Churchill, and Stalin: The War They Waged and the Peace They Sought.* Princeton, N.J.: Princeton University Press, 1967.

Indicates the degree of disagreement between Anglo-American military planners concerning strategy in the Middle East and Europe.

350 Fields, Harvey Joseph. "Pawn of Empires: A Study of United States Middle East Policy, 1945-1953." Ph.D. dissertation, Rutgers University, 1975. (DA 36, p3068)

Although this dissertation primarily examines U.S.-Middle East policy during the Truman years, it also analyzes U.S. interests before, during, and after the war. It develops allied rivalries in Iran, Greece, Saudi Arabia, and the Levant.

351 Fisher, Sydney Nettleton. *The Middle East: A History.* New York: Knopf, 1960.

Contains one brief chapter on World War II which highlights Anglo-American differences in Turkey, Syria and Lebanon, and Saudi Arabia.

352 Gallagher, Charles F. *United States and North Africa: Morocco, Algeria and Tunisia.* Cambridge, Mass.: Harvard University Press, 1963.

Discusses the growth of nationalism in North Africa and the American impact thereon.

353 Gardner, Lloyd C. *Architects of Illusion: Men and*

Ideas in American Foreign Policy, 1941-1949. Chicago: Quadrangle, 1970.
Repeats the thesis set forth in item 354, with further emphasis on policy in Iran.

354 ________. Economic Aspects of New Deal Diplomacy. Madison: University of Wisconsin Press, 1964.
Takes the New Left position that American wartime Middle Eastern policy was motivated by the quest for economic gain in the region's oil fields and not by considerations of defense.

355 Haley, P. Edward. "Britain and the Middle East," in Tareq Y. Ismael, ed., The Middle East and World Politics. Syracuse, N.Y.: Syracuse University Press, 1974.
Suggests that U.S. policy tended to advance American economic interests, to oppose imperialism and colonialism, and to eliminate British influence.

356 Hall, Luella J. The United States and Morocco, 1776-1956. Metuchen: Scarecrow Press, 1971.
Moroccan nationalism was seemingly encouraged by President Franklin D. Roosevelt's words to the Sultan in 1943.

357 Halperin, Samuel. The Political World of American Zionism. Detroit: Wayne State University Press, 1961.
This author indicates the rapidity with which American Jews endorsed Zionist goals during World War II.

358 Halpern, Ben. The Idea of a Jewish State. Cambridge, Mass.: Harvard University Press, 1969.
A general study of the background on the rise of a Jewish state in Palestine.

359 Hamburger, Robert Lee. "Franco-American Relations, 1940-1962: The Role of United States anti-Colonialism and anti-Communism in the Formulation of United States Policy on the Algerian Question." Ph.D. dissertation, Notre Dame University, 1970. (DA 32, p519)
Suggests that President Roosevelt's opposition to the French position in Algeria was hedged about with reservations.

360 Helseth, William Arthur. "The United States and

Turkey: Their Relations from 1784 to 1962." Ph.D. dissertation, Fletcher School of Law and Diplomacy, 1962.

Contains a chapter on American wartime relations with Turkey, dealing with Lend Lease, Turkish neutrality, and the Anglo-American difference of opinion on Turkish entry into the war.

361 Hoskins, Halford L. The Middle East: Problem Area in World Politics. New York: Macmillan, 1957.

Suggests that U.S. policy vis-à-vis Iran did not always follow a British initiative.

362 Howard, Harry N. "The Bicentennial in American-Turkish Relations," Middle East Journal, 30 (summer 1976), 291-310.

Reasserts the thesis set forth in item 364.

363 ________. "The Great Powers and the Middle East," in Tareq Y. Ismael, ed., The Middle East in World Politics. Syracuse, N.Y.: Syracuse University Press, 1974.

Reasserts the thesis set forth in item 364.

364 ________. Turkey, the Straits and U.S. Policy. Baltimore: Johns Hopkins University Press, 1974.

Considers the Anglo-American negotiations with Turkey during the war; asserts that U.S. and Russian military chiefs, plus those of Britain, actually opposed Turkish entry into the war. It was only in 1943-44 that British leaders desired Turkish entry into the conflict.

365 Hull, Cordell. The Memoirs of Cordell Hull. 2 vols. New York: Macmillan, 1948.

The second volume of this significant memoir furnishes important insights into U.S. Middle-Eastern policy in World War II. Author declares that policy was anti-imperial, yet pursued an aggressive course to secure oil in Saudi Arabia and Iran. Critical of Roosevelt for talking on "both sides of the question" on creation of a Jewish state in Palestine.

366 Hurewitz, Jacob C. Middle East Dilemmas: The Background of United States Policy. New York: Harper, 1953.

During World War II United States regarded the Middle East, with the exception of Saudi Arabia and Palestine, as an area in which British influence was predominant. An excellent analysis of U. S. policy considerations during the war and postwar eras.

367 _______. "The Road to Partition: The Palestine Problem, 1936-1948." Ph. D. dissertation, Columbia University, 1950. (W 1951, p198, DDAU) [Abstract not available.]

368 _______. The Struggle for Palestine. New York: Greenwood Press, 1968.
Describes the rise of Zionist sentiment in the U. S. during the war and concludes that the President made contradictory pledges to Jews and Arabs concerning a Jewish national home in Palestine.

369 Ismael, Tareq Y. The Middle East in World Politics: A Study in Contemporary International Relations. Syracuse, N. Y.: Syracuse University Press, 1974.
Contains a number of essays relating to the American role in the Middle East during World War II.

370 Issa, Mahmoud K. "Trade between Egypt and the United States." Ph. D. dissertation, University of Minnesota, 1953. (DA 13, p690)
Claims that World War II advanced American sales in Egypt, and the U. S. became the second largest supplier of Egypt's manufacturing needs.

371 al-Jazairi, Mohamed Zayyan. "Saudi Arabia: A Diplomatic History, 1924-1964." Ph. D. dissertation, University of Utah, 1971. (DA 32, p868)
Author asserts that Saudi Arabia maintained a neutralist policy during World War II, but declared war on Axis powers when victory for the Allies seemed certain.

372 Kabbani, Rashid. "Morocco: From Protectorate to Independence, 1912-1956." Ph. D. dissertation, American University, 1957. (DA 17, p2051)
An analysis of the origins of international problems in Morocco and a study of Morocco in contemporary world affairs. Views the rise of urban problems and the irrelevance of French urban life to young Moroccans as the chief source of Franco-Moroccan conflicts between 1944 and 1956.

373 Kazdal, Mustafa N. "Trade Relations between the United States and Turkey, 1919-1944." Ph. D. disser-

tation, Indiana University, 1946. (W 1946, p40, DDAU) [Abstract not available.]

374 Kirk, George E. The Middle East in the War. London: Oxford University Press, 1952.

An excellent treatment of Anglo-American diplomatic differences. Asserts that while U.S. was anti-imperial vis-à-vis people contained in European empires, it nevertheless pursued an aggressive policy to acquire new oil concessions in the region.

375 Klebanoff, Shoshana. Middle East Oil and U.S. Foreign Policy with Special Reference to the U.S. Energy Crisis. New York: Praeger, 1974.

Contains a brief chapter on the American wartime quest for oil in the Middle East. Emphasizes efforts in Saudi Arabia where Petroleum Reserves Corporation tried to obtain government ownership of that country's oil reserves.

376 Kolko, Gabriel. The Politics of War: The World and United States Foreign Policy, 1943-1945. New York: Random House, 1968.

An aggressive American quest for Middle-Eastern oil caused the Soviet Union to respond with a move to achieve access to oil in Iran.

377 Kolko, Joyce, and Gabriel Kolko. The Limits of Power: The World and United States Foreign Policy, 1945-1954. New York: Harper & Row, 1972.

A New Left view that asserts that American wartime Middle-Eastern policy was aggressive and aimed to supplant British supremacy in the region.

378 Lenczowski, George. The Middle East in World Affairs. Ithaca, N.Y.: Cornell University Press, 1956.

Gives broad-brush treatment to American wartime problems in Turkey, Saudi Arabia, Palestine, Iran, Syria and Lebanon, and Egypt, and suggests that the U.S. did pursue an independent policy that frequently was at odds with Britain.

379 ________. Russia and the West in Iran, 1918-1948. Ithaca, N.Y.: Cornell University Press, 1949.

Critical of U.S. wartime policy in Iran, asserting that it was passive and encouraged Russian aggressive moves in postwar era.

380 Lilienthal, Alfred M. The Other Side of the Coin: An American Perspective of the Arab-Israeli Conflict. New York: Devin-Adair, 1965.

An anti-Zionist view of American reaction to the Palestine question. Critical of President Roosevelt who was motivated by political considerations.

381 Lohbeck, Don. Patrick J. Hurley. Chicago: Henry Regnery, 1956.

Author claims that General Hurley's fact-finding mission in the Middle East influenced President Roosevelt's policy vis-à-vis Iran.

382 McNeill, William Hardy. America, Britain, and Russia: Their Cooperation and Conflict, 1941-1946. New York: Johnson Reprint Corp., 1970.

Gives background to Anglo-American tensions over strategic considerations that involved the Middle East.

383 El Mallakh, Ragaei William. "The Effects of the Second World War on the Economic Development of Egypt." Ph.D. dissertation, Rutgers University, 1955. (DA 15, p2435)

Asserts that the war had a profound effect on Egypt's economy by increasing industrial production by more than 50 percent. The Middle East Supply Center's activities are treated.

384 Malone, Joseph J. "America and the Arabian Peninsula: The First Two Hundred Years," Middle East Journal, 30 (summer 1976), 406-24.

Treats briefly American wartime concern for future petroleum reserves to supplant domestic sources depleted by the needs of war.

385 Manuel, Frank E. The Realities of American-Palestine Relations. Washington, D.C.: Public Affairs Press, 1949.

Describes the growth of the Zionist movement in the U.S., and concludes that President Roosevelt's statements on the Palestine question were contradictory.

386 Mark, Eduard M. "Allied Relations in Iran, 1941-1947: The Origins of a Cold War Crisis," Wisconsin Magazine of History, 59 (autumn 1975), 51-63.

A revisionist essay that asserts that Russia's quest

for a sphere in Northern Iran came in response to earlier American efforts to obtain a concession in Iran.

387 Melka, Robert L. "The Axis and the Arab Middle East, 1930-1945." Ph. D. dissertation, University of Minnesota, 1966. (DA 27, p1762)

Treats the British success in thwarting a German effort to obtain power in Iraq. The Axis powers were unsuccessful in the Middle East, and Nazi policies led to the eventual triumph of Zionism.

388 Mikesell, Raymond F., and Hollis B. Chenery. Arabian Oil: America's Stake in the Middle East. Chapel Hill: University of North Carolina Press, 1949.

The authors analyze the Petroleum Reserve Corporation's efforts to obtain access to Saudi Arabian Oil, and describe the events leading to the Anglo-American Petroleum Agreement and Congressional disapproval thereof.

389 Millspaugh, Arthur C. Americans in Persia. Washington, D. C.: Brookings Institution, 1946.

Highly critical of American wartime policy in Iran, where weakness and vacillation gave encouragement to the Soviets to pursue an aggressive policy.

390 Mojdehi, Hassan. "Arthur C. Millspaugh's Two Missions to Iran and Their Impact on American-Iranian Relations." Ph. D. dissertation, Ball State University, 1975. (DA 36, p5472)

This dissertation is critical of the State Department's handling of the second Millspaugh Mission to Iran. Conclusions seem to reflect those contained in item 389.

391 Morison, Elting E. Turmoil and Tradition: A Study of the Life and Times of Henry L. Stimson. New York: Atheneum, 1964.

Gives some attention to Anglo-American differences over a wartime strategy that extended to North Africa.

392 Morison, Samuel E. History of United States Naval Operations in World War II. 15 vols. Boston: Little, Brown, 1947-1962.

Volume II of this series, Operations in North African Waters, October 1942-June 1943, concerns Allied strategical aims and the efforts to achieve these aims in the Middle East by means of Operation TORCH.

393 Mosley, Leonard. Power Play: Oil in the Middle

East. New York: Random House, 1973.

A readable work that gives slim treatment to American wartime diplomatic negotiations with Saudi Arabia.

394 Motter, T. H. Vail. The Persian Corridor and Aid to Russia. Washington, D. C.: U. S. Government Printing Office, 1952.

Describes evolution of wartime policy in Iran where U. S. hoped to achieve a stable government that could withstand the pressures of the Soviet Union and Britain.

395 Murphy, Robert. Diplomat Among Warriors. New York: Doubleday, 1964.

A very readable memoir that describes the complexities of American dealings with the French in North Africa prior to and after the landings in North Africa.

396 Nash, Gerald D. United States Oil Policy, 1890-1964. Pittsburgh: University of Pittsburgh Press, 1968.

A brief, but penetrating account of American wartime oil policy in the Middle East. Demonstrates the interaction between oil companies and government officials to achieve access to oil in Saudi Arabia.

397 Nolte, R. H. "The United States and the Middle East," in Georgianna S. Stevens, ed., The United States and the Middle East (Englewood Cliffs, N. J.: Prentice-Hall, 1964).

Asserts that American wartime Middle-Eastern policy was "innocent of policy objectives" and its whole purpose was to win the war.

398 Oder, Irwin. "The United States and the Palestine Mandate, 1920-1948: A Study of the Impact of Interest Groups on Foreign Policy." Ph. D. dissertation, Columbia University, 1956. (DA 16, p2507)

Describes the rise of Zionist pressure on U. S. government, but says that President Roosevelt was unable "to reach a satisfactory solution to the Palestine dilemma."

399 Peck, Malcolm Cameron. "Saudi Arabia in United States Foreign Policy to 1958: A Study in the Sources and Determinants of American Policy." Ph. D. dissertation, Fletcher School of Law and Diplomacy, 1970. (X 1970, p286, ADD) [Abstract not available.]

400 Pfau, Richard Anthony. "Avoiding the Cold War: The

United States and the Iranian Oil Crisis, 1944," Essays in History, XVIII (1974), 104-14.

This essay treats the tension between U.S. and Russian policy-makers in wartime Iran over the latter's quest for an oil concession. Concludes that U.S. did not permit competition for oil to threaten wartime cooperation with the Soviets.

401 _______. "The United States and Iran, 1941-1947: Origins of Partnership." Ph.D. dissertation, University of Virginia, 1975. (DA 36, p6245)

Treats the evolutionary process of American policy in wartime Iran, including the effort of American oil interests to obtain a concession.

402 Pogue, Forrest C. George C. Marshall. 4 vols. New York: Viking Press, 1973.

Indicates General Marshall's hard feelings toward British strategists who favored a North African operation, thus delaying the cross-channel invasion of Europe. Also shows his opposition to bringing Turkey into the war.

403 Raleigh, Edward A. "An Inquiry into the Influences of American Democracy on the Arab Middle East, 1819-1958." Ph.D. dissertation, Pacific University, 1960. (X 1960, p111, ADD) [Abstract not available.]

404 Ramazani, Rouhollah K. "Iran and the United States: An Experiment in Enduring Friendship," Middle East Journal, 30 (summer 1976), 322-34.

A brief look at wartime relations.

405 _______. Iran's Foreign Policy, 1941-1973: A Study of Foreign Policy in Modernizing Nations. Charlottesville: University Press of Virginia, 1975.

Presents a view of American policy from an Iranian perspective. Iranians wanted U.S. to serve as a makeweight against Russia and Britain.

406 Ray, Deborah Wing. "The Takoradi Route: Roosevelt's Prewar Venture beyond the Western Hemisphere," Journal of American History, LXII (September 1975), 340-58.

American planners established an air route to the Middle East that greatly enhanced the Allied war effort.

407 Reitzel, William. The Mediterranean: Its Role in

America's Foreign Policy. New York: Harcourt-Brace, 1948.

During World War II, the U.S. viewed the Middle East as an area where military considerations were of primary concern. But oil was also a factor in policy-making.

408 Rivlin, Helen Anne B. "American Jews and the State of Israel: A Bicentennial Perspective," Middle East Journal, 30 (summer 1976), 369-89.

A brief sketch of the reaction of American Jews to the Palestine question.

409 Sachar, Howard M. Europe Leaves the Middle East, 1936-1954. New York: Knopf, 1972.

This study describes a broad range of U.S. Middle-East activities during the war, but concludes that the U.S. recognized the primacy of Great Britain in the region.

410 Safran, Nadav. The United States and Israel. Cambridge, Mass.: Harvard University Press, 1963.

While this work gives some space to U.S. consideration of the Palestine question during the war, it attempts to provide the reader with a broad view of life in Israel.

411 Shaheen, Ghaleb S. "The Foreign Policy of Lebanon." Ph.D. dissertation, Syracuse University, 1959. (DA 20, p2879)

An interesting study of domestic influences on Lebanese foreign policy. Treats this small state's effort to remain independent.

412 Sheehan, M. K. Iran: Impact of United States Interests and Policies. Brooklyn: Theo Gaus, 1968.

Develops the evolution of American policy in Iran; the second Millspaugh mission is treated; views wartime cooperation as a foundation for postwar rapprochement.

413 Shwadran, Benjamin. The Middle East, Oil and the Great Powers. New York: Praeger, 1955.

A good account of the aggressive American oil policy in World War II which was initiated by a government concerned about American oil reserves being replaced by Saudi Arabian oil.

414 Simpson, Dwight J. "British Palestine Policy, 1939-1949." Ph.D. dissertation, Stanford University, 1950. (DD 17, p180) [Abstract not available.]

415 Smith, Gaddis. American Diplomacy During the Second World War, 1941-1945. New York: Wiley, 1966.

An excellent work that asserts that the U. S. opposed British imperial aspirations in the Middle East and sought to expand American influence at every opportunity. Stresses that an independent American policy crossed British aims in Saudi Arabia, Turkey, Syria and Lebanon, and Iran.

416 Speiser, Ephraim. The United States and the Near East. Cambridge, Mass.: Harvard University Press, 1952.

An excellent study that posits that the United States had no comprehensive policy for the Mideast during World War II but deferred to the British lead.

417 Stackman, Ralph R. "Laurence A. Steinhardt: New Deal Diplomat, 1933-1945." Ph. D. dissertation, Michigan State University, 1967. (DA 28, p4106)

This New-Deal diplomat served as U. S. Ambassador to wartime Turkey and sought to keep Turkey neutral, in spite of British efforts to force her into war. Also treats economic warfare that sought to deny strategic materials to the Axis.

418 Stevens, Richard P. American Zionism and the United States Foreign Policy. New York: Pageant Press, 1962.

A well-written account that describes the growth of Zionist influence on the U. S. government and President Roosevelt's reaction thereto. Concludes that he made contradictory statements to both Arabs and Jews on the Palestine question.

419 Stocking, George W. Middle East Oil: A Study in Political and Economic Controversy. Nashville: Vanderbilt University Press, 1970.

Author gives an account of the U. S. government's efforts to aid Saudi Arabia in order to preserve American ascendancy in the Saudi oil fields.

420 Stookey, Robert W. America and the Arab States: An Uneasy Encounter. New York: Wiley, 1975.

Gives slim treatment to American wartime activities in the Middle East.

421 Sykes, Christopher. Crossroads to Israel, 1917-1948. Bloomington: Indiana University Press, 1973.

Worthwhile reading for further understanding of the growing crisis in Palestine during the war years.

422 Tabari, Keyvan. "Iran's Policies Toward the United States During the Anglo-Russian Occupation, 1941-1946." Ph.D. dissertation, Columbia University, 1967. (DA 28, p1881)
Views this relationship in terms of the interaction between Iran's domestic and external politics and a need to find a makeweight to balance against Britain and Russia. Also treats the evolution of U.S. policy in Iran.

423 Thomas, Lewis V., and Richard N. Frye. The United States and Turkey and Iran. Cambridge, Mass.: Harvard University Press, 1951.
Affords a brief sketch of U.S. activities in Iran during the war and an even briefer treatment of relations with Turkey.

424 Thorpe, James Arthur. "The Mission of Arthur C. Millspaugh to Iran, 1943-1945." Ph.D. dissertation, University of Wisconsin, 1973. (DA 35, p387)
Critical of the State Department's treatment of Millspaugh's mission which was doomed from the outset because of the growth of Iranian nationalism.

425 Twitchell, K.S. Saudi Arabia: With an Account of the Development of Its Natural Resources. Princeton, N.J.: Princeton University Press, 1958.
Sets the stage for the great American oil investment in Saudi Arabia.

426 Walt, Joseph William. "Saudi Arabia and the Americans, 1928-1951." Ph.D. dissertation, Northwestern University, 1960. (DA 21, p1548)
This account encompasses the extension of Lend Lease to Saudi Arabia, the effort of the Petroleum Reserves Corporation to acquire control over American oil interests, and the sending of a U.S. military mission to train the Saudi army.

427 Weisband, Edward. Turkish Foreign Policy, 1943-1945. Princeton, N.J.: Princeton University Press, 1973.
An excellent treatment of Anglo-American-Turkish negotiations during the war. American opposition to Turkish entry into the war was based on strategic considerations,

while the Turks feared Russian incursion into Anatolia. Also treats the economic facet and the importance of the Straits.

428 Welles, Sumner. Where Are We Heading? New York: Harper Bros., 1946.
Asserts that President Roosevelt discussed the Palestine question with King Ibn Saud, but never swerved from his promise to help create a Jewish state in Palestine.

429 Wilmington, Martin W. The Middle East Supply Centre. Albany: State University of New York Press, 1971.
Chronicles Anglo-American cooperation in administering the MESC. Asserts that U. S. withdrew because it resented Britain's effort to control Middle Eastern economics in the postwar era.

430 ________. "The Middle East Supply Centre," Middle East Journal, 6 (1952), 144-66.
An excellent synopsis of item 429.

431 Wilson, Evan M. "The Palestine Papers, 1943-1947," Journal of Palestine Studies, II (summer 1973), 33-54.
A good account of the evolution of U. S. policy vis-à-vis the Palestine question. Claims that President Roosevelt made contradictory statements on the Palestine question.

432 Yale, William. The Near East: A Modern History. Ann Arbor: University of Michigan Press, 1958.
A thumbnail sketch of U. S. wartime Middle-East activities, with particular emphasis on the Palestine issue.

L

CONTAINMENT, FOREIGN AID, NATIONALISM AND MODERNIZATION, 1945-1955

433 Abbas, Jabir Ali. "Points of Departure in Egypt's Foreign Policy: The Essence of Nasser's Power." Ph.D. dissertation, Indiana University, 1969. (DA 32, p5846)

Author selects a number of issues in the period 1952 to 1956 to demonstrate the power of Nasser and his impact on the Arab world.

434 Abu-Diab, Fawzi. "Lebanon and the United Nations, 1945-1958." Ph.D. dissertation, University of Pennsylvania, 1965. (DA 26, p3464)

An account of Lebanon's actions and reactions in the United Nations Organization, with emphasis on its opposition to the creation of Israel, the Palestinian Arab refugee problem, and its request for U.S. aid in the 1958 crisis.

435 Abu-Jaber, Faiz Saley. "Egypt and the Cold War, 1952-1956: Implications for American Policy." Ph.D. dissertation, Syracuse University, 1966. (DA 27, p4306)

Explores the Eisenhower administration's efforts to create a Middle-Eastern alliance with emphasis on the Baghdad Pact, and Egypt's reaction.

436 Abu Salih, Abbas Said. "History of the Foreign Policy of Lebanon, 1943-1958." Ph.D. dissertation, University of Texas, 1971. (DA 32, p6325)

Examines Lebanon's position on a number of issues, with emphasis on her acceptance of the Eisenhower Doctrine, a position that jeopardized her position with other Arab states.

437 Acheson, Dean. _Present at the Creation: My Years at the State Department._ New York: Norton, 1969.

Discusses his role in the formulation of the Truman Doctrine and his efforts to create a Middle-East alliance.

438 Agwani, Mohammed Shafi. The United States and the Arab World, 1945-1952. Aligarh, India: Institute of Islamic Studies, 1955.

Concentrates on U.S. effort to erect a defense posture in the Middle East, but concludes that this policy failed due to American involvement with Zionism and association with the imperialist powers.

439 al-Akhrass, Mouhamad Safouh. "Revolutionary Change and Modernization in the Arab World: A Case from Syria." Ph.D. dissertation, University of California, Berkeley, 1969. (DA 31, p833)

This study analyzes the sharp, rapid change in Syria as it moved toward a more modern society--a change from agrarian-feudalism to socialism.

440 Alberts, Darlene Jean. "King Hussein of Jordan: The Consummate Politician." Ph.D. dissertation, Ohio State University, 1973. (DA 34, p692)

This study examines the rise of Jordanian nationalism in view of the policies and actions of King Hussein.

441 Albion, Robert Greenhalgh, and R. H. Connery. Forrestal and the Navy. New York: Columbia University Press, 1962.

The author demonstrates Forrestal's efforts to found the Sixth Fleet to protect American Mediterranean and Middle-Eastern interests in the early years of the Cold War.

442 Alvarez, David Joseph. "The United States and Turkey, 1945-1946: The Bureaucratic Determinants of Cold War Diplomacy." Ph.D. dissertation, University of Connecticut, 1975. (DA 36, p6859)

Concentrates on the State Department's Office of Near Eastern and African Affairs, which was the principal office in forming a policy toward Turkey. Focuses on the bureaucratic role in policy-making.

443 Amouzegar, Jahanigir. "The Role of the United States Technical Assistance in the Development of Underdeveloped Countries with Special Reference to Iran." Ph.D. dissertation, University of California, Los Angeles, 1955. (W 1955, p164, DDAU)

Inquires into the effectiveness of the United States' Point Four Program in Iran to determine its long-range influence on economic problems.

444 Arcilesi, Salvatore Alfred. "Development of United

States Foreign Policy in Iran, 1949-1960." Ph.D. dissertation, University of Virginia, 1965. (DA 26, p6144)

This dissertation describes and analyzes the development of U.S. policy in Iran and concludes that it was successful in stimulating economic development and political stability.

445 Avery, Peter. Modern Iran. New York: Praeger, 1965.

Focuses attention on the U.S. role in ousting the Soviets from Iran in 1946 crisis.

446 Badeau, John S. American Approach to the Arab World. New York: Harper, 1968.

An outstanding study that provides a frame of reference for understanding an American role in a changing Arab world.

447 El-Behairy, Mohamed Mohamed. "The Suez Canal in World Politics, 1945-1961." Ph.D. dissertation, Ohio State University, 1961. (DA 22, p3724)

Demonstrates the manner in which the Suez Canal acquired new significance as a military bastion for Western defense of the Middle East.

448 Bernstein, Barton J. Politics and Policies of the Truman Administration. Chicago: Quadrangle Books, 1970.

A New Left view of the Truman Doctrine as a tool of economic and political expansion.

449 Blessing, James Alan. "The Suspension of Foreign Aid by the United States, 1948-1972." Ph.D. dissertation, State University of New York, Albany, 1975. (DA 36, p4001)

The United States has been most likely to suspend aid to Middle Eastern and African countries for military and political reasons and also to appease domestic critics of policy.

450 Bose, Tarun Chandra. The Superpowers and the Middle East. New York: Asia Publishing House, 1973.

The first portion of this book concentrates on the U.S. effort to erect a defense policy in the Middle East; it also examines the American role in the birth of Israel.

451 Brown, L. Carl. "The United States and the Maghrib," *Middle East Journal*, 30 (summer 1976), 273-90.
A brief sketch of postwar policy determinants.

452 Bryson, Thomas A. *American Diplomatic Relations with the East, 1784-1975: A Survey.* Metuchen, N.J.: Scarecrow Press, 1977.
Concludes that the postwar American policy of defense was in response to aggressive Soviet actions in the Middle East. Describes the making of the Truman Doctrine and efforts to erect a defense structure.

453 ________. *American Middle Eastern Diplomacy.* St. Charles, Mo.: Forum Press, 1974.
A thumbnail sketch of postwar diplomacy.

454 Burke, Mary Patrice. "United States Aid to Turkey: Foreign Aid and Foreign Policy," Ph.D. dissertation, University of Connecticut, 1977. (DA 38, p5030)
This study examines and analyzes United States Economic aid to Turkey in an effort to gain insights into the aid relationships.

455 Burnett, John Howard, Jr. "Soviet-Egyptian Relations during the Khrushchev Era: A Study in Soviet Foreign Policy." Ph.D. dissertation, Emory University, 1966. (DA 27, p2187)
Examines the techniques used by the Soviet Union--trade, aid, exchange programs, propaganda, and others--to align Egypt with the Soviet bloc.

456 Byrnes, James. *All in One Lifetime.* New York: Harper, 1958.
This memoir describes policy-making with respect to the employment of the U.S. Navy in the Mediterranean to support foreign policy and sheds light on U.S. support of Turkey, Greece, and Iran.

457 Campbell, John C. *Defense of the Middle East: Problems of American Policy.* New York: Harper, 1960.
A classic study that is necessary to an understanding of American problems and dilemmas in forming a policy for the postwar Middle East. U.S. policy responded to an aggressive Soviet move, concludes this author.

458 Cottam, Richard W. *Nationalism in Iran.* Pittsburgh: University of Pittsburgh Press, 1964.

Concludes that the United States assumed the British position of western leadership in Iran to oppose a Soviet takeover.

459 ________. "The United States, Iran, and the Cold War," Journal of Iranian Studies, III (winter 1970), 2-22.

American policy in postwar Iran was defensive in nature and designed to thwart a Soviet thrust in the direction of the Persian Gulf.

460 Curry, George. James F. Byrnes. New York: Cooper Square Publishers, 1965.

Indicates the importance of this Secretary of State in the Iranian crisis of 1945-1946.

461 Daniel, Robert L. American Philanthropy in the Near East, 1820-1960. Athens: Ohio University Press, 1970.

Concludes that early American philanthropic ventures were precursors to Point Four and other American foreign-aid programs.

462 Darvich-Kodjouri, Djamchid. "Images and Perception in International Relations: A Case Study of Relationships between Iran and the Great Powers, 1919-1953." Ph. D. dissertation, Miami University, 1976. (DA 37, p4600)

Assesses the image of Iran held by the Great Powers during the postwar era.

463 Decker, Donald James. "U. S. Policy Regarding the Baghdad Pact." Ph. D. dissertation, American University, 1975. (DA 36, p1786)

This dissertation concludes that in 1953 Secretary Dulles correctly analyzed the components of a successful defense of the Middle East, but because of other factors the policy failed, although it did strengthen some of the member nations.

464 deRiencourt, Amaury. The American Empire. New York: Dell Books, 1968.

Takes the New Left position that U. S. foreign aid was based on a policy of economic and political penetration of the Middle East.

465 Doenecke, Justus D. "Iran's Role in Cold War Re-

visionism," Journal of Iranian Studies, V (spring-summer 1972), 96-111.
Examines various interpretations of the Russian gambit in postwar Iran.

466 _______. "Revisionists, Oil and Cold War Diplomacy," Journal of Iranian Studies, III (winter 1970), 23-33.
Assesses revisionist view of the origins of the Cold War in Iran.

467 Elfiky, Hassan Salama. "A History of Teacher In-Service Education in the United States: With Recommendations for Egyptian Education." Ph. D. dissertation, University of Minnesota, 1961. (DA 22, p3916)
To apply American use of in-service training to the Egyptian program, with a view to improving the latter.

468 Ellis, Harry B. Challenge in the Middle East: Communist Influence and American Policy. New York: Ronald Press, 1960.
Asserts that Arabs were more concerned with the Communist menace than is commonly realized.

469 Erden, Deniz A. "Turkish Foreign Policy Through the United Nations." Ph. D. dissertation, University of Massachusetts, 1974. (DA 36, p1077)
This dissertation also includes an analysis of Turkey's relations with the U. S. in the early postwar era.

470 Faddah, Mohammad Ibrahim. "The Foreign Policy of Jordan, 1947-1967." Ph. D. dissertation, Oklahoma University, 1971. (DA 32, p2770)
This is a political analysis of Jordan's foreign policy.

471 Fakhsh, Mahmud A. "Education and Political Modernization and Change in Egypt." Ph. D. dissertation, University of Connecticut, 1973. (DA 34, p832)
Investigates the role which modern education has played in bringing about political modernization and socio-economic change in Egypt.

472 Farzanegan, Bahram. "United States Response and Reaction to the Emergence of Arab and African States in International Politics." Ph. D. dissertation, American University, 1966. (DA 27, p1886)
U. S. no longer tries to shape events in the Middle

East, thus departing from a vociferous opposition to the Soviets in the early Cold-War era.

473 Fatemi, Faramarz. "The U. S. S. R. in Iran: The Irano-Soviet Dispute and the Pattern of Azerbaijan Revolution, 1941-1947." Ph. D. dissertation, New School of Social Research, 1976. (DA 38, p3712)

This dissertation analyzes Soviet motives for moving into Northern Iran, the evolution of policy, the expected goals, and the eventual Russian withdrawal.

474 Faulkner, Constance Parry. "The Economic Effects of United States Public Law 480 in the United Arab Republic." Ph. D. dissertation, University of Utah, 1969. (DA 30, p1694)

This study investigates the impact of U. S. foreign aid on Egypt.

475 Fields, Harvey Joseph. "Pawn of Empires: A Study of United States Middle East Policy, 1945-1953." Ph. D. dissertation, Rutgers University 1975. (DA 36, p3068)

This work examines the combination of factors in the policy-making process during the Truman years. Concludes that oil and Western hegemony in the region motivated policy.

476 Firoozi, Ferydoon. "The United States Economic Aid to Iran, 1950-1960." Ph. D. dissertation, Dropsie University, 1966. (X 1966, p46, ADD) [Abstract not available.]

477 Fisher, Carol A., and Fred Krinsky. Middle East in Crisis: A Historical and Documentary Review. Syracuse, N. Y.: Syracuse University Press, 1959.

A broadbrush treatment of U. S. and Soviet goals in the postwar Middle East.

478 Fisher, Sydney Nettleton. The Middle East: A History. New York: Knopf, 1960.

Provides backdrop for postwar American policy.

479 Fleming, D. F. The Cold War and Its Origins. 2 vols. Garden City, N. Y.: Doubleday, 1961.

Presents a revisionist view of the origins of the Cold War in Turkey and Iran.

480 Fort, Raymond. "A Study of the Development of the

American Technical Assistance Program in Iran." Ph. D. dissertation, Cornell University, 1961. (DA 22, p2276)

The United States undertook technical assistance in Iran because of political and economic factors, and utilized programs already underway in Europe to serve as models for those used in Iran.

481 Fouad, Mahmoud Hassan. "The Economics of Foreign Aid: The U. A. R. Experience with the U. S. and U. S. S. R. Programs, 1952-1965." Ph. D. dissertation, University of Southern California, 1968. (DA 29, p1999)

Author argues that foreign aid is an important tool in the foreign policy of the two nations and has played an important role in the development of Egypt. Suggests that the U. S. should resume its program of aid.

482 Freeland, Richard M. The Truman Doctrine and the Origins of McCarthyism: Foreign Policy, Domestic Politics, and Internal Security, 1946-1948. New York: Knopf, 1972.

Concludes that the enunciation of the Truman Doctrine must be viewed in terms of domestic politics.

483 Frye, Richard N., ed. The Near East and the Great Powers. Port Washington, N. Y.: Kennikat Press, 1951.

This work contains an interesting collection of essays relative to the East-West conflict.

484 Gaddis, John Lewis. The United States and the Origins of the Cold War, 1941-1947. New York: Columbia University Press, 1972.

Concludes that the origins of the Cold War must be seen in light of domestic politics.

485 Gallagher, Charles F. United States and North Africa: Morocco, Algeria, and Tunisia. Cambridge, Mass.: Harvard University Press, 1963.

Sees the Maghreb in terms of nationalism in the postwar era when the U. S. exerted some influence on the course of events.

486 Gardiner, Arthur Z. "Point Four and the Arab World," Middle East Journal, 4 (1950), 296-306.

This very compact essay presents an overview of the Point Four program, concentrating on its purposes, criticisms of the program, motives of the U. S., the need for the program, and the opportunity for American capital investment in the Middle East.

487 Gardner, Lloyd C. Architects of Illusion: Men and Ideas in American Foreign Policy, 1941-1949. Chicago: Quadrangle, 1970.

This author views the origins of the Cold War in Iran as a Soviet response to an American aggressive move to acquire an oil concession.

488 ________. "From Liberation to Containment, 1945-1953," in William Appleman Williams, ed., From Colony to Empire: Essays in the History of American Foreign Relations. New York: Wiley, 1972.

Concludes that economic motivations underlay the enunciation of the Truman Doctrine. Access to Middle-Eastern oil was a factor to be considered.

489 Garrett, James Madison, II. "Assistance to Turkey as an Instrument of United States Foreign Policy, with Emphasis on Military Assistance, 1947-1955." Ph. D. dissertation, Columbia University, 1960. (DA 21, p1990)

An analysis of assistance to Turkey that concludes that U. S. policy-makers used this as a tool in the power struggle with the Soviets.

490 Gartner, Joseph F. "America's Defense Policy in the Middle East, 1953-1958." Ph. D. dissertation, University of Chicago, 1962. (X 1962, p182, ADD) [Abstract not available.]

491 Gerteiny, Alfred George. "The Concept of Positive Neutralism in the United Arab Republic." Ph. D. dissertation, St. Johns University, 1963. (Index, 1962, p118, ADD) [Abstract not available.]

492 Glassman, Jon David. "Arms for the Arabs: The Soviet Union and War in the Middle East." Ph. D. dissertation, Columbia University, 1976. (DA 37, p6038)

This study examines the quantity and quality of Soviet weapons delivered, the military supervision provided, and the causes for Soviet actions.

493 Gurpinar, Nevzat. "Short-Term Agricultural Coopera-

tive Credit in the United States and Turkey and Suggestions for the Improvement of the Turkish System." Ph. D. dissertation, Ohio State University, 1950. (W 1950, p140, DDAU)

Using the American experience in extending agricultural short-term credit, the author presents a case for the improvement of the Turkish system.

494 Hackley, Lloyd V. "Soviet Behavior in the Middle East as a Function of Change, 1950-1970." Ph. D. dissertation, University of North Carolina, 1976. (DA 37, p4340)

The Soviet Union and the United States were inexperienced in dealing with client states and were compelled to evolve new behavior patterns in international relations.

495 Hahn, Lorna Joan. "North Africa: Nationalism to Nationhood." Ph. D. dissertation, University of Pennsylvania, 1962. (DA 24, p5521)

This study discusses nationalism in the Maghreb in the post-World War II era.

496 Hakim, George. "Point Four and the Middle East," Middle East Journal, 4 (1950), 183-95.

This essay presents the purposes of Point Four and some of the problems incurred in implementing the program.

497 Haley, P. Edward. "Britain and the Middle East," in Tareq Y. Ismael, ed., The Middle East and World Politics. Syracuse, N. Y.: Syracuse University Press, 1974.

Discusses Britain's declining role in the Middle East in the post-World War II period.

498 Hall, Luella J. The United States and Morocco, 1776-1956. Metuchen, N. J.: Scarecrow Press, 1971.

Accounts for the rise of Moroccan nationalism in the period following World War II.

499 Hamburger, Robert Lee. "Franco-American Relations, 1940-1962: The Role of United States anti-Colonialism and anti-Communism in the Formulation of United States Policy on the Algerian Question." Ph. D. dissertation, Notre Dame University, 1970. (DA 32, p519)

The U. S. was cautious in abetting anti-colonialism because of the increasingly hostile Soviet attitude toward the changing Middle East in the postwar ear.

500 Harbutt, Fraser J. "The Fulton Speech and the Iran Crisis of 1946: A Turning Point in American Foreign Policy." Ph. D. dissertation, University of California, Berkeley, 1976. (DA 37, p6011)

The confused American policy began to take form following Winston Churchill's Fulton speech. The incident marked a turning point for U. S. policy vis-à-vis Iran and the Soviet Union and was more decisive than the Truman Doctrine.

501 Harris, George S. "A Political History of Turkey, 1945-1950." Ph. D. dissertation, Harvard University, 1957. (X 1957, p110, ADD) [Abstract not available.]

502 ________. Troubled Alliance: Turkish-American Problems in Historical Perspective, 1945-1971. Stanford, Calif.: Hoover Institution on War, Revolution and Peace, 1972.

This writer suggests that U. S. policy was already supportive of Turkey prior to the enunciation of the Truman Doctrine. An excellent description of the evolution of U. S. policy.

503 Harris, Jonathan. "Communist Strategy Toward the 'National Bourgeoisie' in Asia and the Middle East." Ph. D. dissertation, Columbia University, 1966.

Treats Soviet efforts to develop a coherent policy toward the Middle East in the postwar era.

504 Harsaghy, Fred Joseph. "The Administration of American Cultural Projects Abroad: A Developmental Study with Case Histories of Community Relations in Administering Educational and Informational Projects in Japan and Saudi Arabia." Ph. D. dissertation, New York University, 1965. (DA 27, p1899)

This work attempts a case study of U. S. cultural projects in a number of communities in Saudi Arabia.

505 Hatzilambrou, Lambros. "Soviet Foreign Policy in the Eastern Mediterranean: A Systematic Approach." Ph. D. dissertation, Howard University, 1976. (DA 37, p4603)

Assesses Soviet policy in the Eastern Mediterranean and concludes that the Soviets have effected a major disturbance in the area by their support of various Arab regimes.

506 Helseth, William Arthur. "The United States and

Turkey: Their Relations from 1784 to 1962." Ph.D. dissertation, Fletcher School of Law and Diplomacy, 1962.

Describes the evolution of policy from the end of World War II through the enunciation of the Truman Doctrine to Turkey's joining NATO.

507 Hess, Gary R. "The Iranian Crisis of 1945-1946," *Political Science Quarterly*, 89 (March 1974), 117-46.

This essay surveys U.S. support for Iran and claims that it was a "confluence of national security and domestic considerations that caused the American government to take the tough stand that led to one of the first United States-Soviet conflicts of the cold war."

508 Horowitz, David. *The Free World Colossus: A Critique of American Foreign Policy in the Cold War.* New York: Hill and Wang, 1956.

A revisionist study that concludes that American foreign aid was extended to the Middle East and elsewhere as a means of economic penetration and political domination.

509 Hoskins, Halford L. *The Middle East: Problem Area in World Politics.* New York: Macmillan, 1957.

Discusses the evolution of U.S. policy in the early Cold War era, and asserts that it was designed to contain Soviet incursion into the region. Provides a good analysis of U.S. foreign aid to the Middle East.

510 ________. "Some Aspects of the Security Problem in the Middle East," *American Political Science Review*, 47 (1953), 188-98.

Views the enunciation of the Truman Doctrine as a hallmark in the course of increasing American involvement in the Middle East.

511 Hourani, Albert. "The Decline of the West in the Middle East," *International Affairs*, XXIX (January 1953), 22-42; and (April 1953), 156-83.

Declares that the Arabs' espousal of anti-Western sentiment was a problem to Anglo-American military planners who worked on a defense of the Middle East. Sentiment based on nationalism and anti-colonialism.

512 Howard, Harry N. "The Bicentennial in American-Turkish Relations," *Middle East Journal*, 30 (summer 1976), 291-310.

Describes the enunciation of the Truman Doctrine and the fashioning of the troubled Turkish-American alliance.

513 ________. Turkey, the Straits and U. S. Policy. Baltimore: Johns Hopkins University Press, 1974.

Asserts that U. S. concern over Turkish control of the Straits was central to U. S. support for Turkey in the immediate Cold War era.

514 ________. "The United States and the Middle East," in Tareq Y. Ismael, ed., The Middle East in World Politics. Syracuse, N. Y.: Syracuse University Press, 1974.

A brief essay that highlights U. S. interests and problems in the postwar Middle East.

515 ________. "The United States and the Problem of the Turkish Straits," Middle East Journal, 1 (January 1947), 59-72.

This essay provides a summary of American involvement at the Straits and asserts that the Soviet effort to dominate the Straits led to U. S. opposition and support for Turkey.

516 ________. "The United States and the Soviet Union in the Middle East," in Ernest Jackh, ed., Background in the Middle East. Ithaca, N. Y.: Cornell University Press, 1952.

Provides a brief sketch of the growing Soviet-American conflict in the postwar Middle East.

517 Hurewitz, J. C. Middle East Dilemmas: The Background of United States Policy. New York: Harper, 1953.

This author provides a classic study that concludes that American policy-makers had basic dilemmas in making policy because of the association with Britain, the growth of Arab nationalism, and association with Israel.

518 ________. Middle East Politics: The Military Dimension. New York: Praeger, 1972.

U. S. policy to contain Russia grew slowly from crisis to crisis and U. S. arms aid was designed to contain the Soviet thrust at the Middle East.

519 ________. Soviet-American Rivalry in the Middle East. New York: Praeger, 1969.

The purpose of this work is to examine Soviet-American rivalry in terms of military might, economic leverage, cultural penetration, and exchange.

520 Ibrahim, Saad Eddin Mohamed. "Political Attitudes of an Emerging Elite: A Case Study of the Arab Students in the United States." Ph. D. dissertation, University of Washington, 1968. (DA 29, p2380)

The purpose of this study is to describe, analyze, and explain the ideological orientations of Arab students in the United States.

521 Ismael, Tareq Y., ed. The Middle East in World Politics. Syracuse, N. Y.: Syracuse University Press, 1974.

This collection of essays provides sweeping insights into the U. S. role in the Cold War in the Middle East.

522 Issa, Mahmoud K. "Trade between Egypt and the United States." Ph. D. dissertation, University of Minnesota, 1953. (DA 13, p690)

American trade with Egypt continued to grow in the postwar era.

523 Jackh, Ernest, ed. Background of the Middle East. Ithaca, N. Y.: Cornell University Press, 1952.

This collection of essays is important to an understanding of U. S. -Middle East relations in the Cold War period.

524 ________. "The Geostrategic Uniqueness of the Middle East," in his Background ... (item 523).

Demonstrates that the Middle East became important to American national security interests after 1947, because the vital communication-transportation routes and reserves of oil fitted into this country's national interests.

525 al-Jazairi, Mohamed Zayyan. "Saudi Arabia: A Diplomatic History, 1924-1964." Ph. D. dissertation, University of Utah, 1971. (DA 32, p868)

This is a detailed account of the history of a country that looms large in American vital interests in view of the growing energy crisis.

526 Jones, Joseph Marion. The Fifteen Weeks. New York: Harcourt, Brace & World, 1955.

This important study presents much of the activity in high levels of government that preceded the enunciation of the Truman Doctrine and reveals the importance of the State Department bureaucracy in policy-making.

527 Kabbani, Rashid. "Morocco: From Protectorate to Independence, 1912-1956." Ph.D. dissertation, American University, 1957. (DA 17, p2051)
Describes the continued growth of Moroccan nationalism in the postwar era.

528 Kazemian, Gholam Hossein. "The Impact of United States Technical and Financial Aid on the Rural Development of Iran." Ph.D. dissertation, American University, 1967. (DA 28, p3328)
This investigation studies the overall effects of the U.S. technical assistance programs in the upgrading of farming technology in the rural areas of Iran.

529 Kennan, George F. Memoirs, 1925-1950. 2 vols. New York: Little, Brown, 1967.
Offers pungent criticism of the broad scope of the Truman Doctrine that is typical of the realist critique of American diplomacy.

530 Kermani, Taghi. "The United States Participation in the Economic Development of the Middle East, with Special Reference to Iran, Iraq, and Jordan." Ph.D. dissertation, University of Nebraska, 1959. (DA 20, p550)
An analysis of American foreign aid which sought to bring about political stability and social reforms so necessary for progress.

531 Kerwin, Harry Wayne. "An Analysis and Evaluation of the Program of Technical Assistance to Education Conducted in Iran by the Government of the United States from 1952-1962." Ph.D. dissertation, American University, 1964. (DA 26, p5820)
The purpose of this work is to review the technical assistance offered to the Iranian education program from 1952 to 1962.

532 Khadduri, Majid. "The Problem of Regional Security in the Middle East: An Appraisal," Middle East Journal, XI (winter 1957), 12-22.
Surveys the many factors that militated against the erection of a regional security structure.

533 ________. Republican Iraq. London: Oxford Univer-

sity Press, 1969.
Provides interesting background to the course of Iraqi development in the postwar era.

534 Khouri, Fred John. "The Arab States in the United Nations: A Study of Political Relations, 1945-1950." Ph. D. dissertation, Columbia University, 1953. (DA 14, p177)
This is a study of Arab actions and reactions to those political issues of paramount importance to the Arab world.

535 Khoury, Angela Jurdak. "The Foreign Policy of Lebanon." Ph. D. dissertation, American University, 1968. (DA 29, p947)
This dissertation studies and evaluates the historical background leading to Lebanese independence and analyzes her foreign policy from 1943 to 1963.

536 Kianfar, Mehdi. "Arab Unity and Collective Security of the Middle East." Ph. D. dissertation, American University, 1956. (Index, 1955, 126, ADD) [Abstract not available.]

537 Kirk, George E. The Middle East, 1945-50. London: Oxford University Press, 1954.
An excellent study of the period that tends to view American policy from a British perspective. Views American policy as aggressive and determined by aspirations of economic aggrandizement.

538 Knight, Jonathan. "American Statecraft and the 1946 Black Sea Straits Controversy," Political Science Quarterly, 90 (fall 1975), 451-75.
This essay treats the American support for Turkey during this crisis and provides a good view of the foundation of the United States Sixth Fleet which played such an important role in U.S. diplomacy.

539 Kolko, Joyce, and Gabriel Kolko. The Limits of Power: The World and United States Foreign Policy, 1945-1954. New York: Harper & Row, 1972.
This is a revisionist study that asserts that American postwar Middle-Eastern policy was aggressive and evoked a Soviet response that initiated the Cold War.

540 al-Kubaisi, Basil Raouf. "The Arab Nationalist Move-

ment, 1951-1971: From Pressure Group to Socialist Party." Ph.D. dissertation, American University, 1971. (DA 33, p792)

This account treats the conditions affecting the emergence of Arab Nationalists Movement (ANM) and the impact which that movement has had upon the goals of the Arab nationalist movement in general.

541 Kuniholm, Bruce R. "The United States, the Northern Tier, and the Origins of the Cold War: Great Power Conflict and Diplomacy in Iran, Turkey, and Greece." Ph.D. dissertation, Duke University, 1976. (DA 38, p2304)

The purpose of this work is to demonstrate how historical development along the Northern Tier evolved into the postwar conflict between the United States and the Soviet Union.

542 LaCouture, Jean. Nasser: A Biography. New York: Knopf, 1973.

An excellent study of a historical figure who loomed large in American Middle-Eastern policy considerations and alternatives.

543 LaFeber, Walter. America, Russia, and the Cold War, 1945-1960. New York: Wiley, 1967.

This is a revisionist critique of the origins of the Cold War.

544 Lederer, Ivo J., and Wayne S. Vucinich, eds. The Soviet Union and the Middle East: The Post-World War II Era. Stanford, Calif.: Hoover Institution Press, 1974.

A collection of essays that highlights Soviet foreign-policy objectives in the postwar Middle East.

545 Lenczowski, George. Middle East in World Affairs. Ithaca, N.Y.: Cornell University Press, 1956.

Provides a good general background to the area during the early years of the Cold War.

546 ________. "Tradition and Reform in Saudi Arabia," Current History, 52 (February 1967), 98-104.

Provides an insight into the historical background of a nation with whom the U.S. has vital interests.

547 Lens, Sidney. The Forging of the American Empire

from the Revolution to Vietnam: A History of American Imperialism. New York: Crowell, 1971.

A revisionist study that views the origins of the Cold War in the Middle East in terms of Soviet responses to American aggressive actions.

548 Lewis, Bernard. The Middle East and the West. Bloomington: Indiana University Press, 1965.

Suggests that American defense of the Middle East was impaired by its association with imperial Britain and by a divergence of Eastern and Western civilizations with their different value systems.

549 ________. "The Middle Eastern Reaction to Soviet Pressures," Middle East Journal, 10 (spring 1956), 125-37.

Claims the Arabs are anti-Western and apply a double standard to the West and to Russia, because the clash of civilizations and imperialism color their world view.

550 Lewis, Jesse W., Jr. The Strategic Balance in the Mediterranean. Washington, D.C.: American Enterprise Institute for Public Policy Research, 1976.

An excellent study of the complex strategic considerations necessary to a formulation of an American Middle-East defense posture against Soviet incursion into the region.

551 Libby, Ruthven E. "Strategic Military Importance of the Middle East," in Philip W. Thayer, ed., Tensions in the Middle East. Baltimore: Johns Hopkins University Press, 1958.

Identifies the strategic importance of the Middle East in terms of important mineral resources necessary to Western industrial nations.

552 Madadi, Gol-Agha. "American Foreign Policy Through Alliance and Its Application in the Middle East." Ph.D. dissertation, Indiana University, 1967. (DA 28, p4693)

This study demonstrates that American policy in the Cold-War era was based on alliance to achieve collective security in the Middle East.

553 Malone, Joseph J. "America and the Arabian Peninsula: The First Two Hundred Years," Middle East Journal, 30 (summer 1976), 406-24.

Demonstrates the importance of Saudi Arabia to the United States in the postwar era.

554 Mansour, Hussein Omar. "The Discovery of Oil and Its Impact on the Industrialization of Saudi Arabia." Ph.D. dissertation, Arizona University, 1973. (DA 34, p2522)

Demonstrates the impact of American oil development on the economy of Saudi Arabia.

555 Mark, Eduard M. "Allied Relations in Iran, 1941-1947: The Origins of a Cold War Crisis," Wisconsin Magazine of History, 59 (autumn 1975), 51-63.

Asserts that Russian aggressive actions in Iran were in response to an earlier American quest for an oil concession in that country's northern reaches.

556 Marlowe, John. Arab Nationalism and British Imperialism: A Study in Power Politics. London: Cresset Press, 1961.

Traces the rise of Arab nationalism and relates it to the British imperial position in the Middle East.

557 Masannat, George Suleiman. "Aspects of American Policy in the Arab Middle East, 1947-1957, with Emphasis on United States Egyptian Relations." Ph.D. dissertation, University of Oklahoma, 1964. (DA 25, p4803)

This study is an attempt to describe American-Egyptian relations since 1947, to analyze the underlying rationale behind policies, and to emphasize American efforts to prevent Soviet intrusions in the Arab Middle East.

558 Millis, Walter, and E. S. Duffield, eds. The Forrestal Diaries. New York: Viking, 1951.

This diary provides an insight into Secretary Forrestal's reasons for founding the Sixth Fleet, the high-level talks necessary to achieve this goal, and the early operations of the Fleet.

559 Murad, Ahmad Asad. "Egypt's Economic Relations with the Soviet Bloc and the United States." Ph.D. dissertation, University of Wisconsin, 1961. (DA 22, p1846)

This work concentrates on the American and Soviet economic rivalry in Egypt with a view to influencing that country's policy.

560 Muzaffar, Jamal E. "American-Soviet Policy in the Arab East, 1939-1957." Ph.D. dissertation, George-

town University, 1964. (Index, 1963, p124, ADD) [Abstract not available.]

561 Nasir, Sari Jamil. "The Image of the Arab in American Popular Culture." Ph. D. dissertation, University of Illinois, 1962. (DA 23, p4003)
This study investigates the portrayal of the Arab in American popular culture with emphasis on motion pictures and men's magazines.

562 Nolte, R. H. "The United States and the Middle East," in Georgianna G. Stevens, ed., _The United States and the Middle East._ Englewood Cliffs, N. J.: Prentice-Hall, 1964.
Discusses American efforts to erect a defense structure in the Middle East.

563 Nuseibeh, Hazem Zaki. "The Ideas of Arab Nationalism." Ph. D. dissertation, Princeton University, 1954. (DA 14, p1787)
An account of Arab nationalism which views it in relationship to the process of westernization.

564 Oguzkan, Abdulbaki Turhan. "The University Extension Movement in the United States and its Implications for the Middle East Technical University, Turkey." Ph. D. dissertation, Ohio State University, 1965. (DA 27, p371)
Suggests that several ideas were developed in the growth of extension movement in the United States that can be utilized in Turkey.

565 O'Hali, Abdulaziz A. "Saudi Arabia in the United Nations General Assembly, 1946-1970." Ph. D. dissertation, Claremont Graduate School, 1974. (DA 36, p1792)
Attempts to determine Saudi Arabia's degree of participation in the General Assembly plenary meetings.

566 Partin, Michael Wayne. "United States-Iranian Relations, 1945-47." Ph. D. dissertation, North Texas State University, 1977. (DA 38, p4331)
This is an analysis of relations in a crucial time in the early years of the Cold War.

567 Patai, Raphael. _The Arab Mind._ New York: Scribner's, 1973.

This study presents some interesting observations on the operation of the Arab mind, some of which must be accepted with reservation.

568 Patrick, Robert Bayard. "Iran's Emergence as a Middle Eastern Power." Ph.D. dissertation, University of Utah, 1973. (DA 34, p2001)

An attempt to gauge the relative weight of Iran's influence in recent crises and to formulate conclusions relative to likely future developments.

569 Peck, Malcolm Cameron. "Saudi Arabia in United States Foreign Policy to 1958: A Study in the Sources and Determinants of American Policy." Ph.D. dissertation, Fletcher School of Law and Diplomacy, 1970. (X 1970, p286, ADD) [Abstract not available.]

570 Perry, Glenn Earl. "United States Relations with Egypt, 1951-1963: Egyptian Neutralism and the American Alignment Policy." Ph.D. dissertation, University of Virginia, 1964. (DA 25, p3670)

This study explains the deterioration of U.S.-Egyptian relations which thwarted the American attempt to erect a defense structure in the Middle East.

571 Pfau, Richard Anthony. "Containment in Iran, 1946: The Shift to an Active Policy," Diplomatic History, 1 (fall 1977), 359-372.

Indicates the manner in which an American diplomat shored up an Iranian government standing athwart Soviet attempts to obtain a sphere of influence in that country.

572 ________. "The Legal Status of American Forces in Iran," Middle East Journal, 28 (spring 1974), 141-53.

This essay describes the Status of Forces Agreement covering American troops in Iran and the State Department effort to obtain exclusive jurisdiction over its forces.

573 ________. "The United States and Iran, 1941-1947." Ph.D. dissertation, University of Virginia, 1975. (DA 36, p6245)

This work chronicles U.S. support for Iran in 1946 when the Soviets attempted to establish a satellite state in Iran and suggests that Ambassador Allen's efforts were a determining factor.

574 Polk, William R. "The Nature of Modernization: The

Middle East and North Africa," Foreign Affairs, 44 (October 1965), 100-110.

This essay gives an account of the "new men" that emerged in the Middle East to create a new society in the Middle Eastern region in the postwar era. Modernization was their goal.

575 ________. The United States and the Arab World. Cambridge, Mass.: Harvard University Press, 1965.

An excellent study that is most necessary to an understanding of the American role in the Arab world in the postwar era.

576 Quandt, William B. "United States Policy in the Middle East: Constraints and Choices," in Paul Y. Hammond and Sidney S. Alexander, eds., Political Dynamics in the Middle East. New York: American Elsevier, 1972.

This is a comprehensive essay that characterizes the American policy of defense of the Middle East as a failure. An excellent study that provides an overview of U.S.-Mideast policy from 1945 to the late 1960s.

577 Raleigh, Edward A. "An Inquiry into the Influences of American Democracy on the Arab Middle East, 1819-1958." Ph.D. dissertation, Pacific University, 1960. (X 1960, p111, ADD) [Abstract not available.]

578 Ramazani, Rouhollah K. "Iran and the United States: An Experiment in Enduring Friendship," Middle East Journal, 30 (summer 1976), 322-34.

This account describes the growing partnership between the United States and Iran in the postwar era.

579 ________. Iran's Foreign Policy, 1941-1973: A Study of Foreign Policy in Modernizing Nations. Charlottesville: University Press of Virginia, 1975.

A comprehensive work that views American policy from an Iranian perspective. Focuses on U.S. opposition to Soviet thrust into Iran in 1946.

580 Reitzel, William. "The Importance of the Mediterranean," in Jackh, Ernest, ed., The Background in the Middle East. Ithaca, N.Y.: Cornell University Press, 1952.

Asserts that the Middle East and the Mediterranean became vital to American security during the Cold War era.

581 Ricks, Eldin. "United States Economic Assistance to Israel, 1949-1960." Ph.D. dissertation, Dropsie University, 1970. (X 1970, p73, ADD) [Abstract not available.]

582 Rifai, Abdul Halim. "The Eisenhower Administration and the Defense of the Arab Middle East." Ph.D. dissertation, American University, 1966. (DA 27, p3101)
Concludes that the Baghdad Pact failed as evidenced by all of the Arab states leaving the U.S. security system and/or rejecting it outright, a failure due to historical, economic, psychological, and political factors.

583 Rogow, Arnold. James Forrestal: A Study of Personality, Politics and Policy. New York: Macmillan, 1963.
Author provides an analysis of Forrestal's motives in forming the Sixth Fleet in response to Soviet policy in the Middle East.

584 al-Rubaiy, Abdul Amir. "Nationalism and Education: A Study of Nationalistic Tendencies in Iraq Education." Ph.D. dissertation, Kent State University, 1972. (DA 33, p5027)
This dissertation examines the relationship between education and the forces of nationalism in Iraq.

585 Rubinstein, Alvin Z. "The Soviet Union in the Middle East," Current History, 63 (October 1972), 165-69.
Describes the growing Soviet role in this ever-changing region.

586 Rustow, Dankwart A. "Defense of the Near East," Foreign Affairs, XXXIV (January 1956), 271-86.
This article describes factors such as oil, geography, and regional disunity that bear on the effort to improvise a defense policy in the Middle East.

587 Sachar, Howard M. Europe Leaves the Middle East, 1936-1954. New York: Knopf, 1972.
Describes the advent of a full-blown U.S. Middle-East policy that developed as the European powers departed from the area in the postwar period.

588 el-Saghieh, Khaled I. "Nationalism in Morocco: A Study of Recent Developments with Special Reference to

the Moroccan Question in the United Nations." Ph. D. dissertation, American University, 1955. (22, p229, DDAU) [Abstract not available.]

589 Samii, Cyrus B. "The Arab-Asian Bloc in the United Nations." Ph. D. dissertation, University of Kansas, 1955. (22, p234, DDAU) [Abstract not available.]

590 Sam'o, Elias. "The Arab States in the United Nations: A Study of Voting Behavior." Ph. D. dissertation, American University, 1967. (DA 28, p1489)
Examines 72 votes to determine Arab behavior on questions of great moment during the Cold War era.

591 Sands, William. "Middle East Background," in Georgianna Stevens, ed., _The United States and the Middle East._ Englewood Cliffs, N.J.: Prentice-Hall, 1964.
Describes the flow of nationalism among the Arab states and their struggle for modernization.

592 Shaheen, Ghaleb S. "The Foreign Policy of Lebanon." Ph. D. dissertation, Syracuse University, 1959. (DA 20, p2879)
Describes this country's effort to maintain its sovereignty while working through the League of Arab States and cooperating with the U. S.

593 Shaker, Fatina Amin. "Modernization of the Developing Nations: The Case of Saudi Arabia." Ph. D. dissertation, Purdue University, 1972. (DA 34, p433)
This study investigates the struggle for modernization in Saudi Arabia, a land which retains a conservative monarchy and many traditions at variance with modernity.

594 Sheehan, M. K. _Iran: Impact of United States Interests and Policies, 1941-1954._ Brooklyn, N. Y.: Theo Gaus, 1972.
Describes the evolution of U. S. policy in Iran from one of disinterest to actual support in the Cold War era.

595 Smith, Gaddis. _Dean Acheson._ New York: Cooper Square Publishers, 1972.
Focuses on this cold warrior's efforts to formulate a policy that would meet the demands of the postwar era.

596 Smolansky, Oles M. "The Soviet Union and the Arab

East, 1947-1957: A Study in Diplomatic Relations." Ph.D. dissertation, Columbia University, 1959. (DA 20, p1424)

This study of Arab-Soviet relations concludes that the Soviets between 1947 and 1957 desired to eliminate the West from the Middle East and to dominate that region.

597 Spain, James W. "Middle East Defense: A New Approach," Middle East Journal, VIII (summer 1954), 251-66.

This essay describes the adverse Arab reaction to the Baghdad Pact which departed from previous efforts to erect a defense structure based on the Suez.

598 Speiser, Ephraim. The United States and the Near East. Cambridge, Mass.: Harvard University Press, 1952.

This early study of the subject focuses on the evolutionary process of American policy in the postwar era when national security interests took precedence over all other considerations.

599 Spielman, William C. The United States in the Middle East: A Study of American Foreign Policy. New York: Pageant Press, 1959.

A brief study that provides a bare outline of the transition of American policy in the postwar era when national security interests became paramount.

600 Stevens, Georgianna G. "Arab Neutralism and Bandung," Middle East Journal, 11 (1957), 139-52.

Describes the adherence of Arab states to neutralism as a response to the American effort to erect a defense structure in the Middle East.

601 ________, ed. The United States and the Middle East. Englewood Cliffs, N.J.: Prentice-Hall, 1964.

This collection of essays is necessary to an understanding of the American role in the defense of the Middle East in the Cold War era.

602 Stookey, Robert W. America and the Arab States: An Uneasy Encounter. New York: Wiley, 1975.

Describes the climate of Arab nationalism in which the U.S. attempted to create a defense structure and the Arab reaction to this effort.

603 Strausz-Hupé, Robert. "The United States and the

Middle East," in Philip W. Thayer, ed., Tensions in the Middle East. Baltimore: Johns Hopkins Press, 1958.

This essay views American Middle-Eastern policy as an effort to replace Britain in the regional conflict in order to bar Soviet intrusion into the region.

604 Swomley, John M. American Empire: The Political Ethics of Twentieth Century Conquest. New York: Macmillan, 1970.

This is a revisionist study that views American foreign aid in the Middle East in terms of a quest for economic and political hegemony.

605 Tabari, Keyvan. "Iran's Policies Toward the United States during the Anglo-Russian Occupation, 1941-1946." Ph. D. dissertation, Columbia University, 1967. (DA 28, p1881)

Describes the evolution of American policy from the simple effort to protect traditional American interests to the complex desire to contain a Soviet intrusion into the country.

606 Tansky, Leo. "Comparative Impact of United States and U. S. S. R. Economic Aid to Underdeveloped Countries with Special Reference to India, Turkey, and the United Arab Republic." Ph. D. dissertation, American University, 1964. (DA 26, p746)

This study investigates the contribution of economic aid programs to determine the impact of these programs on the public-private investment relationship in the respective countries.

607 Tarr, David W. "American Power and Diplomacy in the Middle East." Ph. D. dissertation, University of Chicago, 1961. (X 1961, p160, ADD) [Abstract not available.]

608 Thayer, Philip W., ed. Tensions in the Middle East. Baltimore: Johns Hopkins Press, 1958.

This collection of essays bears upon the U. S. effort to create a defense posture in the postwar Middle East.

609 Thomas, Lewis V., and Richard N. Frye. The United States and Turkey and Iran. Cambridge, Mass.: Harvard University Press, 1951.

Describes the emergence of an American Middle-East defense policy in these two countries in the immediate postwar era.

610 Torrey, Gordon H. *Syrian Politics and the Military.* Columbus: Ohio State University Press, 1964.
Provides good background material for the consideration of Syrian foreign policy during the early Cold-War era.

611 Truman, Harry S. *Memoirs.* 2 vols. New York: Doubleday, 1955.
This readable memoir provides interesting insights into the foreign policy-making process in the early Cold-War period when problems and events created the need to formulate a new policy toward the Middle East.

612 Turner, Jack Justin. "Arab-Asian Positive Neutralism and United States Foreign Policy." Ph.D. dissertation, University of Kentucky, 1969. (DA 30, p3532)
This study describes the problem that United States policy-makers had with those Arab states that opted for neutralism and a position outside the American Middle-East defense structure.

613 Ulam, Adam. *Expansion and Coexistence: The History of Soviet Foreign Policy, 1917-1967.* New York: Praeger, 1968.
Focuses on Soviet policy in the postwar era and shows it to have pursued an aggressive course which provoked an American response that aimed to contain a Soviet incursion into the region.

614 Utley, Freda. *Will the Middle East Go West?* Chicago: Henry Regnery, 1957.
Asserts that the American policy of defense was impaired by association with Great Britain whose imperial past compromised the American position. Too, the U.S. upheld traditional regimes that were associated with the old social order.

615 Warne, William E. *Mission for Peace: Point 4 in Iran.* New York: Bobbs-Merrill, 1956.
An excellent study that concentrates on Point Four objectives and successes in Iran. Concludes that successes were widespread and a vindication of the program's advocates.

616 Weems, Miner Lile. "The Propaganda Struggle in the Middle East, 1955-1958." Ph.D. dissertation, Georgetown University, 1962. (Index, 1961, p180, ADD) [Abstract not available.]

617 Weisband, Edward A. "Anticipating the Cold War:

Turkish Foreign Relations, 1943-1945." Ph. D. dissertation, Johns Hopkins University, 1970. (DA 34, p844)

Sets forth the variables that impinged on Turkish foreign policy-making just prior to the advent of the Cold War.

618 Wendzel, Robert Leroy. "United States National Interests and the Middle East, 1955-1958." Ph. D. dissertation, University of Florida, 1965. (DA 26, p4790)

Concentrates on the course of United States relations with Egypt in the aftermath of the formation of the Baghdad Pact.

619 Wilber, Donald N. Iran: Past and Present. Princeton, N. J.: Princeton University Press, 1948.

Provides a brief background of the events relative to Iran's role in the Cold War.

620 Xydis, Stephen. "The American Naval Visits to Greece and the Eastern Mediterranean in 1946." Ph. D. dissertation, Columbia University, 1956.

This dissertation provides an account of early American naval visits to the Middle East in the dawning years of the Cold War.

621 _______. "The Genesis of the 6th Fleet," U. S. Naval Institute Proceedings, 84 (August 1958), 41-50.

This essay describes the events leading up to the founding of the Sixth Fleet to protect American interests in the Middle East.

622 _______. Greece and the Great Powers, 1944-1947: Prelude to the "Truman Doctrine." Thessaloniki: Institute for Balkan Studies, 1963.

An excellent study that sets forth the events concerning Greece and Turkey that preceded the enunciation of the Truman Doctrine. Concentrates on the factors relating to the abrupt change in U. S. policy vis-à-vis the Middle East.

623 Yale, William. The Near East: A Modern History. Ann Arbor: University of Michigan Press, 1958.

Provides a sketch of the course of events that involved the U. S. in the postwar Middle East.

624 Younis, Adele Linda. "The Coming of the Arabic-Speaking People to the United States." Ph. D. disser-

tation, Boston University, 1961. (DA 22, p1151)

Focuses on the arrival of an ethnic group which has an interest in the formation of an American foreign policy for the Middle East.

625 Zakhem, Samir Hanna. "Lebanon between East and West: Big Power Politics in the Middle East." Ph. D. dissertation, University of Colorado, 1970. (DA 31, p3006)

Describes problems relative to a small state caught up in the complexities of the Cold War in the Middle East.

626 Zindani, Abdul Wahed Aziz. "Arab Politics in the United Nations." Ph. D. dissertation, Notre Dame University, 1976. (DA 37, p3891)

Deals with Arab behavior in the United Nations where many problems of the postwar Middle East were settled.

M

ISRAEL AND THE ARAB-ISRAELI CONFLICT TO 1955

627 Abboushi, W. F. The Angry Arabs. Philadelphia: Westminster Press, 1974.
The author points out the Zionist influence on U. S. policy-making, but declares that the growing American economic dependence on Arab oil is a factor that must be considered.

628 Abu-Lughod, Ibrahim, and Baha Abu-Laban, eds. Settler Regimes in Africa and the Arab World: The Illusion of Endurance. Wilmette, Ill.: Medina University Press International, 1974.
A collection of essays that presents an Arab perception of the creation of Israel, one that views this act as a piece of European imperialism.

629 Acheson, Dean. Present at the Creation: My Years at the State Department. New York: Norton, 1969.
Asserts that President Truman had tight control over policy-making vis-à-vis the Palestine question.

630 Agwani, Mohammed Shafi. The United States and the Arab World, 1945-1952. Aligarh, India: Institute of Islamic Studies, 1955.
States that Truman acted contrary to American national interests in supporting partition of Palestine.

631 Arakie, Margaret. The Broken Sword of Justice: America, Israel, and the Palestine Tragedy. London: Quartet Books, 1973.
Points to the powerful Zionist influence on the U. S. government in the partition of Palestine.

632 Badeau, John S. American Approach to the Arab World. New York: Harper, 1968.
Suggests that the American tie to Israel prevents the

initiation of an American Middle-Eastern policy that seeks goals in the national interest. Sees Israel as a liability to the U. S.

633 Balboni, Alan Richard. "A Study of the Efforts of the American Zionists to Influence the Formulation and Conduct of United States Policy during the Roosevelt, Truman, and Eisenhower Administrations." Ph. D. dissertation, Brown University, 1973. (DA 34, p6056)
Truman acted for Israel and contrary to best advice from the State, War, and Navy Departments due to an articulate public opinion and strong support for Zionist goals among key figures in American society.

634 Batal, James. "Truman Chapters on the Middle East," Middle East Forum, XXXI (December 1956), 11-13 et seq.
President Truman's support for Zionist goals was based on political expedience according to this author.

635 Bickerton, Ian J. "President Truman's Recognition of Israel," American Jewish Historical Quarterly, LVIII (December 1968), 173-239.
Declares that President Truman's policy vis-à-vis Israel was balanced between the opposing forces of Zionism and the State Department and that his policy fell far short of Zionist goals.

636 Bose, T. C. The Superpowers and the Middle East. New York: Asia Publishing House, 1973.
Focuses attention on the plight of the Arab refugees following the creation of Israel.

637 Botsai, Sarah Lillian. "The United States and the Palestine Refugees." Ph. D. dissertation, American University, 1972. (DA 33, p4508)
This study analyzes the effects of American support both for Israeli sovereignty and for justice for the Palestinians in the pursuit of regional stability.

638 Brook, David. "The United Nations and the Arab-Israeli Armistice System, 1949-1959." Ph. D. dissertation, Columbia University, 1961. (DA 22, p4069)
The purpose of this study is to examine the functioning of the Arab-Israeli armistice system with a view to ascertaining whether this regime has contributed toward a lessening of tensions.

639 Bryson, Thomas A. American Diplomatic Relations with the Middle East, 1784-1975: A Survey. Metuchen, N.J.: Scarecrow Press, 1977.

Views President Truman's support for the creation of Israel as an aberration in the total context of U.S. response to the desires of Middle-Eastern ethnic minorities for self-determination.

640 Campbell, John C. Defense of the Middle East: Problems of American Policy. New York: Harper, 1960.

This author contends that American policy toward Israel is not tied to the national interests, for political considerations were paramount in the decision to create Israel.

641 Crum, Bartley C. Behind the Silken Curtain. New York: Simon & Schuster, 1947.

Critical of American policy toward the Palestine issue, claiming that it has been characterized by duplicity.

642 Davis, John H. The Evasive Peace: A Study of the Zionist/Arab Problem. London: John Murray, 1968.

Discusses the plight of Palestinian refugees in the international context of the Arab-Israeli struggle.

643 Dohse, Michael A. "American Periodicals and the Palestine Triangle, 1936-1947." Ph.D. dissertation, Mississippi State University, 1966. (DA 27, p3395)

This study attempted to determine how objectively the leading non-Jewish American periodicals presented the Palestine problem during the period 1936 to 1947.

644 Ellis, Harry B. Challenge in the Middle East: Communist Influence and American Policy. New York: Ronald Press, 1960.

A critical account of U.S. policy on the Palestine question. Asserts that this policy might result in the loss of the Middle East to Russia.

645 Feis, Herbert. The Birth of Israel: The Tousled Diplomatic Bed. New York: Norton, 1969.

An account of American support for the partition of Palestine. Concludes that politics did force Truman to support Zionist goals.

646 Fisher, Carol A.; and Fred Krinsky. Middle East in Crisis: A Historical and Documentary Review.

Syracuse, N.Y.: Syracuse University Press, 1959.
A narrative account of U.S. support for the partition of Palestine.

647 Fisher, Sydney Nettleton. The Middle East: A History. New York: Knopf, 1960.
Provides a good chapter on the American role in the partition of Palestine.

648 Fishman, Hertzel. "American Protestantism and the State of Israel, 1937-1967." Ph.D. dissertation, New York University, 1972. (1971, p22, ADD) [Abstract not available.]

649 Forsythe, David Prevatt. "The United Nations and the Peaceful Settlement of Disputes: The Case of the Conciliation Commission for Palestine." Ph.D. dissertation, Princeton University, 1968. (DA 29, p2775)
This study draws attention to the United Nations Conciliation Commission for Palestine as a case study of the United Nations role in peacemaking.

650 Frye, Richard N., ed. The Near East and the Great Powers. Port Washington, N.Y.: Kennikat Press, 1951.
Contains two essays that are highly critical of U.S. policy on the creation of Israel.

651 Galbraith, M. Rita Francis. "The Arab-Jewish Conflict in a World Power Setting." Ph.D. dissertation, St. John's University, 1963. (X 1963, p118, ADD) [Abstract not available.]

652 Gama, Abid Husni. "The United Nations and the Palestinian Refugees: An Analysis of the United Nations Relief and Works Agency in the Near East, 1 May 1950-30 June 1971." Ph.D. dissertation, University of Arizona, 1972. (DA 33, p695)
This study describes the efforts of United Nations Relief and Works Agency to implement an economic solution to the Palestine refugee problem.

653 Ganin, Zvi. "The Diplomacy of the Weak: American Zionist Leadership during the Truman Era, 1945-1948." Ph.D. dissertation, Brandeis University, 1975. (DA 36, p480)
The aim of this work is to describe and analyze the

formulation and the effectiveness of Zionist policies on critical issues with reference to Palestine during the Truman years.

654 Gidney, James. "The Middle East: The Last Crusade," West Georgia College: Studies in the Social Sciences, XI (June 1970), 16-29.
This essay is critical of U. S. policy toward the Palestine question, asserting that domestic politics rather than considerations of the national interest determined policy.

655 Golding, David. "United States Policy in Palestine and Israel, 1945-1949." Ph. D. dissertation, New York University, 1961. (DA 27, p1887)
This study places U. S. policy toward Palestine in the context of American foreign policy and concludes that many other factors determined this policy other than domestic politics alone.

656 Gottlieb, Paul H. "The Commonwealth of Nations at the United Nations." Ph. D. dissertation, Boston University, 1962. (DA 23, p1003)
Provides some insights into the Commonwealth of Nations reaction to the Palestine problem.

657 Grand, Samuel. "A History of Zionist Youth Organizations in the United States from Their Inception to 1940." Ph. D. dissertation, Columbia University, 1958. (DA 18, p1777)
Provides a description of these organizations which form a part of the Zionist lobby that brought pressure to bear on the U. S. government in 1947-1948.

658 Gruen, George Emanuel. "Turkey, Israel and the Palestine Question, 1948-1960: A Study in the Diplomacy of Ambivalence." Ph. D. dissertation, Columbia University, 1970. (DA 34, p2737)
This study determines that Turkey's pro-Arab stance on the Palestine-Israel question was determined not by U. S. pressure but by Turkey's national interests.

659 Haddad, William Woodrow. "Arab Editorial Opinion Toward the Palestine Question, 1947-1958." Ph. D. dissertation, Ohio State University, 1970. (DA 31, p4673)
This study is a survey of Arab newspapers and editorials in over 60 newspapers in Lebanon, Syria, Pales-

tine-Jordan, and Egypt, and concludes that the Zionist threat did not unify Arab editorial opinion.

660 Halperin, Samuel. The Political World of American Zionism. Detroit: Wayne State University Press, 1961.
Describes the force of Zionist propaganda to shape Jewish and American public opinion on the Palestine question.

661 Halpern, Ben. The Idea of a Jewish State. Cambridge, Mass.: Harvard University Press, 1969.
Provides little or no treatment of the U.S. role in the creation of Israel.

662 Hamdan, Zuhair. "A Study of the Arab-Israeli Conflict in the United Nations during the Period between 1947 and 1957." Ph.D. dissertation, Union Graduate School, 1976. (DA 37, p6737)
This study examined the effectiveness of Arab policies in the United Nations with respect to Israel in a number of situations calling for political action.

663 Hamlet, Bruce D. "A Comparative Analysis of British Foreign Relations: The Palestine War, 1947-1949; the Suez Crisis, 1956; the Arab-Israeli Crisis, 1967." Ph.D. dissertation, Claremont Graduate School, 1971. (DA 32, p1049)
Author presents an analysis of British policy in three crisis situations and concludes that in all three instances British domestic opinion was the most important factor in policy-making.

664 Hordes, Jess N. "Evolving U.N. Approaches to and the Role of U.N. Machinery in the Arab-Israeli Conflict, 1947-1956." Ph.D. dissertation, Johns Hopkins University, 1974. (DA 38, p1008)
This dissertation attempts to define the nature and evolution of the U.N.'s overall approach between 1947 and 1956, while also touching on the changing role of U.N. instrumentalities in the process.

665 Hoskins, Halford L. The Middle East: Problem Area in World Politics. New York: Macmillan, 1957.
Questions U.S. pro-Israeli policy that jeopardizes real interests in the Arab world.

666 Howard, Harry N. "Conflicts of Interest," in Alan R.

Taylor and Richard N. Tetlie, eds., Palestine: A Search for Truth. Approaches to the Arab-Israeli Conflict. Washington, D.C.: Public Affairs Press, 1970.

Refutes Zionist claim of an identity of interests between the United States and Israel.

667 Huff, Earl Dean. "Zionist Influences Upon U.S. Foreign Policy: A Study of American Policy Toward the Middle East from the Time of the Struggle for Israel to the Sinai Conflict." Ph.D. dissertation, University of Idaho, 1971. (DA 32, p3400)

This dissertation is a study of the extent to which the American Zionist movement has been successful in influencing American foreign policy toward the Middle East over the decades 1947-1967.

668 Hurewitz, J. C. Middle East Dilemmas: The Background of United States Policy. New York: Harper, 1953.

A classic, this work demonstrates the dilemma that American policy-makers had in trying to contain the Soviet Union, win Arab support, and at the same time assist the State of Israel.

669 _______. "The Road to Partition: The Palestine Problem, 1936-1948." Ph.D. dissertation, Columbia University, 1950. (W 1951, p198, DDAU) [Abstract not available.]

670 _______. The Struggle for Palestine. New York: Greenwood Press, 1968.

Critical of U.S. policy on the creation of Israel, which he characterizes as ambiguous because of the bureaucratic differences of opinion shared by State, War, Navy Departments, the Joint Chiefs, and the White House.

671 Hyatt, David Mayer. "The United Nations and the Partition of Palestine." Ph.D. dissertation, Catholic University, 1973. (DA 34, p5281)

Studies the Palestine question in the United Nations in 1947.

672 Isaacs, Stephen D. Jews and American Politics. New York: Doubleday, 1974.

An excellent study of the effectiveness and method of operation of the Zionist lobby in American politics.

673 Ismael, Tareq. "The Soviet Union and the Middle East," in Tareq Y. Ismael, ed., The Middle East in World Politics. Syracuse, N. Y.: Syracuse University Press, 1974.
A short summary of Soviet interests in the Middle East that reflects upon U. S. interests in Israel.

674 Jafari, Lafi Ibrahim. "Migration of Palestinian Arab and Jordanian Students and Professionals to the United States." Ph. D. dissertation, Iowa State University, 1971. (DA 32, p4722)
A study about the migration of a certain group of Arabs to the United States who have formed an ethnic lobby affecting U. S. -Israeli relations.

675 Kennan, George F. Memoirs, 1925-1950. 2 vols. New York: Little, Brown, 1967.
Critical of the Truman Doctrine and of U. S. support of Israel--a policy that could open the door to Soviet intrusion into the Middle East.

676 Khouri, Fred John. The Arab-Israeli Dilemma. Syracuse, N. Y.: Syracuse University Press, 1968.
An indictment of U. S. support for the creation of Israel.

677 ________. "The Arab States in the United Nations: A Study of Political Relations, 1945-1950." Ph. D. dissertation, Columbia University, 1953. (DA 14, p177)
This study investigates the role of the Arab states in the United Nations from 1945 to 1950.

678 Kirk, George E. The Middle East, 1945-1950. London: Oxford University Press, 1954.
Provides a view of American involvement with the Palestine problem from a British perspective.

679 Koch, Howard Everard, Jr. "Permanent War: A Reappraisal of the Arab-Israeli War." Ph. D. dissertation, Stanford University, 1973. (DA 34, p3505)
This study is an inquiry into the 25-year-old Arab-Israeli confrontation.

680 El-Kordy, Abdul-Hafez M. "The United Nations Peace-Keeping Functions in the Arab World." Ph. D. dissertation, American University, 1967. (DA 28, p3743)
This dissertation examines the United Nations' peace-

keeping function. Concludes that the Arab-Israeli impasse continues to challenge the functions of the U. N. because of Israeli refusal to implement U. N. resolutions.

681 Krammer, Arnold P. "Soviet Bloc Relations with Israel, 1947-1953." Ph. D. dissertation, University of Wisconsin, 1970. (DA 31, p5323)
Provides insight into the changing Soviet policy vis-à-vis Zionism and Israel.

682 Lenczowski, George. Middle East in World Affairs. Ithaca, N. Y.: Cornell University Press, 1956.
Contains a good synoptic chapter on the growth of Zionism, its coming to fruition in the United States, and early American policy toward Israel.

683 Lewis, Bernard. The Middle East and the West. Bloomington: Indiana University Press, 1965.
Concludes that Zionism and imperialism are chief factors for Arab hatred of the West. Concludes U. S. should disassociate itself from the British and Israel.

684 Lewis, Evelyn. "The Jewish Vote: Fact or Fiction: Trends in Jewish Voting Behavior." Ph. D. dissertation, Ball State University, 1976. (DA 37, p6704)
This is a study of Jewish voting behavior that concludes that the Jewish vote is an anachronism and that Jews vote their own individual interests as do other Americans.

685 Lilienthal, Alfred M. The Other Side of the Coin: An American Perspective of the Arab-Israeli Conflict. New York: Devin-Adair, 1965.
This is an anti-Zionist work that is critical of American policy-makers for permitting the Zionist lobby to dominate the formulation of policy toward Israel.

686 Lipstadt, Deborah E. "The Zionist Cause of Louis Lipsky, 1900-21." Ph. D. dissertation, Brandeis University, 1977. (DA 37, p7921)
An account of an early American Zionist.

687 McDonald, James G. My Mission in Israel, 1948-1951. New York: Simon & Schuster, 1951.
Critical of the American State Department's handling of policy-making vis-à-vis Israel.

688 Mallison, W. T., Jr. "The Legal Problems Concern-

ing the Juridicial Status and Political Activities of the Zionist Organization/Jewish Agency: A Study in International and United States Law," William and Mary Law Review, 9 (spring 1968), 556-629.

An interesting essay that delineates the method of operation used by the Zionist lobby in the United States.

689 ________. "The Zionist-Israel Juridicial Claims to Constitute 'the Jewish People' Nationality Entity and to Confer Membership in It: Appraisal in Public International Law," George Washington Law Review, 32 (June 1964), 983-1075.

This essay indicts the State of Israel for using the "Jewish people" concept to maintain an exclusivity about the Jewish state, one that precludes Palestinian Arabs from taking up their land on returning to Israel.

690 Mansy, Thomas M. "Palestine in the United Nations." Ph.D. dissertation, Georgetown University, 1950. (17, p179, DDAU) [Abstract not available.]

691 Manuel, Frank E. The Realities of American-Palestine Relations. Washington, D.C.: Public Affairs Press, 1949.

Critical of the early U.S. policy toward the Palestine question.

692 Marlowe, John. Arab Nationalism and British Imperialism: A Study in Power Politics. London: Cresset Press, 1961.

An interesting study of two conflicting forces which impinged on American support for Zionist goals in Palestine.

693 Mazuzan, George T. "United States Policy toward Palestine at the United Nations, 1947-1948: An Essay," Prologue, 7 (1975), 163-76.

This essay views U.S. policy toward Palestine within the larger context of Soviet-American relations which found the U.S. trying to contain a Soviet intrusion into the Middle East.

694 ________. "Warren R. Austin: A Republican Internationalist and United States Foreign Policy." Ph.D. dissertation, Kent State University, 1969. (DA 30, p5389)

This is a biographic account of the U.S. Ambassador at the United Nations during the years 1946 to 1952 when the questions of Palestine and Israel were frequently before that body.

695 Miller, Merle. Plain Speaking: An Oral Biography of Harry S. Truman. New York: Putnam, 1974.
Sets forth Harry Truman's personal views on the creation of Israel which included both Biblical and political influences.

696 Millis, Walter, and E. S. Duffield, eds. The Forrestal Diaries. New York: Viking, 1951.
Critical of President's handling of the Palestine question which was decided on the basis of political considerations. Viewed the Palestine question in terms of American petroleum needs which could be met from Middle-Eastern oil reserves.

697 Moskovits, Shlomo. "The United States Recognition of Israel in the Context of the Cold War, 1945-1948." Ph. D. dissertation, Kent State University, 1976. (DA 37, p7923)
Rejects the view that American decisions on Palestine were based on political considerations. Posits that the U. S. recognized Israel because of the need to bar possible Soviet entry into the Middle East, and because Israel had declared its independence.

698 Mustafa, Urabi S. "The United States and Jordan with Special Reference to the Palestine Question." Ph. D. dissertation, American University, 1966. (DA 28, p279)
This author declares that the Arab-Israeli problem greatly complicated American relations with Jordan. Asserts that the U. S. could end the Arab-Israeli impasse by an impartial policy that would stabilize Jordan and establish better relations with Arab states.

699 Oder, Irwin. "The United States and the Palestine Mandate, 1920-1948: A Study of the Impact of Interest Groups on Foreign Policy." Ph. D. dissertation, Columbia University, 1956. (DA 16, p2507)
Suggests that American Zionists did not achieve all of their goals and that their influence on American policy has been exaggerated.

700 Peretz, Don. "Israel and the Arab Refugees." Ph. D. dissertation, Columbia University, 1955. (DA 16, p563)

Traces the development of Israel's policy toward the Arab refugee problem and the efforts of the United Nations to settle it.

701 Phillips, William. Ventures in Diplomacy. London: John Murray, 1955.
Very critical of the Truman administration's handling of the Palestine issue, which is characterized as being politically motivated. Author favored a bi-national solution.

702 Polk, William R. The United States and the Arab World. Cambridge, Mass.: Harvard University Press, 1965.
Claims that the Palestine problem was settled on the basis of domestic politics.

703 Quandt, William B. "United States Policy in the Middle East: Constraints and Choices," in Paul Y. Hammond and Sidney S. Alexander, eds., Political Dynamics in the Middle East. New York: American Elsevier, 1972.
Concludes that domestic politics and not foreign policy imperatives determined Truman's decision on the Palestine question.

704 Rahinsky, Herbert. "United States Foreign Policy and the Arab Refugees." Ph. D. dissertation, New York University, 1971. (DA 32, p2616)
This dissertation evaluates the significance and implications of American foreign policy in relation to the problem of the Arab refugees and to the efforts of UNRWA to settle it.

705 Reich, Bernard. "Israel's Foreign Policy: A Case Study of Small State Diplomacy." Ph. D. dissertation, University of Virginia, 1964. (DA 25, p3670)
This study is an analysis of Israel's diplomacy in several major areas: security, economic development, and the promotion of Jewish-Zionist ideology.

706 Richardson, Chaning Bulfinch. "The United Nations and Arab Refugee Relief, 1948-1950: A Case Study in International Organization." Ph. D. dissertation, Columbia University, 1951. (DA 11, p1089)
This work is a description and analysis of the manner in which the United Nations met the problems posed by the flight of Arabs from Palestine in 1948.

707 Ricks, Eldin. "United States Economic Assistance to Israel, 1949-1960." Ph. D. dissertation, Dropsie University, 1970. (X 1970, p73, ADD) [Abstract not available.]

708 Rivlin, Helen Anne B. "American Jews and the State of Israel: A Bicentennial Perspective," Middle East Journal, 30 (summer 1970), 369-89.

This essay is a synopsis of American Jewish feeling toward the Holy Land and the State of Israel which emerged there in 1948.

709 Roosevelt, Kermit. "The Partition of Palestine: A Lesson in Pressure Politics," Middle East Journal, 11 (January 1948), 1-16.

Concludes that American recognition of Israel was not supportive of U. S. national interests.

710 Rowland, Howard Douglas. "The Arab-Israeli Conflict as Represented in Arabic Fictional Literature." Ph. D. dissertation, University of Michigan, 1971. (DA 32, 4021)

This dissertation analyzes the works of a large number of Arab writers of fiction to determine their perspective on the conflict between Arabs and Jews.

711 Sachar, Howard M. Europe Leaves the Middle East, 1936-1954. New York: Knopf, 1972.

This work contains two excellent chapters on the end of the British mandate in Palestine and the Arab-Israeli war that followed.

712 Safran, Nadav. From War to War: The Arab-Israeli Confrontation, 1948-1967. New York: Pegasus, 1969.

Treats the 1948 Arab-Israeli war in detail, pointing out the Arabs preferred a policy of no war and no peace.

713 ________. "The Soviet Union and Israel," in Ivo J. Lederer and Wayne S. Vucinich, eds., The Soviet Union and the Middle East: The Post-World War II Era. Stanford, Calif.: Hoover Institution Press, 1974.

This is an excellent short treatment of the radical changes that accompanied Soviet policy toward the goals of Zionism and the State of Israel.

714 ________. The United States and Israel. Cambridge,

Mass.: Harvard University Press, 1963.
Provides a critical analysis of the U.S. involvement in the creation of the State of Israel.

715 Samii, Cyrus B. "The Arab-Asian Bloc in the United Nations." Ph.D. dissertation, University of Kansas, 1955. (22, p234, DDAU) [Abstract not available.]

716 Sam'o, Elias. "The Arab States in the United Nations: A Study of Voting Behavior," Ph.D. dissertation, American University, 1967. (DA 28, p1489)
Examines Arab voting on 72 issues to determine their voting behavior.

717 Sankari, Farouk Ali. "The United Nations Truce Supervision Organization in Palestine." Ph.D. dissertation, Claremont Graduate School, 1968. (DA 29, p4081)
This work describes and analyzes the work of the UNTSO, founded following the creation of Israel in 1948.

718 Selzer, Michael. "Sources of Conflict," in Alan R. Taylor and Richard N. Tetlie, ed., Palestine: A Search for Truth: Approaches to the Arab-Israeli Conflict. Washington, D.C.: Public Affairs Press, 1970.
Discusses the influence of the Zionist lobby on the U.S. government in matters pertaining to Israel.

719 Simpson, Dwight J. "British Palestine Policy, 1939-1949." Ph.D. dissertation, Stanford University, 1950. (17, p180, DDAU) [Abstract not available.]

720 Smith, Gaddis. Dean Acheson. New York: Cooper Square Publishers, 1972.
A short biography of an American who figured largely in the making of the Truman Doctrine.

721 Smith, Gary V., ed. Zionism: The Dream and the Reality. New York: Barnes & Noble, 1974.
This is an excellent series of essays dealing with American perceptions of Israel.

722 Snetsinger, John. Truman, the Jewish Vote and the Creation of Israel. Stanford, Calif.: Hoover Institution Press, 1974.
This author concludes that President Truman's decision on the Palestine question was motivated wholly by political considerations.

723 Snider, Lewis. "Middle East Maelstrom: The Impact of Global and Regional Influences on the Arab-Israeli Conflict, 1947-1973." Ph. D. dissertation, University of Michigan, 1975. (DA 36, p6940)

Examines the relative impact of global power rivalries and of inter-Arab political conflicts and bloc alignments on the intensity of the Arab-Israeli conflict.

724 Sowayyegh, Abdul-Aziz Hussein. "Oil and the Arab-Israeli Conflict: A Study in Arab Oil Strategy between 1948-1973." Ph. D. dissertation, Claremont Graduate School, 1977. (DA 37, p7302)

This study examines the Arab oil-producing countries' use of oil as political leverage from the early 1940s to the 1973 October war.

725 Spielman, William C. The United States in the Middle East: A Study of American Foreign Policy. New York: Pageant Press, 1959.

Asserts that Israel has proven to be a liability to American foreign policy-makers concerned with formulating a Middle-East policy.

726 Stevens, Richard P. American Zionism and United States Foreign Policy. New York: Pageant Press, 1962.

An excellent study of the efforts of American Zionists to use U.S. government aid in achieving the goals necessary to the creation of the State of Israel.

727 Stookey, Robert W. America and the Arab States: An Uneasy Encounter. New York: Wiley, 1975.

Declares that American support for the creation of Israel ran athwart a rising tide of Arab nationalism and suggests that this support was based on political considerations.

728 Suleiman, Fuad K. "The Arab Boycott of Israel." Ph. D. dissertation, Fletcher School of Law and Diplomacy, 1966. (Selim, p116) [Abstract not available.]

729 Sykes, Christopher. Crossroads to Israel, 1917-1948. Bloomington: Indiana University Press, 1973.

A lengthy study that carries American reaction to the Zionist movement from noninvolvement through full support for the creation of Israel.

730 Taylor, Alan, and Richard N. Tetlie, eds. Palestine:

A Search for Truth: Approaches to the Arab-Israeli Conflict. Washington, D.C.: Public Affairs Press, 1970.
This collection of essays sheds light on Zionist influence on American Middle East policy and on the American perceptions of Israel.

731 Truman, Harry S. Memoirs. 2 vols. New York: Doubleday, 1955.
This memoir reveals the Zionist pressure on Truman, the bureaucratic split over the Palestine question, and the President's own personal feelings on the matter.

732 Welles, Sumner. We Need Not Fail. Boston: Houghton Mifflin, 1948.
Shows the bureaucratic differences in the Truman administration on the Palestine question and the efforts to find a solution.

733 ______. Where Are We Heading? New York: Harper Bros., 1946.
Very critical of President Truman whose policy on the Palestine question was based on political considerations.

734 Wilson, Evan M. "The Palestine Papers, 1943-1947," Journal of Palestine Studies, 2 (summer 1973), 33-54.
An excellent synoptic article that shows the evolution of American policy on Palestine during the Roosevelt and Truman administrations.

735 Windmueller, Steven Fred. "American Jewish Interest Groups: Their Roles in Shaping United States Foreign Policy in the Middle East; A Study of Two Time Periods: 1945-1948, 1955-1958." Ph.D. dissertation, University of Pennsylvania, 1973. (DA 34, p5288)
This work studies the operation of the Jewish community on policy-making.

736 Yale, William. The Near East: A Modern History. Ann Arbor: University of Michigan Press, 1958.
A good chapter is presented on the U.S. involvement with the Palestine question.

737 Zindani, Abdul Wahed Aziz. "Arab Politics in the United Nations." Ph.D. dissertation, Notre Dame University, 1976. (DA 37, p3891)
A portion of this work deals with the Arab political reaction to the birth of Israel and Arab diplomacy in the first Arab-Israeli war of 1948.

N

THE EISENHOWER ERA, 1952-1960

738 Abbas, Jabir Ali. "Points of Departure in Egypt's Foreign Policy: The Essence of Nasser's Power." Ph. D. dissertation, Indiana University, 1969. (DA 32, p5846)

This dissertation deals with a figure whose adversary relationship with the United States had a striking impact on American foreign policy-making.

739 Adams, Michael. Suez and After: Years of Crisis. Boston: Beacon Press, 1958.

Critical of American foreign policy-making during the Suez crisis. Concludes the Eisenhower Doctrine had little merit to it.

740 Badeau, John S. American Approach to the Arab World. New York: Harper, 1968.

Concludes that after the Suez crisis the United States assumed the role of custodian of Western interests in the Middle East.

741 Barker, A. J. Suez: The Seven Day War. London: Faber & Faber, 1964.

This is primarily a military study that rejects the thesis that Britain and France operated in collusion with Israel in the Suez operation in 1946.

742 Beal, John Robinson. John Foster Dulles, 1888-1959. New York: Harper Bros., 1951.

A semi-official biography that presents Dulles as a cold warrior who viewed the Middle East in terms of the on-going conflict between the United States and the Soviet Union.

743 El-Behairy, Mohamed Mohamed. "The Suez Canal in World Politics, 1945-1961." Ph. D. dissertation, Ohio State University, 1961. (DA 22, p2724)

This work covers the Suez crisis and concludes that its effects were felt in the Arab world after the crisis had subsided.

744 Bose, Tarun Chandra. The Superpowers and the Middle East. New York: Asia Publishing House, 1973.
Concludes that the Baghdad Pact led to Russian entry into the Middle East, that U.S. policy in the Suez crisis was proper, but that the Eisenhower Doctrine nullified the gains made in 1956.

745 Broad, Lewis. Anthony Eden: Chronicles of a Career. New York: Crowell, 1955.
A biography of a figure who figures largely in U.S. policy-making during the Suez crisis.

746 Bromberger, Merry, and Serge Bromberger. Secrets of Suez. London: Sidgwick & Jackson, 1957.
Critical of British diplomatic and military planning in the entire Suez crisis.

747 Bryson, Thomas A. American Diplomatic Relations with the Middle East, 1784-1975: A Survey. Metuchen, N.J.: Scarecrow Press, 1977.
Views the Baghdad Pact as dysfunctional to American vital interests and concludes that the Eisenhower Doctrine erased diplomatic gains achieved by American policy during the Suez crisis.

748 Campbell, John C. Defense of the Middle East: Problems of American Policy. New York: Harper, 1960.
Arab nationalism is viewed as a force that countered the Baghdad Pact and provided the wave that led to Nasser's nationalization of the Suez, a crisis that resulted in the rise of U.S. prestige. Eisenhower's Doctrine nullified this rapid rise.

749 Decker, Donald James. "U.S. Policy Regarding the Baghdad Pact." Ph.D. dissertation, American University, 1975. (DA 36, p1786)
This study concludes that Dulles correctly assessed the defense needs of the Middle East, but that numerous factors beyond his control resulted in the Pact's failure to prevent Soviet intrusion into the Middle East.

750 Dougherty, J. E. "The Aswan Decision in Perspec-

tive," Political Science Quarterly, LXXXIV (1959), 21-45.

Concludes that Dulles' renege on the Aswan Dam might not have been the only factor causing President Nasser to nationalize the Suez Canal.

751 Drummond, Roscoe, and Gaston Coblentz. Duel at the Brink: John Foster Dulles' Command of American Power. New York: Doubleday, 1960.

This study of Dulles declares that psychological factors caused the breach in Anglo-American relations during the Suez crisis, because neither Dulles nor Eden had a proper appreciation of the other's constraints and predilections.

752 Eagleton, Clyde. "The United Nations and the Suez Crisis," in Philip W. Thayer, ed., Tensions in the Middle East. Baltimore: Johns Hopkins Press, 1958.

Suggests that the Eisenhower Doctrine was not in conformity with past American diplomatic experience which had utilized the United Nations to achieve diplomatic goals.

753 Eden, Anthony. Full Circle: The Memoirs of Anthony Eden. Boston: Houghton Mifflin, 1960.

Suggests that Eisenhower and Dulles did not fully communicate with Eden during the Suez crisis, thus leading the latter to believe that he might rely on U.S. support for British reliance on force.

754 Eisenhower, Dwight D. Waging Peace, 1956-1961: The White House Years. New York: Doubleday, 1965.

This interesting memoir presents insights into the formation of policy with respect to the Baghdad Pact, the decision to cancel the Aswan Dam pledge, the opposition to the use of force at Suez, and the decisions to intervene in Lebanon pursuant to the Eisenhower Doctrine.

755 Ellis, Harry B. Challenge in the Middle East: Communist Influence and American Policy. New York: Ronald Press, 1960.

A critical view of Eisenhower's Middle East policy in the case of the Baghdad Pact and the Eisenhower Doctrine.

756 Epstein, Leon D. British Politics in the Suez Crisis. Urbana: University of Illinois Press, 1963.

This is an excellent study of British domestic policy and public opinion during the Suez crisis.

757 Finer, Herman. Dulles over Suez: The Theory and Practice of His Diplomacy. Chicago: Quadrangle, 1964.
This is a lengthy, detailed study of Dulles' diplomacy that views his policies as being counterproductive to America's best interests.

758 Fisher, Carol A., and Fred Krinsky. Middle East in Crisis: A Historical and Documentary Review. Syracuse, N.Y.: Syracuse University Press, 1959.
Contains a brief narrative chapter on the Suez crisis.

759 Fisher, Sydney Nettleton. The Middle East: A History. New York: Knopf, 1960.
This work contains a critical analysis of the Eisenhower Middle East policy.

760 Fitzsimons, M. A. "The Suez Crisis and the Containment Policy," Review of Politics, XIX (October 1957), 419-45.
Shows that the United States has vital interests in the Middle East that conflict with those of Great Britain and Israel.

761 Fredericks, Edgar Jesse. "Soviet-Egyptian Relations, 1955-1965, and Their Effect on Communism in the Middle East and the International Position of the Soviet Union." Ph. D. dissertation, American University, 1968. (DA 29, p1265)
This dissertation examines the relationship between the Soviet Union and Egypt, with particular emphasis on the military relationship that developed in 1955 just prior to the Suez crisis.

762 Gallman, Waldemar J. Iraq Under General Nuri. Baltimore: Johns Hopkins Press, 1964.
This work suggests that the United States had good cause not to join the Baghdad Pact, the creature of John Foster Dulles.

763 Gelber, Lionel. America in Britain's Place: The Leadership of the West and Anglo-American Unity. New York: Praeger, 1961.
Asserts that Dulles' renege on Aswan was not the cause of Nasser's nationalization of Suez but does conclude that Dulles' pronouncements ruined negotiations to settle the Suez issue.

764 Gerson, Louis. John Foster Dulles. New York: Cooper Square Publishers, 1967.
Laudatory of Dulles, concluding that Dulles was not responsible for the nationalization of Suez and that he did not sabotage British negotiations with Egypt.

765 Gerteiny, Alfred George. "The Concept of Positive Neutralism in the United Arab Republic." Ph. D. dissertation, St. Johns University, 1963. (Index, 1962, p118, ADD) [Abstract not available.]

766 Glassman, Jon David. "Arms for the Arabs: The Soviet Union and War in the Middle East." Ph. D. dissertation, Columbia University, 1976. (DA 37, p6038)
This study examines the weapons delivered by the Soviets during the period since 1955, but it does give emphasis to the arms deal made just prior to the Suez crisis.

767 Goodhart, A. L. "Some Legal Aspects of the Suez Situation," in Philip W. Thayer, ed., Tensions in the Middle East. Baltimore: Johns Hopkins Press, 1958.
Declares that the United States made its position clear on the possible use of force by Britain and France.

768 Goold-Adams, Richard. The Time of Power: Reappraisal of John Foster Dulles. London: Weidenfeld & Nicolson, 1962.
Critical of Dulles for causing the Suez crisis and then impeding negotiations to bring about a settlement of the issue.

769 Gottlieb, Paul H. "The Commonwealth of Nations at the United Nations." Ph. D. dissertation, Boston University, 1962. (DA 23, p1003)
Deals with the Suez question before the United Nations.

770 Guhin, Michael A. John Foster Dulles: A Statesman and His Times. New York: Columbia University Press, 1972.
This biography is very complimentary of Dulles and presents his diplomatic career in a laudatory light.

771 Hackley, Lloyd V. "Soviet Behavior in the Middle East as a Function of Change, 1950-1970." Ph. D. dissertation, University of North Carolina, 1976. (DA

37, p4340)

Says that Soviet deliveries of arms has often brought slim dividends in terms of policy goals.

772 Haley, P. Edward. "Britain and the Middle East," in Tareq Y. Ismael, ed., The Middle East and World Politics. Syracuse, N.Y.: Syracuse University Press, 1974.

Presents some interesting views of the British motives during the Suez crisis.

773 Hamdan, Zuhair. "A Study of the Arab-Israeli Conflict in the United Nations during the Period between 1947 and 1957." Ph.D. dissertation, Union Graduate School, 1976. (DA 37, p6737)

One portion of this dissertation concerns the Suez crisis in 1956-1957; it concludes that the United Nations was not a useful forum for the Arabs.

774 Hamlet, Bruce D. "A Comparative Analysis of British Foreign Relations: The Palestine War, 1947-1949; the Suez Crisis, 1956; the Arab-Israeli Crisis, 1967." Ph.D. dissertation, Claremont Graduate School, 1971.

This author does deal with the Suez crisis as a facet of British Middle-East relations in these two crucial decades.

775 Hoopes, Townsend. The Devil and John Foster Dulles. Boston: Little, Brown, 1973.

This biography is very critical of Dulles' policy in the Middle East, especially of his Eisenhower Doctrine.

776 Howard, Harry N. "The United States and the Middle East," in Tareq Y. Ismael, ed., The Middle East in World Politics. Syracuse, N.Y.: Syracuse University Press, 1974.

Provides a brief insight into Eisenhower's Middle East policy.

777 Huang, T. T. F. "Some International and Legal Aspects of the Suez Canal Question," American Journal of International Law, LI (1957), 277-307.

Discusses the implications of this crisis in terms of international law. Views nationalization as a violation of public international law.

778 Huff, Earl Dean. "Zionist Influences Upon U.S. For-

eign Policy: A Study of American Policy toward the Middle East from the Time of the Struggle for Israel to the Sinai Conflict." Ph. D. dissertation, University of Idaho, 1971. (DA 32, p3400)

Suggests that Zionist influence on U. S. government diminished considerably during the Eisenhower era.

779 Hurewitz, J. C. Middle East Politics: The Military Dimension. New York: Praeger, 1972.

Discusses Soviet motivation for introducing arms into Egypt during the 1950s.

780 ________, ed. Soviet-American Rivalry in the Middle East. New York: Praeger, 1969.

Several essays in this collection suggest Soviet motives for introducing arms to Egypt just prior to the Suez crisis.

781 Joynt, Carey B. "John Foster Dulles and the Suez Crisis," in Gerald N. Grob, ed., Statesmen and Statecraft of the Modern West. Barre, Mass.: Barre Publishers, 1967.

Claims that Dulles' action on the Aswan Dam was not wholly to blame for Nasser's nationalization. A complimentary study of Dulles' diplomacy in the Suez crisis.

782 ElKashef, Ahmad Refat. "Soviet Policy toward Egypt, 1955-1967." Ph. D. dissertation, Boston University, 1973. (DA 34, p7305)

This work discusses the rise of cordial relations between Egypt and the Soviet Union during the heightened rise of Egyptian nationalism.

783 Kerkheide, Virginia White. "Anthony Eden and the Suez Crisis of 1956." Ph. D. dissertation, Case Western Reserve University, 1972.

Views Eden's actions in terms of the diplomacy of the 1930s when Europe could not stop Adolf Hitler. Eden portrayed as determined to remove Nasser from power.

784 Khalil, Houssam El-Dawla H. "The Soviet Foreign Policy toward Egypt, 1955-1964." Ph. D. dissertation, Howard University, 1970. (DA 31, p6134)

Views Soviet policy as trying to expand Russian prestige, reduce Western influence, and enhance Egypt's positive neutralism.

785 Khan, Rais Ahmad. "Radio Cairo and Egyptian For-

eign Policy, 1956-1959." Ph.D. dissertation, University of Michigan, 1967. (DA 28, p3245)

Deals with the dissemination of information from Cairo in the 1956-1959 era and analyzes it in three crisis situations: Suez, Jordan, and Lebanon.

786 Kline, Earl Oliver. "The Suez Crisis: Anglo-American Relations and the United Nations." Ph.D. dissertation, Princeton University, 1961. (DA 22, p2866)

Critical of Dulles and Eisenhower for bringing about the crisis by rejecting Nasser's bid for aid on the Aswan Dam and for opposing the use of force which torpedoed the London Conference.

787 Lenczowski, George. The Middle East in World Affairs. Ithaca, N.Y.: Cornell University Press, 1962.

Critical of the Eisenhower-Dulles policy in the case of the Baghdad Pact and the Eisenhower Doctrine.

788 ________. United States Interests in the Middle East. Washington, D.C.: American Enterprise Institute, 1968.

Critical of the Eisenhower Doctrine.

789 Love, Kennett. Suez: The Twice Fought War. New York: McGraw-Hill, 1969.

This is perhaps the most detailed analysis of events leading to the Suez crisis and of the course of diplomacy in the aftermath.

790 McCormick, James M. "An Interaction Analysis of International Crises: A Study of the Suez Crisis and the Six Day War." Ph.D. dissertation, Michigan State University, 1973. (DA 34, p6080)

This study examines the foreign policy during these two international crises in the Middle East.

791 Makled, Ismail Sabri Eysa. "Comparative International Behavior in the Suez Crisis: A Perspective Study." Ph.D. dissertation, University of Pittsburgh, 1965. (DA 26, p3468)

Focuses on describing the perceptions of foreign policy elites in the United States, Egypt, Britian, France, the Soviet Union and Israel before and during the Suez crisis.

792 Marlowe, John. Arab Nationalism and British Imperialism: A Study in Power Politics. London: Cresset

Press, 1961.

Demonstrates that the U.S. took Britain's place in the Middle East following the Suez crisis.

793 Masannat, George Suleiman. "Aspects of American Policy in the Arab Middle East, 1947-1957, with Emphasis on United States-Egyptian Relations." Ph. D. dissertation, University of Oklahoma, 1964. (DA 25, p4803)

The main thrust of this dissertation is U.S.-Egyptian relations during the Suez debacle. It examines the American attempt to reach a peaceful settlement in this crisis. It also examines the rationale of the Eisenhower Doctrine.

794 Meo, Leila. Lebanon, Improbable Nation: A Study in Political Development. Bloomington: Indiana University Press, 1965.

An examination of the role of the Eisenhower Doctrine as it applied to Lebanon is the subject of this monograph.

795 Murphy, Robert. Diplomat Among Warriors. New York: Doubleday, 1964.

Discusses the Suez crisis and its causes and the application of the Eisenhower Doctrine to Lebanon.

796 Nolte, Richard H. "Year of Decision in the Middle East," Yale Review, XLVI (winter 1957), 228-44.

Claims that the Suez crisis placed Nasser in closer proximity to the Soviet Union. Critical of U.S. policy in this period.

797 Nutting, Anthony. No End of a Lesson: The Story of Suez. New York: Potter Publishing, 1967.

Is critical of both Eden and Dulles for not clearly communicating their views prior to and during this crisis.

798 Penrose, Stephen B. L. "From Suez to Lebanon: Soviet-American Interaction in the Middle East, 1956-1958." Ph. D. dissertation, Fletcher School of Law and Diplomacy, 1973. (Selim, p92) [Abstract not available.]

799 Perry, Glenn Earl. "United States Relations with Egypt, 1951-1963: Egyptian Neutralism and the American Alignment Policy." Ph. D. dissertation, University

of Virginia, 1964. (DA 25, p3670)

Views this relationship in terms of the U.S. effort to structure a Middle Eastern alliance and Egypt's rebuff and subsequent turn to the Soviet Union.

800 Polk, William R. The United States and the Arab World. Cambridge, Mass.: Harvard University Press, 1965.

Critical of Dulles for his use of imprecise language in the Suez crisis; provides an interesting description of the operation of the Eisenhower Doctrine.

801 Pompa, Edward M. "Canadian Foreign Policy during the Suez Crisis of 1956." Ph.D. dissertation, St. Johns University, 1969. (DA 30, p3406)

A study of the role of Canada in this crisis.

802 Quandt, William B. "United States Policy in the Middle East: Constraints and Choices," in Paul Y. Hammond and Sidney S. Alexander, eds., Political Dynamics in the Middle East. New York: American Elsevier, 1972.

Contains synoptic and analytical treatment of the Baghdad Pact, the Suez crisis, and the Eisenhower Doctrine. Concludes that American policy of defense in the Mideast was not successful.

803 El-Quazzaz, Marwan H. "A Comparative Analysis of United States Policy in the 1956 Suez War and the 1967 Arab-Israeli War." Ph.D. dissertation, Southern Illinois University, 1976. (DA 37, p6037)

This dissertation describes, in part, how the United States took the lead in opposing the Anglo-French, Israeli invasion of the Suez.

804 Rifai, Abdul Halim. "The Eisenhower Administration and the Defense of the Arab Middle East." Ph.D. dissertation, American University, 1966. (DA 27, p3101)

Concludes that the Baghdad Pact and the Eisenhower Doctrine failed and by 1959 all of the Arab world was outside the U.S. security system, a failure due to historic, economic, political, and psychological reasons.

805 Robertson, Terence. Crisis: The Inside Story of the Suez Conspiracy. New York: Atheneum, 1965.

This is very critical of Dulles' actions during the

entire crisis, from his renege on Aswan to his "betrayal" of Eden when the latter tried to resolve the crisis by use of force.

806 Safran, Nadav. From War to War: The Arab-Israeli Confrontation. New York: Pegasus, 1969.
Asserts that the U. S. did not adhere to the Baghdad Pact because of Israeli opposition and that the Iraqi coup spoiled the Eisenhower Doctrine and caused the U. S. to reassess its Mideast policy.

807 ________. The United States and Israel. Cambridge, Mass.: Harvard University Press, 1963.
Presents a sketch of Eisenhower's Middle-East policy.

808 Smolansky, O. M. "Moscow and the Suez Crisis, 1956: A Reappraisal," Political Science Quarterly, 80 (1965), 581-605.
A critical view of Soviet moves during the Suez crisis. Concludes that Russian attempts at intimidation were meaningless and made for propaganda purposes.

809 Snider, Lewis W. "Middle East Maelstrom: The Impact of Global and Regional Influences on the Arab-Israeli Conflict, 1947-1973." Ph. D. dissertation, University of Michigan, 1975. (DA 36, p6940)
This study examines the relative impact of global power rivalries and of inter-Arab political conflicts and bloc alignments on the intensity of the Arab-Israeli conflict.

810 Sowayyegh, Abdul-Aziz Hussein. "Oil and the Arab-Israeli Conflict: A Study in Arab Oil Strategy between 1948-1973." Ph. D. dissertation, Claremont Graduate School, 1977. (DA 37, p7302)
Discusses the Arabs' use of oil as a political lever during the 1956 Suez crisis.

811 Stevens, Georgianna G., ed. The United States and the Middle East. Englewood Cliffs, N. J.: Prentice-Hall, 1964.
Contains several essays on the Eisenhower Middle-East policy that conclude that Soviets made gains after 1958 failure of the Eisenhower Doctrine.

812 Stillman, Arthur McLean. "The United Nations and the Suez Canal." Ph. D. dissertation, American University,

1965. (DA 26, p1754)
The Suez crisis served as a valuable precedent pointing to the possibilities and limitations of the United Nations as a peace-keeping organization.

813 Stock, Ernest. "Israel on the Road to Sinai: A Small State in a Test of Power." Ph.D. dissertation, Columbia University, 1963.
Examines the course of events leading to the Sinai war, suggesting that the Egyptian deal with the Soviets for arms was the turning point for Israel, which then viewed Egypt as a military power and threat to her existence.

814 Stookey, Robert W. America and the Arab States: An Uneasy Encounter. New York: Wiley, 1975.
Discusses briefly the U.S. role in the creation of the Baghdad Pact, in the Suez crisis, and its reasons for the Eisenhower Doctrine.

815 Thayer, Charles W. Diplomat. New York: Harper, 1959.
Discusses American involvement in the Lebanese crisis of 1958 pursuant to the Eisenhower Doctrine.

816 Thayer, Philip W., ed. Tensions in the Middle East. Baltimore: Johns Hopkins Press, 1958.
Contains essays of interest to the formation of policy during the Eisenhower era.

817 Thomas, Hugh. Suez. New York: Harper & Row, 1966.
A readable account of the Suez crisis from a British point of view that is critical of both Eden and Dulles.

818 Turner, Jack Justin. "Arab-Asian Positive Neutralism and United States Foreign Policy." Ph.D. dissertation, University of Kentucky, 1969. (DA 30, p3532)
Discusses Arab neutralism, a factor that figured in Secretary Dulles' consideration of the Aswan Dam.

819 Utley, Freda. Will the Middle East Go West? Chicago: Henry Regnery, 1957.
Critical of Dulles' renege on the Aswan Dam and concludes that the Eisenhower Doctrine was counter-productive due to American association with Britain and Israel.

820 Vatikiotis, P. J. Conflict in the Middle East. London:

Allen & Unwin, 1971.
Sheds some light on the Lebanese civil war and its relation to the Eisenhower Doctrine.

821 Weems, Miner Lile. "The Propaganda Struggle in the Middle East, 1955-1958." Ph. D. dissertation, Georgetown University, 1962. (Index, 1961, p180, ADD) [Abstract not available.]

822 Wendzel, Robert Leroy. "United States National Interests and the Middle East, 1955-1958." Ph. D. dissertation, University of Florida, 1965. (DA 26, p4790)
Concludes that U. S. policy towards Egypt was detrimental to the national interests of the United States.

823 Wint, Guy, and Peter Calvocoressi. _Middle East Crisis._ Harmondsworth, England: Penguin Books, 1957.
Discusses Dulles' renege on Aswan Dam and blames him for eratic behavior during the Suez crisis that led Eden to draw wrong conclusions on the American's views of the problem.

824 Wolf, John Berchmans. "An Interpretation of the Eisenhower Doctrine: Lebanon, 1958." Ph. D. dissertation, American University, 1968. (DA 29, p949)
Provides an account of U. S. reaction and action during the Lebanese crisis which resulted in the decline of the American Middle Eastern posture.

825 Wright, Quincy. "Intervention, 1956," _American Journal of International Law,_ LI (1957), 257-76.
Israeli, British and French aggression at Suez was a violation of international law and was hardly justified by the nationalization of the Suez Canal.

826 ________. "United States Intervention in Lebanon," _American Journal of International Law,_ LIII (1959), 112-25.
Suggests that the United States would not justify its intervention in Lebanon in terms of foreign intervention to subvert the Lebanese government.

827 Wynn, Wilson. _Nasser of Egypt: The Search for Dignity._ Cambridge, Mass.: Harvard University Press, 1959.
A sympathetic study of Nasser whose policies must

be viewed in light of his concern for the Arab in world politics.

828 Yale, William. The Near East: A Modern History. Ann Arbor: University of Michigan Press, 1958.
Provides a sketch of Eisenhower's Middle-East policy that is critical of Secretary Dulles.

829 Yizhar, Michael. "The Eisenhower Doctrine: A Case Study of American Foreign Policy Formulation and Implementation." Ph. D. dissertation, New School, 1969. (DA 30, p5049)
A descriptive analysis of the Doctrine that concludes that not only did it not prevent Soviet intrusion into the Middle East but it contributed to the Arab unrest in the region.

O

THE DECADE OF THE 1960s

830 Abboushi, W. F. The Angry Arabs. Philadelphia: Westminster Press, 1974.
Provides an insight into Arab view of the Arab-Israeli controversy and the American involvement therein.

831 Abu-Jaber, Kamel S. "United States Policy toward the June Conflict," in Ibrahim Abu-Lughod, ed., The Arab-Israeli Confrontation ... (item 832).
Concludes that U.S. policy during the 1967 war was partial to the aims of Israel.

832 Abu-Lughod, Ibrahim, ed. The Arab-Israeli Confrontation of June 1967: An Arab Perspective. Evanston, Ill.: Northwestern University Press, 1970.
This collection of essays aims to present an alternative perspective to the Israeli point of view which has dominated American opinion on the Arab-Israeli conflict.

833 ________, and Baha Abu-Laban, eds. Settler Regimes in Africa and the Arab World: The Illusion of Endurance. Wilmette, Ill.: Medina University Press, 1974.
The authors furnish an interesting view of the Arab-Israeli controversy as it impinges on the Palestinians.

834 Akgonenc, Oya. "A Study of Political Dynamics of Turkish Foreign Policy with Particular Reference to New Trends in Turco-Arab Relations, 1960-1975." Ph.D. dissertation, American University, 1975. (DA 37, p4598)
The author suggests that U.S. congressional attitudes toward the Cyprus problem antagonized the Turks, thus influencing the new direction in Turkish diplomacy.

835 Alberts, Darlene Jean. "King Hussein of Jordan: The Consummate Politician." Ph.D. dissertation, Ohio State University, 1973. (DA 34, p692)

This is a study of a Middle-Eastern figure who has figured large in America's policy for this troubled region.

836 Arakie, Margaret. The Broken Sword of Justice: America, Israel and the Palestine Tragedy. London: Quartet Books, 1973.

Asserts that the U.S. arranged arms sales to Israel in the 1960s and laid the foundation for the 1967 conflict.

837 Badeau, John S. American Approach to the Arab World. New York: Harper, 1968.

This is the best single work on the decade of the 1960s, a period when the U.S. attempted an even-handed policy. Concludes that the 1967 Arab-Israeli war hurt U.S.-Arab relations.

838 ________. "U.S.A. and U.A.R.: A Crisis in Confidence," Foreign Affairs, 43 (January 1965), 281-96.

Describes the hardening of relations between the U.S. and Egypt just prior to the 1967 Arab-Israeli conflict.

839 Beling, Willard A., ed. The Middle East: Quest for an American Policy. Albany: State University of New York Press, 1974.

This collection of essays contains several articles that bear on American involvement in the Middle East in the 1960s.

840 Blessing, James Alan. "The Suspension of Foreign Aid by the United States, 1948-1972." Ph.D. dissertation, State University of New York, Albany, 1975. (DA 36, p4001)

A portion of this work treats the suspension of U.S. foreign aid during the 1960s.

841 Bose, Tarun Chandra. The Superpowers and the Middle East. New York: Asia Publishing House, 1973.

This author provides a critical view of the U.S. involvement in the 1967 Arab-Israeli war.

842 Botsai, Sarah Lillian. "The United States and the Palestine Refugees." Ph.D. dissertation, American University, 1972. (DA 33, p4508)

Critical of U.S. policy for not taking a clear position on the refugee question.

843 Bryson, Thomas A. American Diplomatic Relations

with Middle East, 1784-1975: A Survey. Metuchen, N. J.: Scarecrow Press, 1977.

This work surveys U. S. policy with the Middle East in the 1960s and concludes with the U. S. effort to bring peace to the region following the June War.

844 Campbell, John C. "The Arab-Israeli Conflict: An American Policy," Foreign Affairs, 49 (October 1970), 51-69.

Suggests that the U. S. must support Israel to keep a Middle East balance that would deny Russia hegemony over the region.

845 Chubin, Shahram. "Iran's Foreign Policy, 1958-1972: A Small State's Constraints and Choices." Ph. D. dissertation, Columbia University, 1974. (DA 37, p4600)

The author discusses Iran's diplomacy as that of a small state, strategically located and of significance to the great power rivalry.

846 Dadant, Philip M. "American and Soviet Defense Systems in the Middle East," in Willard A. Beling, ed., The Middle East: Quest for an American Policy. Albany: State University of New York Press, 1973.

This essay discusses the Arab-Israeli 1967 war in terms of Soviet-American relations.

847 Draper, Theodore. Israel and World Politics: Roots of the Third Arab-Israeli War. New York: Viking, 1968.

Views the American involvement in the June War in terms of the on-going U. S. -Soviet rivalry in the Middle East.

848 Erden, Deniz A. "Turkish Foreign Policy Through the United Nations." Ph. D. dissertation, University of Massachusetts, 1974. (DA 36, p1077)

This study treats the Cyprus question in Turkish diplomacy and concludes that the U. S. position on this crisis hurt Turkish-American relations.

849 Faddah, Mohammad Ibrahim. "The Foreign Policy of Jordan, 1947-1967." Ph. D. dissertation, University of Oklahoma, 1971. (DA 32, p2770)

This study covers Jordan's diplomacy during the cricial decade of the 1960s.

850 Fishburne, Charles Carroll, Jr. "United States Policy toward Iran, 1959-1963." Ph. D. dissertation, Florida State University, 1964. (DA 26, p7431)

The author critically analyzes American policy in terms of ends and means with emphasis on the political behavior of American policy-makers--legislative and executive--during the transition from a Republican to a Democratic administration.

851 Fredericks, Edgar Jesse. "Soviet-American Relations, 1955-1965, and Their Effect on Communism in the Middle East and the International Position of the Soviet Union." Ph. D. dissertation, American University, 1968. (DA 29, p1265)

Analyzes Soviet advances in Egypt during this crucial period that precedes the June war.

852 Gama, Abid Husni. "The United Nations and the Palestinian Refugees: An Analysis of the United Nations Relief and Works Agency in the Near East, 1 May 1950-30 June 1971." Ph. D. dissertation, University of Arizona, 1972. (DA 33, p695)

Useful as background to the time when nationalism was growing among the Palestinians.

853 George, Patrick Cyril. "The United States and the Central Treaty Organization." Ph. D. dissertation, University of Virginia, 1968. (DA 29, p2776)

Discusses the American use of CENTO as a defense structure in the Middle East.

854 Hackley, Lloyd V. "Soviet Behavior in the Middle East as a Function of Change, 1950-1970." Ph. D. dissertation, University of North Carolina, 1976. (DA 37, p4340)

An account of the Soviet's use of foreign aid to gain influence and prestige in the Arab world.

855 Hamlet, Bruce D. "A Comparative Analysis of British Foreign Relations: The Palestine War, 1947-1949; the Suez Crisis, 1956; the Arab-Israeli Crisis, 1967." Ph. D. dissertation, Claremont Graduate School, 1971. (DA 32, p1049)

Declares that British popular sentiment determined the course of British action in the 1967 crisis.

856 Harris, George S. Troubled Alliance: Turkish-

American Problems in Historical Perspective, 1945-1971. Stanford, Calif.: Hoover Institution, 1972.

The author asserts that the Turco-American alliance suffered much wear and tear during the troubled decade of the 1960s over Cyprus, narcotics, the status of U. S. forces, missiles, and leftist sentiment in Turkey.

857 Hatzilambrou, Lambros. "Soviet Foreign Policy in the Eastern Mediterranean: A Systematic Approach." Ph. D. dissertation, Howard University, 1976. (DA 37, p4603)

Suggests that Soviet approach to the Arabs was ideologically oriented and utilized massive infusions of arms to win Arab support.

858 Hensel, Howard M. "Soviet Policy in the Persian Gulf, 1968-1975." Ph. D. dissertation, University of Virginia, 1976. (DA 37, p6738)

In 1968 the British government announced its intention to withdraw from the Persian Gulf in 1971, and this study examines the reaction of the Soviets to this move and the course of action that followed.

859 Howard, Harry N. "The Bicentennial in American-Turkish Relations," Middle East Journal, 30 (summer 1976), 291-310.

Points out some difficulties that marred the good feeling between Turkey and the U. S. during the 1960s.

860 ________. "Continuing Trouble in the Turkish Republic," Current History, 64 (January 1973), 26-29.

Alludes to the growing troubles that emerged in Turkey during the 1960s.

861 ________. "Jordan in Turmoil," Current History, 63 (January 1972), 14-19.

Focuses on the difficulties in Jordan following the 1967 Arab-Israeli war.

862 ________. "The United States and the Middle East," in Tareq Y. Ismael, ed., The Middle East in World Politics. Syracuse, N. Y.: Syracuse University Press, 1974.

Asserts that there was little real change in U. S. policy during the 1960s and that American policy-makers did try to affect a peaceful settlement after the 1967 war.

863 Huff, Earl Dean. "Zionist Influences Upon U. S. For-

eign Policy: A Study of American Policy Toward the Middle East from the Time of the Struggle for Israel to the Sinai Conflict." Ph.D. dissertation, University of Idaho, 1971. (DA 32, p3400)

The Zionist movement was most effective during the decade in question in arousing popular sentiment for a pro-Israeli policy.

864 Hurewitz, J. C. Middle East Politics: The Military Dimension. New York: Praeger, 1972.

Discusses the military aspects of the Soviet-American rivalry in the Middle East.

865 ______, ed. Soviet-American Rivalry in the Middle East. New York: Praeger, 1969.

A series of essays that sheds light on the U.S.-Soviet rivalry that continued during the 1960s.

866 Ince, Nurhan. "Problems and Politics in Turkish Foreign Policy, 1960-1966: With Emphasis on Turkish-United States Relations, the Cyprus Question, and the Leftist Movement." Ph.D. dissertation, University of Kentucky, 1974. (DA 36, p4730)

This study draws attention to numerous problems, mainly the Cyprus question, that tended to dampen U.S.-Turkish relations during the first half of the decade.

867 Jabara, Abdeen. "The American Left and the June Conflict," in Ibrahim Abu-Lughod, ed., The Arab-Israeli Confrontation of June 1967: An Arab Perspective. Evanston, Ill.: Northwestern University Press, 1970.

Suggests that the American Left condemned the war of 1967 and took issue with the majority opinion in the U.S. that was pro-Israeli.

868 Jamjoom, Mohamed Abdulwahid. "International Trade and Balance of Payments of a Mono-Product Economy: A Case Study of the Saudi Arabian Kingdom." Ph.D. dissertation, University of Southern California, 1970. (DA 31, p2565)

The purpose of this study is to provide an analytical examination of the foreign trade and balance of payments of the Saudi Arabian Kingdom for the period 1958-1967.

869 al-Jazairi, Mohamed Zayyan. "Saudi Arabia: A Diplomatic History, 1924-1964." Ph.D. dissertation,

University of Utah, 1971. (DA 32, p868)
The latter part of this study is relevant to this era.

870 Johnson, Lyndon B. The Vantage Point: Perspectives of the Presidency, 1963-1969. New York: Holt, Rinehart, & Winston, 1971.
Provides an excellent description of high-level U. S. policy-making during the 1967 June War, and the effort to secure a peace.

871 Jureidini, Paul A. "The Relationship of the Palestinian Guerrilla Movement with the Government of Jordan, 1967-1970." Ph. D. dissertation, American University, 1975. (DA 36, p3108)
The purpose of this dissertation is to provide a clearer understanding of the evolution of the relationships of the government of Jordan with the Palestinian guerrilla movement.

872 ElKashef, Ahmad Refat. "Soviet Policy toward Egypt, 1955-1967." Ph. D. dissertation, Boston University, 1973. (DA 34, p7305)
This is a study of the Soviet's policy vis-à-vis Egypt between the arms deal in 1955 and the 1967 June War.

873 Kerr, Malcolm H. The Arab Cold War, 1958-1964: A Study of Ideology in Politics. London: Oxford University Press, 1967.
This study examines the internecine strife in the Arab world during a time when the U. S. had to make readjustments in its Middle East policy.

874 Khalil, Houssam El-Dawla H. "The Soviet Foreign Policy toward Egypt, 1955-1964." Ph. D. dissertation, Howard University, 1970. (DA 31, p6134)
This study examines the Soviet-Egyptian rapprochement that the Soviets used to reduce Western prestige in the Arab world.

875 Khouri, Fred J. The Arab-Israeli Dilemma. Syracuse, N. Y.: Syracuse University Press, 1968.
This work is critical of U. S. policy in the 1960s which was politically motivated and was partially responsible for the 1967 war, an event that caused a decline in American prestige in the Middle East.

876 Kikoski, John Frank, Jr. "The United Nations Security Council Resolution of November 22, 1967: International

Politics and Law in an Organizational Setting." Ph. D. dissertation, University of Massachusetts, 1972. (DA 33, p3001)

The purpose of this work is to demonstrate how the United Nations was used in a crisis and to trace the interactions of states, international law and organization which resulted in the passage of this resolution.

877 Koch, Howard Everard, Jr. "Permanent War: A Reappraisal of the Arab-Israeli War." Ph. D. dissertation, Stanford University, 1973. (DA 34, p3505)

This dissertation examines the 25-year-old Arab-Israeli confrontation.

878 El-Kordy, Abdul-Hafez M. "The United Nations Peace-Keeping Function in the Arab World." Ph. D. dissertation, American University, 1967. (DA 28, p3743)

This work examines the United Nations peace-keeping function and concludes that the Arab-Israeli impasse continues to challenge this function because Israel will not implement U. N. resolutions.

879 al-Kubaisi, Basil Raouf. "The Arab Nationalist Movement, 1951-1971: From Pressure Group to Socialist Party." Ph. D. dissertation, American University, 1971. (DA 33, p792)

This study examines the emergence of the Arab Nationalists Movement (ANM) and the impact it had on the Arab nationalist movement in general.

880 Lacouture, Jean. Nasser: A Biography. New York: Knopf, 1973.

A brief biography of a major historical figure during this period.

881 Laqueur, Walter. The Road to War: The Origin and Aftermath of the Arab-Israeli Conflict, 1967-1968. New York: Penguin Books, 1968.

A complete study of the U. S. involvement in the crisis leading to the June War, and the American effort to affect a ceasefire and permanent peace settlement.

882 ________. The Struggle for the Middle East: The Soviet Union in the Mediterranean, 1958-1968. New York: Macmillan, 1969.

This study investigates the Soviet attempt to remove Western influence from the Middle East and to expand its own position in the troubled region.

883 Lederer, Ivo J., and Wayne S. Vucinich. The Soviet Union and the Middle East: The Post-World War II Era. Stanford, Calif.: Hoover Institution Press, 1974.

Several of the essays in this volume deal with the Middle East during the decade of the 1960s, indicating the Soviet Union's new position in the area.

884 Lenczowski, George. "Arab Radicalism: Problems and Prospects," Current History, 60 (January 1971), 32-37.

Describes the growth of Arab radicalism in the aftermath of the 1967 Arab-Israeli war, giving special emphasis on growth of revolutionary sentiment among Palestinians.

885 ________. "Iraq: Seven Years of Revolution," Current History, 48 (May 1965), 281-89.

This essay treats the political evolution in Iraq following the 1958 revolution.

886 ________. "Tradition and Reform in Saudi Arabia," Current History, 52 (February 1967), 98-104.

This essay discusses the stable, conservative regime of Saudi Arabia as it contrasts with the revolutionary states in the Arab world.

887 ________. United States Interests in the Middle East. Washington, D.C.: American Enterprise Institute for Public Policy Research, 1968.

Provides a brief sketch of U.S. involvement in the 1967 war.

888 Lewis, Bernard. "The Arab-Israeli War: The Consequences of Defeat," Foreign Affairs, 46 (January 1968), 321-35.

Suggests that the Soviets manufactured the crisis that led to the 1967 Arab-Israeli war.

889 ________. "The Great Powers, the Arabs and the Israelis," Foreign Affairs (July 1969), 642-52.

Discusses the growth of Soviet prestige in the Arab world following the 1967 war.

890 ________. "The Middle Eastern Reaction to Soviet Pressures," Middle East Journal, X (spring 1956), 125-37.

Treats the inroads made by the Soviets following the 1955 arms deal with the Egyptians.

891 McCormick, James M. "An Interaction Analysis of International Crises: A Study of the Suez Crisis and the Six Day War." Ph.D. dissertation, Michigan State University, 1973. (DA 34, 6080)
A comparison of policy goals and results between the Suez and Six Day War crises.

892 Naber, Anton Ayed. "The Arab-Israeli Water Conflict." Ph.D. dissertation, American University, 1968. (DA 29, p1269)
The study of the Arab-Israeli water conflict is the history of the different plans that were evolved to exploit the waters of the Jordan River and its tributaries.

893 O'Hali, Abdulaziz A. "Saudi Arabia in the United Nations General Assembly, 1946-1970." Ph.D. dissertation, Claremont Graduate School, 1974. (DA 36, p1792)
The purpose of this quantitative study is to determine the degree of Saudi Arabia's participation in the United Nations General Assembly.

894 Patrick, Robert Bayard. "Iran's Emergence as a Middle Eastern Power." Ph.D. dissertation, University of Utah, 1973. (DA 34, p2001)
The work describes the emergence of Iran's power base which is grounded on political, economic, and military considerations.

895 Perry, Glenn Earl. "United States Relations with Egypt, 1951-1963: Egyptian Neutralism and the American Alignment Policy." Ph.D. dissertation, University of Virginia, 1964. (DA 25, p3670)
This study treats in part the normalization of U.S.-Egyptian relations after 1958 when the U.S. began to give economic assistance to Egypt.

896 Polk, William R. The United States and the Arab World. Cambridge, Mass.: Harvard University Press, 1965.
Gives an excellent description of President Kennedy's even-handed Middle-East policy in the early 1960s.

897 Quandt, William B. Decade of Decisions: American Policy toward the Arab-Israeli Conflict, 1967-1976. Berkeley: University of California Press, 1977.
An excellent treatment of U.S. involvement in the

1967 crisis and the efforts to affect a peace settlement in the aftermath of the war.

898 ________. "Domestic Influences on United States Foreign Policy in the Middle East: The View from Washington," in Willard A. Beling, ed., *The Middle East: Quest for an American Policy.* Albany: State University of New York Press, 1973.
Discusses the domestic constraints on U.S. Middle-Eastern policy-makers.

899 ________. "United States Policy in the Middle East: Constraints and Choices," in Paul Y. Hammond and Sidney S. Alexander, eds., *Political Dynamics in the Middle East.* New York: American Elsevier, 1972.
Describes President Kennedy's Middle-East policy and the efforts of President Johnson to prevent the outbreak of war in 1967 and his attempt to achieve a peace settlement following the conflict.

900 El-Quazzaz, Marwan H. "A Comparative Analysis of United States Policy in the 1956 Suez War and the 1967 Arab-Israeli War." Ph.D. dissertation, Southern Illinois University, 1976. (DA 37, p6037)
Concludes that the U.S. in the 1967 war supported the Israeli position that troop withdrawal must be a part of an overall peace settlement.

901 Rahinsky, Herbert. "United States Foreign Policy and the Arab Refugees." Ph.D. dissertation, New York University, 1971. (DA 32, p2616)
Discusses American support of the U.N.'s efforts to care for the Palestinian refugees, victims of the Arab-Israeli confrontation.

902 Ramazani, Rouhollah K. "Iran and the United States: An Experiment in Enduring Friendship," *Middle East Journal*, 30 (summer 1976), 322-34.
Discusses a temporary cooling of relations between the two countries in the 1960s.

903 ________. *Iran's Foreign Policy, 1941-1973: A Study of Foreign Policy in Modernizing Nations.* Charlottesville: University Press of Virginia, 1975.
Asserts that the course of events during the 1960s led Iran to question the firm relationship with the United States, a turn that led to closer ties with the Soviets.

904 Reich, Bernard. "Israel's Quest for Security," Current History, 62 (January 1972), 1-5.
Discusses Israel's pursuit of stability in the aftermath of the 1967 war.

905 _______. "United States Policy in the Middle East," Current History, 60 (January 1971), 1-6.
This essay treats U. S. efforts after 1967 to find a Middle-Eastern settlement.

906 Rubinstein, Alvin Z. Red Star on the Nile: The Soviet Egyptian Influence Relationship Since the June War. Princeton, N. J.: Princeton University Press, 1977.
Treats the massive influx of Soviet arms and advisers following Egypt's defeat in the 1967 war with Israel.

907 _______. "The Soviet Union in the Middle East," Current History, 63 (October 1972), 165-69.
An account of the Soviet objectives and influences in the Middle East.

908 Al-Saadi, Mohammed Ali. "The Jordan River Dispute: A Case Study in International Conflicts." Ph. D. dissertation, University of Massachusetts, 1969. (DA 30, p784)
This dissertation aims at providing a comprehensive and systematic treatment of the Arab-Israeli dispute over the waters of the Jordan River.

909 Safran, Nadav. From War to War: The Arab-Israeli Confrontation, 1948-1967. New York: Pegasus, 1969.
A balanced account of the 1967 Arab-Israeli war that accounts for an American tilt toward Israel based on wide public support for that country's cause.

910 Saliba, Samir Nicholas. "The Jordan River Dispute." Ph. D. dissertation, Tulane University, 1966. (DA 27, p1423)
Says the dispute was bound up in the Arab-Israeli conflict and must be considered in context with the various political questions bearing on the problem.

911 Sam'o, Elias. "The Arab States in the United Nations: A Study of Voting Behavior," Ph. D. dissertation, American University, 1967. (DA 28, p1489)

Examines Arab voting on 72 issues, to determine their voting behavior on questions of great moment to them during the Cold War era.

912 Sankari, Farouk Ali. "The United Nations Truce Supervision Organization in Palestine." Ph. D. dissertation, Claremont Graduate School, 1968. (DA 29, p4081)

Treats U. N. efforts to maintain stability in the Arab-Israeli disputed region.

913 Sherwin, Ronald Graham. "Structural Balance and the International System: The Middle East Conflict, 1967." Ph. D. dissertation, University of Southern California, 1972. (DA 33, p1807)

This dissertation studies the 1967 war and reports on the efforts to operationalize the notion of balance.

914 Snider, Lewis W. "Middle East Maelstrom: The Impact of Global and Regional Influences on the Arab-Israeli Conflict, 1947-1973." Ph. D. dissertation, University of Michigan, 1975. (DA 36, p6940)

This study examines the relative impact of global power rivalries and of inter-Arab political conflicts and bloc alignments on the intensity of the Arab-Israeli conflict.

915 Sowayyegh, Abdul-Aziz Hussein. "Oil and the Arab-Israeli Conflict: A Study in Arab Oil Strategy between 1948-1973." Ph. D. dissertation, Claremont Graduate School, 1977. (DA 37, p7302)

This dissertation attempts to analyze the Arab's use of oil as a political lever during the postwar era.

916 Stevens, Georgianna, ed. _The United States and the Middle East._ Englewood Cliffs, N. J.: Prentice-Hall, 1964.

This collection of essays contains several articles that treat U. S. relations with the Middle East in the 1960s, with emphasis on the swing toward the even-handed policy.

917 Stookey, Robert W. _America and the Arab States: An Uneasy Encounter._ New York: Wiley, 1975.

Discusses the American role during the Arab Cold War, and the U. S. effort to maintain peace prior to, during, and after the 1967 Arab-Israeli conflict.

918 Suleiman, Michael W. "American Mass Media and the

June Conflict," in Ibrahim Abu-Lughod, ed., The Arab-Israeli Confrontation of June 1967: An Arab Perspective. Evanston, Ill.: Northwestern University Press, 1970.

Argues that the American press was reluctant to criticize Israel during the 1967 Arab-Israeli war. It employed a double standard toward Arabs and Jews.

919 Sutcliffe, Claud R. "Change in the Jordan Valley: The Impact and Implications of the East Ghor Canal Project, 1961-1966." Ph.D. dissertation, Princeton University, 1970. (DA 31, p4238)

The East Ghor Canal, a U.S.A.I.D.-financed irrigation project in the Jordan Valley, was officially opened in 1961, and this study attempts to analyze its impact on the region.

920 Taylor, Alan, and Richard N. Tetlie, eds. Palestine: A Search for Truth: Approaches to the Arab-Israeli Conflict. Washington, D.C.: Public Affairs Press, 1970.

This collection of essays contains numerous articles relative to the American perception of Arabs and Israelis during this crucial decade.

921 Tennenboim, Mark. "Soviet-Egyptian Relations, October 1964-September 1970: Brezhnev and Abd al-Nasir." Ph.D. dissertation, New York University, 1977. (DA 38, p2283)

This study attempts to analyze the development of Soviet-Egyptian relations from 1964 to 1970, a period in which the U.S. position in the Mideast was very low.

922 Trice, Robert Holmes, Jr. "Domestic Political Interests and American Policy in the Middle East: Pro-Arab and Corporate Non-Governmental Actors and the Making of American Foreign Policy, 1966-1971." Ph.D. dissertation, University of Wisconsin, 1974. (DA 35, p6790)

The purpose of this work is to develop a better understanding of the role played by non-governmental actors--private individuals, voluntary membership associations and corporations--in the foreign policy-making process.

923 Turner, Jack Justin. "Arab-Asian Positive Neutralism and United States Foreign Policy." Ph.D. dissertation, University of Kentucky, 1969. (DA 30, p3532)

Arab neutralism has been a source of concern for the United States during the period of the Cold War, and this study attempts to analyze this force as a factor in policy-making.

924 Turner, Michael Allan. "The International Politics of Narcotics: Turkey and the United States." Ph. D. dissertation, Kent State University, 1975. (DA 36, p6295)
This study analyzes the American attempt to persuade Turkey in the 1960s to control its opium production, much of which was smuggled into the United States.

925 Wagner, Abraham R. "The Six Day War: A Study in Crisis, Decision-Making." Ph. D. dissertation, University of Rochester, 1973. (Selim, p121) [Abstract not available.]

926 el-Yacoubi, Hassan Hassan Shekih Salim. "The Evolution of Palestinian Consciousness." Ph. D. dissertation, University of Colorado, 1973. (DA 34, p7858)
Analyzes the evolution of Palestinian consciousness.

927 Yost, Charles W. "The Arab-Israeli War: How It Began," Foreign Affairs, 46 (January 1968), 305-20.
Concludes that neither side plotted war, but that both committed blunders making war inevitable.

928 Zindani, Abdul Wahed Aziz. "Arab Politics in the United Nations." Ph. D. dissertation, Notre Dame University, 1976. (DA 37, p3891)
Deals with Arab politics at the U. N.

P

POSTWAR OIL DIPLOMACY AND THE ENERGY CRISIS

929 Abbass, Abdul Majid. "Oil Diplomacy in the Near East." Ph. D. dissertation, University of Chicago, 1940. (DD 7: p93) [Abstract not available.]

930 Ahrari, Mohammed E. "The Dynamics of Oil Diplomacy: Conflict and Consensus." Ph. D. dissertation, Southern Illinois University, 1976. (DA 37, p6037)

This study examines the conflict between oil companies and host countries and shows how OPEC grew out of this conflict and operated to represent the host countries' interests.

931 Akins, James E. "The Oil Crisis: This Time the Wolf Is Here," Foreign Affairs, 51 (April 1973), 462-90.

This is perhaps one of the most important essays to highlight the coming energy crisis in the United States, the growing dependence on Arab oil, and the possible use of oil as a lever to influence U. S. Mideast policy.

932 Ali, Sk. Rustum. Saudi Arabia and Oil Diplomacy. New York: Praeger, 1976.

This study seeks to analyze the use of oil as an instrument of pressure against the United States during the 1973 Arab-Israeli war.

933 Amuzegar, Jahanigir. "The Oil Story: Facts, Fiction and Fair Play," Foreign Affairs, 51 (July 1973), 676-89.

This essay discusses some of the harsh realities of the growing energy crisis and the growing dependence of the U. S. on Middle-East oil.

934 Anbari, Abdul-Amir Ali. "The Law of Petroleum Concession Agreements in the Middle East." Ph. D.

dissertation, Harvard University, 1968. (1968, p234, ADD) [Abstract not available.]

935 Anthony, John Duke, ed. *The Middle East: Oil, Politics, and Development.* Washington, D.C.: American Enterprise Institute, 1975.

This series of essays discusses a wide range of subjects dealing with petroleum and international politics.

936 Barakeh, Abdul Kader. "An Analysis of the Impact of African Oil Development on Middle East Petroleum Exports to Western Europe, 1955-1965." Ph.D. dissertation, Indiana University, 1968. (DA 29, p2847)

This study has determined that African oil has replaced much of Europe's reliance on Middle-Eastern oil which flows from fields owned or controlled by American companies.

937 Bill, James A., and Robert W. Stookey. *Politics and Petroleum: The Middle East and the United States.* Brunswick, Ohio: Kings Court Communications, 1975.

This slim work attempts to introduce the reader to the dynamics of contemporary Middle East politics, giving special emphasis to the growing reliance of the United States upon Middle-Eastern oil.

938 Brown, Robert Eylie. "A Special View of Oil Development in the Desert: Libya in the First Decade, 1955-1965." Ph.D. dissertation, Columbia University, 1970. (DA 31B, p5416)

Discusses the impact of the Libyan Petroleum Law of 1955 on oil development in that country where American developers enjoyed opportunity to develop new reserves of petroleum.

939 Bryson, Thomas A. *American Diplomatic Relations with the Middle East, 1784-1975: A Survey.* Metuchen, N.J.: Scarecrow Press, 1977.

This study surveys the postwar efforts of Americans to develop Middle-Eastern oil reserves and the growing dependence of the United States on Arab oil, coupled with the problems presented by the ongoing Arab-Israeli conflict.

940 Cottam, Richard W. *Nationalism in Iran.* Pittsburgh: University of Pittsburgh Press, 1964.

Discusses the oil crisis in Iran and declares that the CIA did not oust Premier Mossadegh in the 1953 coup d'état.

941 _______. "The United States, Iran and the Cold War," Iranian Studies, III (winter 1970), 2-22.
Asserts that there is no evidence to support the view that American oil interests were a significant factor in U. S. policy-making before 1954.

942 Doenecke, Justus D. "Iran's Role in Cold War Revisionism," Iranian Studies, V (spring-summer 1972), 96-111.
The author presents the revisionist view of oil as a factor in Russo-American relations in the Cold War.

943 _______. "Revisionists, Oil and Cold War Diplomacy," Iranian Studies, III (winter 1970), 23-33.
This essay treats revisionist historians' view of oil as a factor in U. S. diplomacy.

944 Duce, James Terry. "The Changing Oil Industry," Foreign Affairs, 40 (July 1962), 627-34.
An oil official presents some interesting comments on the oil industry in the 1960s.

945 Eisenhower, Dwight D. Mandate for Change, 1953-1956: The White House Years. New York: Doubleday, 1963.
This memoir contains important material relative to the American role in the Iranian oil crisis of the 1950s.

946 _______. Waging Peace, 1956-1961: The White House Years. New York: Doubleday, 1965.
This volume treats the American role in creating the Baghdad Pact, discusses the reasons for withdrawing support on the Aswan Dam and the U. S. reaction to the Suez crisis, and analyzes the reasons for the enunciation of the Eisenhower Doctrine and the subsequent American intervention in Lebanon.

947 Engler, Robert. The Politics of Oil: A Study of Private Power and Democratic Directions. New York: Macmillan, 1961.
This study demonstrates the ties between industry and government in shaping policy and discusses the American role in the Iranian oil crisis of the 1950s.

948 Feis, Herbert. Petroleum and American Foreign Policy. Stanford, Calif.: Stanford University Press, 1944.
A good discussion of a postwar oil policy.

949 Finaish, Mohamed Ali. "Libya's Petroleum Policy." Ph. D. dissertation, University of Southern California, 1972. (DA 33, p4623)

This dissertation analyzes the position of the petroleum industry, of which the U. S. has a considerable stake, in Libya.

950 Finnie, David H. Desert Enterprise: Middle East Oil Industry in Its Local Environment. Cambridge, Mass.: Harvard University Press, 1958.

This work treats the impact of the oil industry on the Middle East, the problems of the companies in their respective host countries, and the relationship between the companies and the U. S. government.

951 Fisher, Carol A., and Fred Krinsky. Middle East in Crisis: A Historical and Documentary Review. Syracuse, N. Y.: Syracuse University Press, 1959.

A brief chapter on the oil industry in the Middle East is presented here.

952 Frank, Helmut Jack. "The Pricing of Middle East Crude Oil." Ph. D. dissertation, Columbia University, 1961. (DA 22, p3023)

This dissertation analyzes the basing-point system for determining the price of Middle East petroleum.

953 Freedman, Robert O. "The Soviet Union and the Politics of Middle Eastern Oil," in Naiem A. Sherbiny and Mark A. Tessler, eds., Arab Oil: Impact on the Arab Countries and Global Implications. New York: Praeger, 1976.

Demonstrates the Soviets' interest in Middle-East oil which is needed by its Eastern bloc allies and as a factor in great-power rivalry.

954 Friedland, Edward, et al. "Oil and the Decline of Western Power," Political Science Quarterly, 90 (fall 1975), 437-50.

Asserts that the U. S. faces a dilemma in the Mideast where the Arabs through oil power and the Israelis through military power can both exert influence on U. S. policy. Suggests the U. S. could use Israeli force in event of future conflict to take over several oil-producing countries to ensure stability and a supply of oil.

955 Garnham, David. "The Oil Crisis and U. S. Attitudes

toward Israel," in Naiem A. Sherbiny and Mark A. Tessler, eds., Arab Oil: Impact on the Arab Countries and Global Implications. New York: Praeger, 1976.

This is an interesting essay on the broad range of American public opinion toward Israel during the energy crisis.

956 Hammad, Mohamed Burham. "Middle Eastern Oil Concessions: Some Legal and Policy Aspects of Relations between Grantors and Grantees." Ph. D. dissertation, Yale University, 1963. (Index 1962, p130, ADD) [Abstract not available.]

957 Ismael, Tareq Y. "Oil: The New Diplomacy," in his The Middle East in World Politics. Syracuse, N. Y.: Syracuse University Press, 1974.

This essay relates the Arab oil weapon to the Arab-Israeli conflict and to the American role therein.

958 Itayim, Fuad. "Arab Oil--The Political Dimension," Journal of Palestine Studies, III (1974), 90-105.

Discusses the Arabs' use of the oil weapon during the October 1973 War.

959 Kaufman, Burton I. "Mideast Multinational Oil, U.S. Foreign Policy, and Antitrust: The 1950s," Journal of American History, LXIII (March 1977), 937-59.

Asserts that the United States used American multinational oil corporations in the Middle East as instruments of U.S. foreign policy.

960 Kayal, Alawi Darweesh. "The Control of Oil: East-West Rivalry in the Persian Gulf." Ph. D. dissertation, University of Colorado, 1972. (DA 33, p4510)

This author discusses the Russo-American rivalry in the Persian Gulf region, an area recently evacuated by the British.

961 Kirk, George E. The Middle East, 1945-50. London: Oxford University Press, 1954.

Relates American aid to Iran to the Iranian nationalization of Anglo-Iranian Oil Co.

962 Klebanoff, Shoshana. Middle East Oil and U.S. Foreign Policy with Special Reference to the U.S. Energy Crisis. New York: Praeger, 1974.

This study relates the American quest for Mideast oil to European recovery, examines the Iranian oil crisis, describes the Suez crisis, summarizes the energy situation in 1967, and concludes with a word on the energy crisis at the time of the 1973 October war.

963 Kolko, Joyce, and Gabriel Kolko. _The Limits of Power: The World and United States Foreign Policy, 1945-1954._ New York: Harper & Row, 1972.
U. S. policy in postwar Iran aimed at securing new sources of petroleum and not at the defense of the country from the Soviets.

964 Landis, Lincoln. "Petroleum in Soviet Middle East Strategy." Ph. D. dissertation, Georgetown University, 1969. (DA 30, p4002)
This dissertation evaluates Soviet interest in Middle-East petroleum, describing it in terms of a long-range, strategic motivation based upon development of a comprehensive pattern of petroleum import and export trade.

965 Lenczowski, George. _Middle East Oil in a Revolutionary Age._ Washington, D. C.: American Enterprise Institute, 1976.
This brief work discusses the relationship between the American oil companies and the host countries, and the latter's efforts to obtain higher economic return on the oil investment.

966 ________. _Oil and State in the Middle East._ Ithaca, N. Y.: Cornell University Press, 1960.
This work is concerned with relations between American and Western oil companies and the various host countries in the Middle East.

967 ________. _United States Interests in the Middle East._ Washington, D. C.: American Enterprise Institute, 1968.
The author presents a concise statement of American Middle-Eastern oil interests to 1968 and suggests that the U. S. would become more dependent on Middle-Eastern oil.

968 Levy, Walter J. "Oil Power," _Foreign Affairs,_ 49 (July 1971), 652-68.
Discusses growing reliance of U. S. on Middle-Eastern oil and the Arab states' increased willingness to obtain greater control over the oil companies.

969 ________. "World Oil Cooperation or International Chaos," Foreign Affairs, 52 (July 1974), 690-713.
This essay asserts the growing dependence of Western industrial countries upon Arab oil.

970 Longrigg, Stephen Hemsley. Oil in the Middle East: Its Discovery and Development. London: Oxford University Press, 1968.
This work addresses the oil companies' quest for oil and is of little use to the diplomatic historian, except when the author discusses American reaction to Iranian nationalization of the Anglo-Iranian Oil Company.

971 Magnus, Ralph. "Middle East Oil and the OPEC Nations," Current History, 70 (January 1976), 22-26.
Relates the difficulties of the OPEC nations in maintaining a solid front against the Western industrial nations.

972 Mansour, Hussein Omar. "The Discovery of Oil and Its Impact on the Industrialization of Saudi Arabia." Ph. D. dissertation, University of Arizona, 1973. (DA 34, p2522)
This work describes the impact of oil discovery on the Saudis and their efforts to capitalize on this rich resource.

973 Mikesell, Raymond F., and Hollis B. Chenery. Arabian Oil: America's Stake in the Middle East. Chapel Hill: University of North Carolina Press, 1949.
The authors discuss the relationship of Middle-Eastern oil to American strategic objectives in the region.

974 Mosley, Leonard. Power Play: Oil in the Middle East. New York: Random House, 1973.
This work describes the American quest for oil in the postwar Middle East, with emphasis on Saudi Arabia, Kuwait, the Arab shekhdoms, Libya, and Iran.

975 Nash, Gerald D. United States Oil Policy, 1890-1964. Pittsburgh: University of Pittsburgh Press, 1968.
Describes ties between oil interests and government officials and the former's quest for oil.

976 Odell, Peter R. Oil and World Power. New York: Taplinger, 1970.
An excellent study of the complexities of the international oil industry and world politics.

977 Pollack, Gerald A. "The Economic Consequences of the Energy Crisis," Foreign Affairs, 52 (April 1974), 452-71.

A discussion of the energy crisis in terms of the balance of payments problem and its effects on the economies of western states.

978 Quandt, William B. "U. S. Energy Policy and the Arab Israeli Conflict," in Naiem A. Sherbiny and Mark A. Tessler, eds., Arab Oil: Impact on the Arab Countries and Global Implications. New York: Praeger, 1976.

This essay discusses the U. S. energy crisis in terms of the Arab-Israeli conflict, with emphasis on the 1973 Arab oil embargo and its repercussions in the U. S.

979 Rustow, Dankwart. "U. S. -Saudi Relations and the Oil Crises of the 1980s," Foreign Affairs, 55 (April 1977), 494-516.

Points out the important interrelationship between the United States and the Saudis and the latter's role in OPEC as it impinges on U. S. energy needs.

980 Al-Sabea, Taha Hussain. "Middle East Oil and Nationalization: An Economic Analysis." Ph. D. dissertation, University of Southern California, 1969. (DA 30, p1717)

Examines the economic feasibility of the nationalization of the oil industry in the Middle-Eastern countries.

981 Sayegh, Kamal S. Oil and Arab Regional Development. New York: Praeger, 1968.

This book discusses the relations between oil companies and host countries and examines the social, economic, and physical impact of oil companies on the Arab lands.

982 Sheehan, M. K. Iran: Impact of United States Interests and Policies. Brooklyn, N. Y.: Theo Gaus, 1968.

Discusses in detail the American role in the Anglo-Iranian oil crisis of the 1950s.

983 Sherbiny, Naiem A., and Mark A. Tessler, eds. Arab Oil: Impact on the Arab Countries and Global Implications. New York: Praeger, 1976.

This collection of essays contains three articles that bear on U. S. diplomatic interests and Middle-East oil.

984 Shwadran, Benjamin. The Middle East, Oil, and the

Great Powers. New York: Praeger, 1955.
This is an excellent study of American diplomacy as it relates to the quest for oil in the postwar era.

985 Sowayyegh, Abdul Aziz Hussein. "Oil and the Arab-Israeli Conflict: A Study in Arab Oil Strategy between 1948-1973." Ph.D. dissertation, Claremont Graduate School, 1977. (DA 37, p7302)
This writer asserts that as long as the Palestinian issue remains unresolved, the Arab oil-producing states would continue to use oil as a lever in international relations.

986 Stocking, George W. Middle East Oil: A Study in Political and Economic Controversy. Nashville: Vanderbilt University Press, 1970.
Treats the Iranian oil controversy of the 1950s; concludes the U.S. acted aggressively in this crisis.

987 Stookey, Robert W. America and the Arab States: An Uneasy Encounter. New York: Wiley, 1975.
The author depicts the ever-changing Middle East as a region vital to American energy needs, both for U.S. allies and for domestic consumption.

988 Tucker, Robert W. "Oil: The Issue of American Intervention," Commentary, 59 (January 1975), 21-31.
Suggests the U.S. consider military intervention as an alternative to future Arab oil embargoes which pose a threat to the well-being of the U.S. and its European and Japanese allies.

989 Tully, Andrew. CIA: The Inside Story. New York: Morrow, 1962.
This author discusses the American role in the 1953 coup d'état that brought down the anti-Western Mossadegh government in Iran.

990 Udovitch, A. L., ed. The Middle East: Oil and Conflict. Lexington, Mass.: Lexington Books, 1976.
This compilation of essays contains numerous articles that relate to the growing American dependence on Middle-Eastern oil.

991 Wise, David, and Thomas B. Ross. The Invisible Government. New York: Random House, 1964.
This book treats the U.S. role in the Iranian political crisis of the 1950s.

Q

THE CRUCIAL DECADE OF THE 1970s

992 Allon, Yigal. "Israel: The Case for Defensible Borders," Foreign Affairs, 55 (October 1976), 38-53.
Presents an interesting solution to the West Bank of the Jordan and the Palestinian issue.

993 AlRoy, Gil Carl. The Kissinger Experience: American Policy in the Middle East. New York: Horizon, 1975.
A critical analysis of Kissinger's diplomacy during the October War and the aftermath.

994 Ball, George W. "How to Save Israel in Spite of Herself," Foreign Affairs, 55 (April 1977), 453-71.
The author presents a method by which the U. S. might urge Israel to take those steps necessary to a Middle-East settlement.

995 Beres, Louis Rene. "Terrorism and the Nuclear Threat in the Middle East," Current History, 70 (January 1976), 27-29.
Suggests that unless the Palestinian issue is settled, the P. L. O. might obtain nuclear weapons and set off a chain of violence that could sweep the Middle East.

996 Bezboruah, Monoranjan. "The United States Strategy in the Indian Ocean, 1968-1976." Ph. D. dissertation, University of Mississippi, 1977. (DA 38, p4357)
This dissertation studies the American effort to bring the Indian Ocean into its strategic concerns following Britain's retreat from that body of water in 1968.

997 Brandon, Henry. "Jordan: The Forgotten Crisis," Foreign Policy, 10 (spring 1973), 158-70.
Assesses U. S. policy in the Jordanian crisis.

998 ________. The Retreat of American Power. New York: Doubleday, 1973.

Provides good treatment of U.S. involvement in the 1970 Jordan crisis.

999 Bryson, Thomas A. American Diplomatic Relations with the Middle East, 1784-1975: A Survey. Metuchen, N.J.: Scarecrow Press, 1977.
Examines American-Middle Eastern diplomacy during and after the 1973 October War as the U.S. sought a new identity in the troubled region.

1000 Campbell, John C. "The Mediterranean Crisis," Foreign Affairs, 53 (July 1975), 605-24.
Views the Mediterranean in terms of the increasing number of political problems that obstruct an American presence in those waters.

1001 Churba, Joseph. The Politics of Defeat: America's Decline in the Middle East. New York: Cyrco Press, 1977.
Posits that the U.S. must support Israel because of that nation's value to American security in the Middle East.

1002 Divine, Donna Robinson. "Why This War ...," International Journal of Middle East Studies, 7 (October 1976), 523-43.
This essay seeks to find a primary motive for President Sadat's decision to make war on Israel in 1973.

1003 Ghareeb, Edmund. "The U.S. Arms Supply to Israel during the October War," Journal of Palestine Studies, III (winter 1974), 114-21.
Treats the American extension of military aid to Israel during the October war.

1004 Golan, Matti. The Secret Conversations of Henry Kissinger: Step-by-Step Diplomacy in the Middle East. New York: Quadrangle, 1976.
This is a critical analysis of Henry Kissinger's diplomacy during and after the October 1973 War.

1005 Hall, Ron, et al. Insight on the Middle East War. London: André Deutsch, 1974.
An excellent narrative account of the war that couples some treatment of diplomacy with extended military coverage.

1006 Hensel, Howard M. "Soviet Policy in the Persian

Gulf, 1965-1975." Ph. D. dissertation, University of Virginia, 1976. (DA 37, p6738)

This study examines Russia's efforts to fill the vacuum brought on by Britain's retreat from the Gulf in 1971.

1007 Herzog, Chaim. The War of Atonement: October, 1973. Boston: Little, Brown, 1975.

A military account of the war by one of its participants.

1008 Hoffman, Stanley. "A New Policy for Israel," Foreign Affairs, 53 (April 1975), 405-31.

Discusses the special relationship between the United States and Israel as it relates to the Arab world and to the Soviet Union.

1009 Holden, David. "The Persian Gulf: After the British Raj," Foreign Affairs, 49 (July 1971), 721-35.

Suggests that unrest will follow the British retreat from the Gulf and points to the Saudi-Iranian competition and the Iraqi quest for Kuwait as examples.

1010 Hottinger, Arnold. "The Depth of Arab Radicalism," Foreign Affairs, 51 (April 1973), 461-504.

This essay treats the intensity and scope of Arab discontent.

1011 Howard, Harry N. "Jordan in Turmoil," Current History, 63 (January 1972), 14-19.

Treats the bad effects that the 1967 war had on Jordan when Israel conquered Jerusalem and the West Bank.

1012 ________. "The United States and the Middle East," in Tareq Y. Ismael, ed., The Middle East in World Politics. Syracuse, N. Y.: Syracuse University Press, 1974.

Critical of the special relationship between the U. S. and Israel and views the "military balance" concept as a euphemism for Israeli military superiority.

1013 Howard, Norman. "Upheaval in Lebanon," Current History, 70 (January 1976), 5-9.

An excellent synopsis of the political problems that led to the Civil War in Lebanon and the international problems that exacerbated it.

1014 Ibrahim, Saad. "American Domestic Forces and the

October War," Journal of Palestine Studies, IV (autumn 1974), 55-81.

This article discusses the various lobbies and inputs that have affected American Middle Eastern policy before and during the October War.

1015 Joyner, Christopher Clayton. "Boycott in International Law: A Case Study of the Arab States and Israel." Ph.D. dissertation, University of Virginia, 1977. (DA 38, p4358)

This study examines the effectiveness of the Arab boycott and its implications for the United States in particular.

1016 Kalb, Marvin, and Bernard Kalb. Kissinger. New York: Dell, 1975.

This biography is lengthy and detailed and focuses on Kissinger's Middle-East diplomacy in a manner complimentary to him.

1017 Kanet, Roger E. "Soviet-American Relations: A Year of Dêtente?" Current History, 63 (October 1972), 156-59.

Soviet-American dêtente is related to the Middle East.

1018 Kennan, George F. The Cloud of Danger: Current Realities of American Foreign Policy. Boston: Little, Brown, 1977.

Suggests that the United States must limit its commitment to Israel and try to achieve an alternative source of petroleum to break the dependence on Arab oil.

1019 Kennedy, Edward M. "The Persian Gulf: Arms Race or Arms Control?," Foreign Affairs, 54 (October 1975), 14-35.

Discusses the American arms flow to the Gulf in terms of a possible Russian incursion and of Iranian and Saudi competition for dominence.

1020 Kent, George. "Congress and American Middle East Policy," in Willard Beling, ed., The Middle East: Quest for an American Policy. Albany: State University of New York Press, 1973.

Discusses the role of Congress in determining American policy vis-à-vis Israel and the Arabs.

1021 Krepon, Michael. "A Navy to Match National Pur-

poses," Foreign Affairs, 55 (January 1977), 356-67.
Discusses the need to review the current world situation as a determinant for a new navy to meet current security needs.

1022 Laqueur, Walter. Confrontation: The Middle East and World Politics. New York: Quadrangle, 1974.
A good narrative account of the October War that divorces the Arab oil embargo from American aid to Israel.

1023 Lenczowski, George. "Egypt and the Soviet Exodus," Current History, 64 (January 1973), 13-16.
An account of the Soviet departure from Egypt and the reasons for American lack of response.

1024 Lewis, Bernard. "The Anti-Zionist Resolution," Foreign Affairs, 55 (October 1976), 52-64.
A brief account of the anti-Zionist resolution that was aired in the United Nations.

1025 Luttwak, Edward N., and Walter Laqueur. "Kissinger and the Yom Kippur War," Commentary, 28 (September 1974), 33-40.
Gives reasons for Kissinger's withholding arms from Israel during the October War.

1026 Morris, Roger. Uncertain Greatness: Henry Kissinger and American Foreign Policy. New York: Harper and Row, 1977.
This work contains a chapter on Kissinger's diplomatic efforts during and after the October War.

1027 Perlmutter, Amos. "Begin's Strategy and Dayan's Tactics: The Conduct of Israeli Foreign Policy," Foreign Affairs, 56 (January 1978), 357-72.
This essay presents the Israeli point of view in reaction to the Sadat November démarche, and it also suggests that the U.S. is playing a conflicting role in acting as Israel's defender and as mediator of the Arab-Israeli dispute.

1028 Platt, Alan R. "The Olympic Games and Their Political Aspects." Ph.D. dissertation, Kent State University, 1976. (DA 37, p5343)
This dissertation touches on the use of terror by Palestinians during the 1972 Olympic Games, an act that aroused American public opinion.

1029 Quandt, William B. Decade of Decisions: American

Policy toward the Arab-Israeli Conflict, 1967-1976. Berkeley: University of California Press, 1977.

The author concentrates on the American role in the Jordanian crisis of 1970, the American role in the October War, and on the effort made by the State Department to arrange a peaceful settlement since the 1973 war.

1030 ________. "Domestic Influences on United States Foreign Policy in the Middle East: The View from Washington," in Willard A. Beling, ed., The Middle East: Quest for an American Policy. Albany: State University of New York Press, 1973.

Asserts that the most important domestic consideration in U.S. Middle-East policy-making is the widespread predisposition of officials in government and the public to favor Israel over the Arab states.

1031 ________. "Kissinger and the Arab-Israeli Disengagement Negotiations," Journal of International Affairs, 29 (spring 1975), 33-48.

A synopsis of Kissinger's efforts to restore peace in the October War and to achieve a settlement in the aftermath.

1032 Ramazani, R. K. The Persian Gulf: Iran's Role. Charlottesville: University Press of Virginia, 1972.

This study concerns Iran's new role in the Persian Gulf, following the British retreat from that region in 1971.

1033 Reich, Bernard. "Israel's Year of Decision," Current History, 74 (January 1978), 15-17.

Presents some of the problems and options that have come Israel's way in 1977.

1034 ________. Quest for Peace: United States-Israel Relations and the Arab-Israeli Conflict. New Brunswick, N.J.: Transaction Books, 1977.

An excellent treatment of the U.S. role in the Arab-Israeli conflict between 1967 and the end of the Nixon administration. Well documented with good bibliography.

1035 ________. "United States Policy in the Middle East," Current History, 70 (January 1976), 1-5.

Assesses the American effort to achieve a Middle Eastern settlement following the October War.

1036 Rouleau, Eric. "The Palestinian Quest," Foreign

Affairs, 53 (January 1975), 264-83.
An excellent discussion of the evolution of Palestinian goals and of the Palestinian's complaint against the course of history that has favored Israel.

1037 Rubin, Barry. "U. S. Policy, January-October 1973," Journal of Palestine Studies, III (1974), 114-21.
A synopsis of American Middle-East policy vis-a-vis the Arab-Israeli conflict just prior to the October War.

1038 Rubinstein, Alvin Z. "Egypt Since the October War," Current History, 70 (January 1976), 14-17.
This essay analyzes President Sadat's tilt toward Washington in the aftermath of the 1973 October War.

1039 _______. Red Star on the Nile: The Soviet-Egyptian Influence Relationship Since the June War. Princeton, N. J.: Princeton University Press, 1977.
The author analyzes Egypt's ejection of the Soviets and President Sadat's attempt to reorient Egyptian foreign policy in the post-Nasser era.

1040 el-Sadat, Anwar. "Where Egypt Stands," Foreign Affairs, 51 (October 1972), 114-23.
The Egyptian President discusses the Egyptian bargaining position in the conflict with Israel.

1041 Safran, Nadav. "Engagement in the Middle East," Foreign Affairs, 53 (October 1974), 45-63.
This essay repeats the thesis set forth in item 1043.

1042 _______. Israel--The Embattled Ally. Cambridge, Mass.: Harvard University Press, 1978.
This book discusses the special relationship between the U. S. and Israel and points out the need for these two states to move toward an equitable settlement in the Middle East.

1043 _______. "The War and the Future of the Arab-Israeli Conflict," Foreign Affairs, 52 (January 1974), 215-36.
The author presents a creditable case for an American-Israeli mutual defense pact as a means of securing Israeli political sovereignty, with a view to bringing Israel to the bargaining table.

1044 Savage, Ralph Lee. "Israeli and American Jewish

Attitudes in 1971 on the Future of Israel's Conquered Territories: A Comparative Analysis." Ph. D. dissertation, University of Southern Mississippi, 1972. (Selim, p. 103-04) [Abstract not available.]

1045 Schulz, Ann T. "A Leadership Role for Iran in the Persian Gulf," Current History, 64 (January 1972), 25-30.

This essay discusses Iran's role in the Gulf following the demise of British hegemony.

1046 ______. "United States Policy in the Middle East," Current History, 74 (January 1978), 1-4.

This essay assesses U. S. policy in terms of objectives that include Israeli security, containment of the Soviets, and access to Arab sources of petroleum.

1047 Sheehan, Edward R. F. The Arabs, Israelis, and Kissinger: A Secret History of American Diplomacy in the Middle East. New York: Crowell, 1976.

This is an account of Kissinger's diplomatic efforts during and after the October War. A readable narrative is coupled with good analysis.

1048 ______. "Step-by-Step Diplomacy in the Middle East," Foreign Policy, II (spring 1976), 4-69.

This is an excerpt from item 1047.

1049 Sim'an, Emile S. "The Persian Gulf as a Subordinate System of World Politics." Ph. D. dissertation, Indiana University, 1977. (DA 38, p5035)

This is a study of the eight oil-producing states of the Persian Gulf and their current, prominent role in world affairs.

1050 Simpson, Dwight James. "Israel after Twenty-five Years," Current History, 64 (January 1973), 1-8.

This article discusses the peace-making efforts that preceded the October War.

1051 ______. "Israel's Year of Decision," Current History, 70 (January 1976), 10-13.

This essay describes the workings of the Jewish lobby in the United States.

1052 Smolansky, O. M. "Soviet Policy in the Middle East," Current History, 74 (January 1978), 5-9.

Assesses Soviet policy goals and successes in the region as of early 1978.

1053 ________. "The Soviet Setback in the Middle East," Current History, 64 (January 1973), 17-20.
Examines the liabilities presented the Soviets by President Sadat's expulsion of Russian advisers in 1972.

1054 Soffer, Ovadia M. "The United Nations Peacemaking Role in the Arab-Israeli Conflict, 1967-1977." Ph. D. dissertation, City University of New York, 1977. (DA 38, p3040)
This study concludes that the U. S. is the primary peacekeeping force in the Middle East because the superpowers are not in accord on the Arab-Israeli dispute.

1055 Sowayyegh, Abdul-Aziz Hussein. "Oil and the Arab-Israeli Conflict: A Study in Arab Oil Strategy Between 1948-1973." Ph. D. dissertation, Claremont Graduate School, 1977. (DA 37, p7302)
Discusses the use of the Arab oil weapon in the 1973 October War.

1056 Stoessinger, John G. Henry Kissinger: The Anguish of Power. New York: Norton, 1976.
This biographical study contains a chapter on Kissinger's Middle-Eastern diplomacy that is both topical and analytical.

1057 Stookey, Robert W. America and the Arab States: An Uneasy Encounter. New York: Wiley, 1975.
This work contains an excellent chapter on U. S. diplomacy during and after the October War.

1058 Szulc, Tad. "Is He Indispensable? Answers to the Kissinger Riddle," New York, July 1, 1974.
Critical of Kissinger's supply of arms to the embattled Israelis during the October War.

1059 Terry, Janice. "1973 U. S. Press Coverage on the Middle East," Journal of Palestine Studies, IV (autumn 1974), 120-33.
This study investigates the attitudes of three U. S. newspapers in 1973 respecting the Arab-Israeli conflict.

1060 Thoman, Roy E. "Iraq and the Persian Gulf Region,"

Current History, 64 (January 1973), 21-38.
This essay discusses Iraq's rivalry with Iran and Kuwait in the aftermath of the British departure from the Gulf.

1061 Trice, Robert H. "Congress and the Arab-Israeli Conflict, Support for Israel in the U.S. Senate, 1970-73," Political Science Quarterly, 92 (fall 1977), 443-63.
Based on seven votes, this article claims that the U.S. Senate is overwhelmingly supportive of Israel's interests.

1062 Turck, Nancy. "The Arab Boycott of Israel," Foreign Affairs, 55 (April 1977), 472-93.
This is an excellent discussion of the Arab economic boycott as it affects U.S. interests with the Arabs.

1063 Turner, Stansfield. "The Naval Balance: Not Just a Numbers Game," Foreign Affairs, 55 (January 1977), 340-54.
This discussion of the future of the U.S. Navy has relevance to the American role in the Mediterranean Sea.

1064 Ullman, Richard H. "After Rabat: Middle East Risks and American Roles," Foreign Affairs, 53 (January 1975), 284-96.
Suggests the U.S. might consider stationing troops in Israel, the better to maintain stability and that country's political sovereignty.

1065 Van der Linden, Frank. Nixon's Quest for Peace. New York: Robert B. Luce, 1972.
Provides excellent treatment of U.S. involvement in the 1970 Jordanian crisis.

1066 Whetten, Lawrence L. The Canal War: Four-Power Conflict in the Middle East. Cambridge, Mass.: MIT Press, 1974.
This is a lengthy narrative account of the military activities of the October War that includes diplomacy preceding, during, and after the war.

1067 Wolfowitz, Paul D. "Nuclear Proliferation in the Middle East: The Politics and Economics of Proposals for Nuclear Desalting." Ph.D. dissertation, University of Chicago, 1972. (1971, p302, ADD) [Abstract not available.]

1068 Xydis, Stephen G. Cyprus: Reluctant Republic. Hague: Mouton, 1973.

This book deals with the dispute over the disposition of Cyprus, but does not devote much space to the U.S. role in problem-solving.

1069 Zoppo, Ciro. "The American-Soviet Mediterranean Confrontation and the Middle East," in Willard Beling, ed., The Middle East: Quest for an American Policy. Albany: State University of New York Press, 1973.

This essay concerns the Soviet-American rivalry in the Mediterranean, with emphasis on the naval race between the two powers.

R

GENERAL

1070 Badeau, John S. American Approach to the Arab World. New York: Harper, 1968.

This is an outstanding study of the American effort to deal with the Arab world in the postwar era when Arab nationalism was on the rise.

1071 Bryson, Thomas A. American Diplomatic Relations with the Middle East, 1784-1975: A Survey. Metuchen, N.J.: Scarecrow Press, 1977.

This is the only survey that attempts to cover the American diplomatic experience from the inception of the republic down to the present time of Arab-Israeli conflict and the energy crisis.

1072 Campbell, John C. Defense of the Middle East: Problems of American Policy. New York: Harper, 1960.

This is an excellent study of American Middle-Eastern diplomacy through the Eisenhower era that also contains an analysis of the numerous problems that perplexed American diplomatists.

1073 Daniel, Robert L. American Philanthropy in the Near East, 1820-1960. Athens: Ohio University Press, 1970.

This is perhaps the best single study of the role of American philanthropy in the Middle East.

1074 DeNovo, John A. American Interests and Policies in the Middle East, 1900-1939. Minneapolis: University of Minnesota Press, 1963.

This work, along with that of James Field (see below), constitute two of the most comprehensive studies of American Middle-Eastern diplomacy, with DeNovo's work covering the period from 1900 to the outbreak of World War II.

1075 Evans, Laurence. United States Policy and the Partition of Turkey, 1914-1924. Baltimore: Johns Hopkins University Press, 1965.

This work covers the period of World War I and the peace conference era to 1924 and delineates the imperatives that shaped diplomacy during this crucial period in the Middle East.

1076 Field, James A., Jr. America and the Mediterranean World, 1776-1882. Princeton, N. J.: Princeton University Press, 1969.

This work is the outstanding study of American diplomacy in the Middle East from the time of the Barbary pirates down to the British occupation of Egypt in 1882.

1077 Gallagher, Charles F. United States and North Africa: Morocco, Algeria, and Tunisia. Cambridge, Mass.: Harvard University Press, 1963.

This effort comprehends an examination of the history and customs of the Maghrebi states along with a sketch of United States diplomacy with them.

1078 Gidney, James B. A Mandate for Armenia. Kent, Ohio: Kent State University Press, 1967.

This is the best single treatment of the Armenian mandate question that influenced U. S. -Turkish relations.

1079 Gordon, Leland James. American Relations with Turkey, 1830-1930: An Economic Interpretation. Philadelphia: University of Pennsylvania, 1932.

An excellent study of American-Turkish diplomatic and economic relations.

1080 Grabill, Joseph L. Protestant Diplomacy and the Near East: Missionary Influence on American Policy, 1810-1927. Minneapolis: University of Minnesota Press, 1971.

This study examines the role of the American missionaries and their influence on U. S. -Middle East relations from earliest times, with emphasis on the Armenian question.

1081 Hall, Ron, et al. Insight on the Middle East War [1973]. London: Andre Deutsch, 1974.

This study of the 1973 October War contains an extensive examination of the military history of the conflict.

1082 Howard, Harry N. The King-Crane Commission:

An American Inquiry in the Middle East. Beirut: Khayats, 1963.

This study, by one of the pioneers in the field, analyzes the problems that beset the Wilson administration in the aftermath of World War I when the Ottoman Empire was being dismantled.

1083 Hull, Cordell. The Memoirs of Cordell Hull. 2 vols. New York: Macmillan, 1948.

This memoir provides excellent treatment of American Middle Eastern diplomacy during World War II.

1084 Hurewitz, J. C. Middle East Dilemmas: The Background of United States Policy. New York: Harper, 1953.

This is an excellent treatment of U. S. relations with the Middle East during the early Cold-War era, and it provides a look at the complexities that beset American diplomatists.

1085 Kirk, George E. The Middle East in the War. London: Oxford University Press, 1952.

This lengthy book provides a look at American diplomacy in the Middle East during World War II and it demonstrates the Anglo-American tensions in the region.

1086 Laqueur. The Road to War: The Origin and Aftermath of the Arab-Israeli Conflict, 1967-8. New York: Penguin, 1968.

This work provides a good look at American diplomacy during the 1967 Arab-Israeli conflict.

1087 Love, Kennett. Suez: The Twice Fought War. New York: McGraw-Hill, 1969.

The author presents a lengthy treatment of the causes of the Suez crisis, of the Anglo-French-Israeli invasion of the Suez, and of the American diplomatic role throughout.

1088 Manuel, Frank E. The Realities of American-Palestine Relations. Washington, D. C.: Public Affairs Press, 1949.

An extended treatment of the American reaction to the Zionist movement from the time of the Wilson Administration's endorsement of the Balfour Declaration until President Truman's endorsement of the Zionist cause.

1089 Polk, William R. The United States and the Arab

<u>World.</u> Cambridge, Mass.: Harvard University Press, 1965.

The author provides an analysis of American diplomacy with the Arab states during the postwar era.

1090 Quandt, William B. <u>Decade of Decisions: American Policy Toward the Arab-Israeli Conflict, 1967-1976.</u> Berkeley: University of California Press, 1977.

This is the best treatment of the subject and it includes an analysis of the American effort to maintain peace before, during, and after the October 1973 War.

1091 Safran, Nadav. <u>The United States and Israel.</u> Cambridge, Mass.: Harvard University Press, 1963.

While providing a sketch of U.S. relations with Israel, this work takes a long look at the country of Israel, with emphasis on its customs, industry, and economy.

1092 Shwadran, Benjamin. <u>The Middle East, Oil and the Great Powers.</u> New York: Praeger, 1955.

A history of the American quest for Middle Eastern oil from the 1920s to the post-World War II era is the subject of this book.

1093 Snetsinger, John. <u>Truman, the Jewish Vote and the Creation of Israel.</u> Stanford, Calif.: Hoover Institution Press, 1974.

This study examines President Truman's consideration of the Palestine question and the creation of the State of Israel.

1094 Speiser, Ephraim. <u>The United States and the Near East.</u> Cambridge, Mass.: Harvard University Press, 1952.

This early effort to examine American-Middle Eastern relations contained a look at the diplomatic problems as well as the cultural, economic, political, and social background of the peoples of the region.

1095 Stevens, Richard P. <u>American Zionism and United States Foreign Policy.</u> New York: Pageant Press, 1962.

The author relates the growth of Zionist sentiment in the United States during World War II that resulted in the U.S. government acting as midwife for the birth of Israel.

1096 Stocking, George W. <u>Middle East Oil: A Study in</u>

Political and Economic Controversy. Nashville: Vanderbilt University Press, 1970.

This is a good treatment of the American quest for Middle Eastern oil from the 1920s through the Iranian oil crisis of the 1950s.

1097 Stookey, Robert W. America and the Arab States: An Uneasy Encounter. New York: Wiley, 1975.

An excellent analysis of American relations with the Arab world is presented in this survey which also provides a good narrative account of the unfolding of this complex relationship.

1098 Thomas, Lewis V., and Richard N. Frye. The United States and Turkey and Iran. Cambridge, Mass.: Harvard University Press, 1951.

Although the authors present a sketch of American diplomatic relations with Turkey and Iran, they are more concerned with providing their readers with a look at life in their respective countries.

1099 Whetten, Lawrence L. The Canal War: Four-Power Conflict in the Middle East. Cambridge, Mass.: MIT Press, 1974.

In addition to presenting a diplomatic history of the October 1973 Arab-Israeli War and its aftermath, this work also examines the interactions among the states of Israel, Egypt, the United States, and the Soviet Union.

1100 Wright, L. C. United States Policy toward Egypt, 1830-1914. New York: Exposition-University Press, 1969.

This study examines American-Egyptian relations down to the outbreak of World War I.

1101 Yeselson, Abraham. United States-Persian Diplomatic Relations, 1883-1921. New Brunswick, N.J.: Rutgers University Press, 1950.

The author examines America's early relations with Persia, a nation whose existence as a sovereign state was complicated by Russian and British aims.

S

DOCTORAL DISSERTATIONS

(See page iv for explanation of symbols)

A good number of the dissertations listed below are not included in the body of this bibliography, in many cases because the authors have published their findings and only the published work (listed in the appropriate section) is annotated. A number of the dissertations below concern the diplomacy of Middle-Eastern countries or other nations, but these are included because they do have a bearing on United States diplomacy. Regardless of the resulting duplication (in that several of the dissertations merely listed here appear also with annotations in the main body), it was thought useful to have one amalgamated list of the doctoral work done in the field, as a convenience to scholars.

1102 Abbas, Jabir Ali. "Points of Departure in Egypt's Foreign Policy: The Essence of Nasser's Power." Indiana University, 1969. DA 32, p5846.

1103 Abbass, Abdul Majid. "Oil Diplomacy in the Near East." University of Chicago, 1940. DD 7:93.

1104 Abbott, Freeland K. "American Policy in the Middle East: A Study of the Attitudes of the United States Toward the Middle East, Especially during the Period 1919-1936." Fletcher School of Law and Diplomacy, 1952. W 1952, p208, ADD.

1105 Abu-Diab, Fawzi. "Lebanon and the United Nations, 1945-1958." University of Pennsylvania, 1965. DA 26, p3464.

1106 Abu-Jaber, Faiz Saley. "Egypt and the Cold War,

1952-1956: Implications for American Policy." Syracuse University, 1966. DA 27, p4306.

1107 Abu Salih, Abbas Said. "History of the Foreign Policy of Lebanon, 1943-1958." University of Texas, 1971. DA 32, p6325.

1108 Ahrari, Mohammed E. "The Dynamics of Oil Diplomacy: Conflict and Consensus." Southern Illinois University, 1976. DA 37, p6037.

1109 Akgonenc, Oya. "A Study of Political Dynamics of Turkish Foreign Policy with Particular Reference to New Trends in Turco-Arab Relations, 1960-1975." American University, 1975. DA 37, p4598.

1110 al-Akhrass, Mouhamad Safouh. "Revolutionary Change and Modernization in the Arab World: A Case from Syria." University of California, Berkeley, 1969. DA 31, p833.

1111 Alberts, Darlene Jean. "King Hussein of Jordan: The Consummate Politician." Ohio State University, 1973. DA 34, p692.

1112 Ali, Sk. Rustum. "The Use of Oil as a Weapon of Diplomacy: A Case Study of Saudi Arabia." American University, 1975. DA 36, p4000.

1113 Alvarez, David Joseph. "The United States and Turkey, 1945-1946: The Bureaucratic Determinants of Cold War Diplomacy." University of Connecticut, 1975. DA 36, p6859.

1114 Amouzegar, Jahanigir. "The Role of the United States Technical Assistance in the Development of Underdeveloped Countries with Special Reference to Iran." University of California, Los Angeles, 1955. W 1955, p164, DDAU.

1115 Anbari, Abdul-Amir Ali. "The Law of Petroleum Concession Agreements in the Middle East." Harvard University, 1968. p234, ADD.

1116 Anderson, Eugene N. "The First Moroccan Crisis, 1904-1906." University of Chicago, 1928. SO 330, p139.

1117 Archon, Dion James. "The United States and the Eastern Mediterranean." Harvard University, 1951. Harvard B., 1950-51, p22.

1118 Arcilesi, Salvatore Alfred. "Development of United States Foreign Policy in Iran, 1949-1960." University of Virginia, 1965. DA 26, p6144.

1119 Bailey, John A., Jr. "Lion, Eagle, and Crescent: The Western Allies and Turkey in 1943: A Study of British and American Diplomacy in a Critical Year of the War." Georgetown University, 1969. DA 31, p1168.

1120 Balboni, Alan Richard. "A Study of the Efforts of the American Zionists to Influence the Formulation and Conduct of United States Policy during the Roosevelt, Truman, and Eisenhower Administrations." Brown University, 1973. DA 34, p6056.

1121 Banani, Amin. "Impact of the West on Iran, 1921-1941: A Study in Modernization of Social Institutions." Stanford University, 1959. DA 20, p3703.

1122 Barakeh, Abdul Kader. "An Analysis of the Impact of African Oil Development on Middle East Petroleum Exports to Western Europe, 1955-1965." Indiana University, 1968. DA 29, p2847.

1123 Bashshur, Munir Antonios. "The Role of Two Western Universities in the National Life of Lebanon and the Middle East: A Comparative Study of the American University of Beirut and the University of Saint-Joseph." University of Chicago, 1964. X 1964, p56, ADD.

1124 El-Behairy, Mohamed Mohamed. "The Suez Canal in World Politics, 1945-1961." Ohio State University, 1961. DA 22, p3724.

1125 Bezboruah, Monoranjan. "The United States Strategy in the Indian Ocean, 1968-1976." University of Mississippi, 1977. DA 38, p4357.

1126 Blair, Leon B. "Western Window in the Arab World." Texas Christian University, 1968. DA 29, p2632.

1127 Blessing, James Alan. "The Suspension of Foreign Aid by the United States, 1948-1972." State University of New York, Albany, 1975. DA 36, p4001.

1128 Botsai, Sarah Lillian. "The United States and the Palestine Refugees." American University, 1972. DA 33, p4508.

1129 Braden, Jean H. "The Eagle and the Crescent: American Interests in the Ottoman Empire, 1861-1870." Ohio State University, 1973. DA 34, p2505.

1130 Brook, David. "The United Nations and the Arab-Israeli Armistice System, 1949-1959." Columbia University, 1961. DA 22, p4069.

1131 Brown, Robert Wylie. "A Special View of Oil Development in the Desert: Libya in the First Decade, 1955-1965." Columbia University, 1970. DA 31B, p5416.

1132 Bryson, Thomas A. "Woodrow Wilson, the Senate, Public Opinion and the Armenian Mandate Question, 1919-20." University of Georgia, 1965. DA 26, p2706.

1133 Burke, Mary Patrice. "United States Aid to Turkey: Foreign Aid and Foreign Policy." University of Connecticut, 1977. DA 38, p5030.

1134 Burnett, John Howard, Jr. "Soviet-Egyptian Relations during the Khrushchev Era: A Study in Soviet Foreign Policy." Emory University, 1966. DA 27, p2187.

1135 Buzanski, Peter Michael. "Admiral Mark L. Bristol and Turkish-American Relations, 1919-1922." University of California, Berkeley, 1960. X 1961, p115, ADD.

1136 Cantor, Milton. "The Life of Joel Barlow." Columbia University, 1954. DA 15, p562.

1137 Chubin, Shahram. "Iran's Foreign Policy, 1958-1972: A Small State's Constraints and Choices." Columbia University, 1974. DA 37, p4600.

1138 Clarfield, Gerard H. "Timothy Pickering and American Foreign Policy, 1795-1800." University of California, Berkeley, 1962. DA 26, p3884.

1139 Cline, Myrtle A. "American Attitude Toward the Greek War of Independence, 1821-1828." Columbia University, 1931. LC 1930, p35.

1140 Collins, George W. "United States-Moroccan Relations, 1904-1912." University of Colorado, 1965. DA 26, p7276.

1141 Conn, Cary Corwin. "John Porter Brown, Father of Turkish-American Relations: An Ohioan at the Sublime Porte, 1832-1872." Ohio State University, 1973. DA 35, p2082.

1142 Cook, Ralph Elliott. "The United States and the Armenian Question, 1894-1924." Fletcher School of Law and Diplomacy, 1957. X 1957, p154, ADD.

1143 Cruickshank, Earl F. "Morocco at the Parting of the Ways: A Study of an Attempt to Reform the System of Native Protection." University of Pennsylvania, 1932. SO 175, p15.

1144 Daniel, Robert Leslie. "From Relief to Technical Assistance in the Near East: A Case Study of Near East Relief and Near East Foundation." University of Wisconsin, 1953. W 1954, p237, DDAU.

1145 Darvich-Kodjauri, Djamchid. "Images and Perception in International Relations: A Case Study of Relationships between Iran and the Great Powers, 1919-1953." Miami University, 1976. DA 37, p4600.

1146 Decker, Donald James. "U.S. Policy Regarding the Baghdad Pact." American University, 1975. DA 36, p1786.

1147 DeNovo, John A. "Petroleum and American Diplomacy in the Near East, 1908-1928." Yale University, 1948. W 1948, p104, DDAU.

1148 Dohse, Michael A. "American Periodicals and the Palestine Triangle, 1936-1947." Mississippi State University, 1966. DA 27, p3395.

1149 Earle, Edward M. "Turkey, the Great Powers, and the Baghdad Railway: A Study in Imperialism." Columbia University, 1923. LC 1923, p39.

1150 Edwards, Rosaline de Gregorio. "Relations between the United States and Turkey, 1893-1897." Fordham University, 1952. W 1952, p208, DDAU.

1151 Elfiky, Hassan Salama. "A History of Teacher In-Service Education in the United States: With Recommendations for Egyptian Education." University of Minnesota, 1961. DA 22, p3916.

1152 Erden, Deniz A. "Turkish Foreign Policy Through the United Nations." University of Massachusetts, 1974. DA 36, p1077.

1153 Evans, Laurence Boyd. "The United States Policy in the Syrian Mandate, 1917-1922." Johns Hopkins University, 1957. X 1957, p154, ADD.

1154 Faddah, Mohammad Ibrahim. "The Foreign Policy of Jordan, 1947-1967." Oklahoma University, 1971. DA 32, p2770.

1155 Fakhsh, Majmud A. "Education and Political Modernization and Change in Egypt." University of Connecticut, 1973. DA 34, p832.

1156 Farzanegan, Bahram. "United States Response and Reaction to the Emergence of Arab and African States in International Politics." American University, 1966. DA 27, p1886.

1157 Fatemi, Faramarz. "The U. S. S. R. in Iran: The Irano-Soviet Dispute and the Pattern of Azerbaijan Revolution, 1941-1947." New School of Social Research, 1976. DA 38, p3712.

1158 Faulkner, Constance Parry. "The Economic Effects of United States Public Law 480 in the United Arab Republic." University of Utah, 1969. DA 30, p1694.

1159 Feinstein, Marnin. "The First Twenty-Five Years of Zionism in the United States, 1882-1906." Columbia University, 1963. DA 24, p4647.

1160 Fields, Harvey Joseph. "Pawn of Empires: A Study of United States Middle East Policy, 1945-1953." Rutgers University, 1975. DA 36, p3068.

1161 Finaish, Mohamed Ali. "Libya's Petroleum Policy." University of Southern California, 1972. DA 33, p4623.

1162 Firoozi, Ferydoon. "The United States Economic Aid to Iran, 1950-1960." Dropsie University, 1966. X 1966, p46, ADD.

1163 Fishburne, Charles Carroll, Jr. "United States Policy Toward Iran, 1959-1963." Florida State University, 1964. DA 26, p7431.

1164 Fishman, Hertzel. "American Protestantism and the State of Israel, 1937-1967." New York University, 1972. 1971, p222, ADD.

1165 Forsythe, David Prevatt. "The United Nations and the Peaceful Settlement of Disputes: The Case of the Conciliation Commission for Palestine." Princeton University, 1968. DA 29, p2775.

1166 Fort, Raymond. "A Study of the Development of the American Technical Assistance Program in Iran." Cornell University, 1961. DA 22, p2276.

1167 Fouad, Mahmoud Hassan. "The Economics of Foreign Aid: The U.A.R. Experience with the U.S. and U.S.S.R. Programs, 1952-1965." University of Southern California, 1968. DA 29, p1999.

1168 Frank, Helmut Jack. "The Pricing of Middle East Crude Oil." Columbia University, 1961. DA 22, p3023.

1169 Fredericks, Edgar Jesse. "Soviet-Egyptian Relations, 1955-1965, and Their Effect on Communism in the Middle East and the International Position of the Soviet Union." American University, 1968. DA 29, p1265.

1170 Galbraith, M. Rita Francis, Sister. "The Arab-Jewish Conflict in a World Power Setting." St. Johns University, 1963. X 1963, p118, ADD.

1171 Gama, Abid Husni. "The United Nations and the Palestinian Refugees: An Analysis of the United Nations Relief and Works Agency in the Near East, 1 May 1950-30 June 1971." University of Arizona, 1972. DA 33, p695.

1172 Ganin, Zvi. "The Diplomacy of the Weak: American Zionist Leadership during the Truman Era, 1945-48." Brandeis University, 1975. DA 36, p480.

1173 Garrett, James Madison, II. "Assistance to Turkey as an Instrument of United States Foreign Policy, with Emphasis on Military Assistance, 1947-55." Columbia University, 1960. DA 21, p1990.

1174 Gartner, Joseph F. "America's Defense Policy in the Middle East, 1953-1958." University of Chicago, 1962. X 1962, p182, ADD.

1175 George, Patrick Cyril. "The United States and the Central Treaty Organization." University of Virginia, 1968. DA 29, p2776.

1176 Gerteiny, Alfred George. "The Concept of Positive Neutralism in the United Arab Republic." St. Johns University, 1963. Index, 1962, 118, ADD.

1177 Gidney, James B. "An American Mandate for Armenia." Case Western Reserve University, 1963. X 1964, p126, ADD.

1178 Gimelli, Louis B. "Luther Bradish, 1783-1863." New York University, 1964. DA 25, p1865.

1179 Glassman, Jon David. "Arms for the Arabs: The Soviet Union and War in the Middle East." Columbia University, 1976. DA 37, p6038.

1180 Golding, David. "United States Policy in Palestine and Israel, 1945-1949." New York University, 1961. DA 27, p1887.

1181 Gossett, Edward Freeman. "The American Protestant Missionary Endeavor in North Africa from Its Origin to 1939." University of California, Los Angeles, 1961. Index, 1960, p115, ADD.

1182 Gottlieb, Paul H. "The Commonwealth of Nations at

the United Nations." Boston University, 1962. DA 23, p1003.

1183 Grabill, Joseph L. "Missionaries Amid Conflict: Their Influence upon American Relations with the Near East, 1914-1917." Indiana University, 1964. DA 26, p334.

1184 Grand, Samuel. "A History of Zionist Youth Organizations in the United States from Their Inception to 1940." Columbia University, 1958. DA 18, p1777.

1185 Gray, Gertrude M. "Oil in Anglo-American Diplomatic Relations, 1920-1928." University of California, Berkeley, 1950. W 1950, p178, DDAU.

1186 Greenwood, Keith M. "Robert College: The American Founders." Johns Hopkins University, 1965. DA 26, p2161.

1187 Gruen, George Emanuel. "Turkey, Israel and the Palestine Question, 1948-1960: A Study in the Diplomacy of Ambivalence." Columbia University, 1970. DA 34, p2737.

1188 Gurpinar, Nevzat. "Short-term Agricultural Cooperative Credit in the United States and Turkey and Suggestions for the Improvement of the Turkish System." Ohio State University, 1950. W 1950, p140, DDAU.

1189 Hackley, Lloyd V. "Soviet Behavior in the Middle East as a Function of Change, 1950-1970." University of North Carolina, 1976. DA 37, p4340.

1190 Haddad, William Woodrow. "Arab Editorial Opinion Toward the Palestine Question, 1947-1958." Ohio State University, 1970. DA 31, p4673.

1191 Hahn, Lorna Joan. "North Africa: Nationalism to Nationhood." University of Pennsylvania, 1962. DA 24, p5521.

1192 Hall, Luella J. "The United States and the Moroccan Problem." Stanford University, 1938. W 1938, p79, DDAU.

1193 Hamburger, Robert Lee. "Franco-American Relations, 1940-1962: The Role of United States anti-Colonialism and anti-Communism in the Formulation of United States Policy on the Algerian Question." Notre Dame University, 1970. DA 32, p519.

1194 Hamdan, Zuhair. "A Study of the Arab-Israeli Conflict in the United Nations during the Period Between 1947 until 1957." Union Graduate School, 1976. DA 37, p6737.

1195 Hamlet, Bruce D. "A Comparative Analysis of British Foreign Relations: The Palestine War, 1947-1949; the Suez Crisis, 1956; the Arab-Israeli Crisis, 1967." Claremont Graduate School, 1971. DA 32, p1049.

1196 Hammad, Mohamed Burham. "Middle Eastern Oil Concessions: Some Legal and Policy Aspects of Relations between Grantors and Grantees." Yale University, 1963. Index, 1962, p130, ADD.

1197 Harbutt, Fraser J. "The Fulton Speech and the Iran Crisis of 1946: A Turning Point in American Foreign Policy." University of California, Berkeley, 1976. DA 37, p6011.

1198 Harmon, Judd Scott. "Suppress and Protect: The United States Navy, the African Slave Trade and Maritime Commerce, 1794-1862." College of William & Mary, 1977. DA 38, p5004.

1199 Harris, George S. "A Political History of Turkey, 1945-1950." Harvard University, 1957. X 1957, p110, ADD.

1200 Harris, Jonathan. "Communist Strategy Toward the 'National Bourgeoisie,' in Asia and the Middle East." Columbia University, 1966. DA 27, p1887.

1201 Harsaghy, Fred Joseph. "The Administration of American Cultural Projects Abroad: A Developmental Study with Case Histories of Community Relations in Administering Educational and Informational Projects in Japan and Saudi Arabia." New York University, 1965. DA 27, p1899.

1202 Hassan, Ragaa Abdel-Rassoul. "An Analysis of the Demand for Food in Egypt." Michigan State University, 1969. DA 30, p5130.

1203 Hatoor Al-Khalidi, Muyhee A. "A Century of American Contribution to Arab Nationalism, 1820-1920." Vanderbilt University, 1959. DA 20, p1340.

1204 Hatzilambrou, Lambros. "Soviet Foreign Policy in the Eastern Mediterranean: A Systematic Approach." Howard University, 1976. DA 37, p4603.

1205 Heggoy, Willy Normann. "Fifty Years of Evangelical Missionary Movement in North Africa, 1881-1931." Hartford Seminary, 1960. DA 22, p238.

1206 Helmreich, Paul C. "The Negotiation of the Treaty of Sèvres, January, 1919-August, 1920." Harvard University, 1964. X 1964, p124, ADD.

1207 Helseth, William Arthur. "The United States and Turkey: Their Relations from 1784 to 1962." Fletcher School of Law and Diplomacy, 1962.

1208 Hensel, Howard M. "Soviet Policy in the Persian Gulf, 1968-1975." University of Virginia, 1976. DA 37, p6738.

1209 Hordes, Jess N. "Evolving U.N. Approaches to and the Role of U.N. Machinery in the Arab-Israeli Conflict, 1947-1956." Johns Hopkins University, 1974. DA 38, p1008.

1210 Hourihan, William James. "Roosevelt and the Sultans: The United States Navy in the Mediterranean, 1904." University of Massachusetts, 1975. DA 36, p1045.

1211 Huff, Earl Dean. "Zionist Influences upon U.S. Foreign Policy: A Study of American Policy toward the Middle East from the Time of the Struggle for Israel to the Sinai Conflict." University of Idaho, 1971. DA 32, p3400.

1212 Hurewitz, Jacob C. "The Road to Partition: The Palestine Problem, 1936-1948." Columbia University, 1950. W 1951, p198, DDAU.

1213 Hyatt, David Mayer. "The United Nations and the Partition of Palestine." Catholic University, 1973. DA 34, p5281.

1214 Ibrahim, Saad Eddin Mohamed. "Political Attitudes of an Emerging Elite: A Case Study of the Arab Students in the United States." University of Washington, 1968. DA 29, p2380.

1215 Ince, Nurhan. "Problems and Politics in Turkish Foreign Policy, 1960-1966: With Emphasis on Turkish-United States Relations, the Cyprus Question, and the Leftist Movement." University of Kentucky, 1974. DA 36, p4730.

1216 Irwin, Ray W. "The Diplomatic Relations of the United States with the Barbary Powers, 1776-1816." New York University, 1929. LC 1931, p95.

1217 Issa, Mahmoud K. "Trade between Egypt and the United States." University of Minnesota, 1953. DA 13, p690.

1218 Jafari, Lafi Ibrahim. "Migration of Palestinian Arab and Jordanian Students and Professionals to the United States." Iowa State University, 1971. DA 32, p4722.

1219 Jamjoom, Mohamed Abdulwahid. "International Trade and Balance of Payments in a Mono-product Economy: A Case Study of the Saudi Arabian Kingdom." University of Southern California, 1970. DA 31, p2565.

1220 al-Jazairi, Mohamed Zayyan. "Saudi Arabia: A Diplomatic History, 1924-1964." University of Utah, 1971. DA 32, p868.

1221 Johnson, Hugh S. "The American Schools in the Republic of Turkey, 1923-1933: A Case Study of Missionary Problems in International Relations." American University, 1975. DA 36, p3107.

1222 Joyner, Christopher Clayton. "Boycott in International Law: A Case Study of the Arab States & Israel." University of Virginia, 1977. DA 38, p4358.

1223 Jureidini, Paul A. "The Relationship of the Palestinian Guerrilla Movement with the Government of Jordan, 1967-1970." American University, 1975. DA 36, p3108.

1224 Kabbani, Rashid. "Morocco: From Protectorate to Independence, 1912-1956." American University, 1957. DA 17, p2051.

1225 ElKashef, Ahmad Refat. "Soviet Policy toward Egypt, 1955-1967." Boston University, 1973. DA 34, p7305.

1226 Kayal, Alawi Darweesh. "The Control of Oil: East-West Rivalry in the Persian Gulf." University of Colorado, 1972. DA 33, p4510.

1227 Kazdal, Mustafa N. "Trade Relations between the United States and Turkey, 1919-1944." Indiana University, 1946. W 1946, p40, DDAU.

1228 Kazemian, Gholam Hossein. "The Impact of United States Technical and Financial Aid on the Rural Development of Iran." American University, 1967. DA 28, p3328.

1229 Kearney, Helen McCready. "American Images of the Middle East, 1824-1924: A Century of Antipathy." University of Rochester, 1976. DA 37, p7250.

1230 Kerkheide, Virginia White. "Anthony Eden and the Suez Crisis of 1956." Case Western Reserve University, 1972. DA 33, p1649.

1231 Kermani, Taghi. "The United States Participation in the Economic Development of the Middle East: With Special Reference to Iran, Iraq, and Jordan." University of Nebraska, 1959. DA 20, p550.

1232 Kerwin, Harry Wayne. "An Analysis and Evaluation of the Program of Technical Assistance to Education Conducted in Iran by the Government of the United States from 1952-1962." American University, 1964. DA 26, p5820.

1233 Khalil, Houssam El-Dawla H. "The Soviet Foreign Policy toward Egypt, 1955-1964." Howard University, 1970. DA 31, p6134.

1234 Khan, Rais Ahmad. "Radio Cairo and Egyptian Foreign Policy, 1956-1959." University of Michigan, 1967. DA 28, p3245.

1235 Khouri, Fred John. "The Arab States in the United Nations: A Study of Political Relations, 1945-1950." Columbia University, 1953. DA 14, p177.

1236 Khoury, Angela Jurdak. "The Foreign Policy of Lebanon." American University, 1968. DA 29, p947.

1237 Kianfar, Mehdi. "Arab Unity and Collective Security of the Middle East." American University, 1956. Index, 1955, p126, ADD.

1238 Kikoski, John Frank, Jr. "The United Nations Security Council Resolution of November 22, 1967: International Politics and Law in an Organizational Setting." University of Massachusetts, 1972. DA 33, p3001.

1239 Klebanoff, Shoshana. "Oil for Europe: American Foreign Policy and Middle East Oil." Claremont Graduate School, 1974. DA 35, p554.

1240 Kline, Earl Oliver. "The Suez Crisis: Anglo-American Relations and the United Nations." Princeton University, 1961. DA 22, p2866.

1241 Koch, Howard Everard, Jr. "Permanent War: A Reappraisal of the Arab-Israeli War." Stanford University, 1973. DA 34, p3505.

1242 El-Kordy, Abdul-Hafez M. "The United Nations Peace-Keeping Functions in the Arab World." American University, 1967. DA 28, p3743.

1243 Krammer, Arnold P. "Soviet Bloc Relations with Israel, 1947-1953." University of Wisconsin, 1970. DA 31, p5323.

1244 al-Kubaisi, Basil Raouf. "The Arab Nationalist Movement, 1951-1971: From Pressure Group to Socialist Party." American University, 1971. DA 33, p792.

1245 Kuniholm, Bruce R. "The United States, the Northern

Tier, and the Origins of the Cold War: Great Power Conflict and Diplomacy in Iran, Turkey, and Greece." Duke University, 1976. DA 38, p2304.

1246 Landis, Lincoln. "Petroleum in Soviet Middle East Strategy." Georgetown University, 1969. DA 30, p4002.

1247 Lewis, Evelyn. "The Jewish Vote: Fact or Fiction: Trends in Jewish Voting Behavior." Ball State University, 1976. DA 37, p6704.

1248 Lewis, Tom T. "Franco-American Diplomatic Relations, 1898-1907." University of Oklahoma, 1970. DA 31, p3475.

1249 Lipstadt, Deborah E. "The Zionist Cause of Louis Lipsky, 1900-1921." Brandeis University, 1977. DA 37, p7921.

1250 McCormick, James M. "An Interaction Analysis of International Crises: A Study of the Suez Crisis and the Six Day War." Michigan State University, 1973. DA 34, p6080.

1251 McDaniel, Robert A. "The Shuster Mission and the Culmination of the Persian Revolution of 1905-1911." University of Illinois, 1966. DA 27, p733.

1252 McDonough, George P. "American Relations with Turkey, 1893-1901." Georgetown University, 1949. W 1951, p205, DDAU.

1253 Madadi, Gol-Agha. "American Foregin Policy Through Alliance and Its Application in the Middle East." Indiana University, 1967. DA 28, p4693.

1254 Makled, Ismail Sabri Eysa. "Comparative International Behavior in the Suez Crisis: A Perspective Study." University of Pittsburgh, 1965. DA 26, p3468.

1255 El Mallakh, Ragaei William. "The Effects of the Second World War on the Economic Development of Egypt." Rutgers University, 1955. DA 15, p2435.

1256 Mansour, Hussein Omar. "The Discovery of Oil and

Its Impact on the Industrialization of Saudi Arabia." University of Arizona, 1973. DA 34, p2522.

1257 Mansy, Thomas M. "Palestine in the United Nations." Georgetown University, 1950. DD 17, p179.

1258 Masannat, George Suleiman. "Aspects of American Policy in the Arab Middle East, 1947-1957, with Emphasis on United States-Egyptian Relations." University of Oklahoma, 1964. DA 25, p4803.

1259 Mazuzan, George T. "Warren R. Austin: A Republican Internationalist and United States Foreign Policy." Kent State University, 1969. DA 30, p5389.

1260 Melka, Robert L. "The Axis and the Arab Middle East, 1930-1945." University of Minnesota, 1966. DA 27, p1762.

1261 Mirak, Robert. "The Armenians in the United States, 1890-1915." Harvard University, 1965. X 1965, p141, ADD.

1262 Mojdehi, Hassan. "Arthur C. Millspaugh's Two Missions to Iran and Their Impact on American-Iranian Relations." Ball State University, 1975. DA 36, p5472.

1263 El-Molla, Yehia Mohamed Saber Salem. "Major Aspects of American-Egyptian Economic Relationships: The Interwar Period." Harvard University, 1951. Harvard B, 1950, 7.

1264 Moore, John H. "America Looks at Turkey, 1876-1909." University of Virginia, 1961. DA 22, p1603.

1265 Morse, Laura L. "Relations between the United States and the Ottoman Empire." Clark University, 1924. SOO 48, p91.

1266 Moskovits, Shlomo. "The United States Recognition of Israel in the Context of the Cold War, 1945-1948." Kent State University, 1976. DA 37, p7923.

1267 Murad, Ahmad Asad. "Egypt's Economic Relations

with the Soviet Bloc and the United States." University of Wisconsin, 1961. DA 22, p1846.

1268 Mustafa, Urabi S. "The United States and Jordan with Special Reference to the Palestine Question." American University, 1966. DA 28, p279.

1269 Muzaffar, Jamal E. "American-Soviet Policy in the Arab East, 1939-1957." Georgetown University, 1964. Index, 1963, p124, ADD.

1270 Naber, Anton Ayed. "The Arab-Israeli Water Conflict." American University, 1968. DA 29, p1269.

1271 Nasir, Sari Jamil. "The Image of the Arab in American Popular Culture." University of Illinois, 1962. DA 23, p4003.

1272 Nordman, Bernard F. "American Missionary Work among Armenians in Turkey, 1830-1923." Illinois University, 1927. LC 1929, p99.

1273 Nuseibeh, Hazem Zaki. "The Ideas of Arab Nationalism." Princeton University, 1954. DA 14, p1787.

1274 O'Brien, Dennis Jay. "The Oil Crisis and the Foreign Policy of the Wilson Administration, 1917-1921." University of Missouri, 1974. DA 36, p489.

1275 Oder, Irwin. "The United States and the Palestine Mandate, 1920-1948: A Study of the Impact of Interest Groups on Foreign Policy." Columbia University, 1956. DA 16, p2507.

1276 Oguzkan, Abdulbaki Turhan. "The University Extension Movement in the United States and Its Implications for the Middle East Technical University, Turkey." Ohio State University, 1965. DA 27, p371.

1277 O'Hali, Abdulaziz A. "Saudi Arabia in the United Nations General Assembly, 1946-1970." Claremont Graduate School, 1974. DA 36, p1792.

1278 Partin, Michael Wayne. "United States-Iranian Relations, 1945-1947." North Texas State University, 1977. DA 38, p4331.

1279 Patrick, Robert Bayard. "Iran's Emergence as a Middle Eastern Power." University of Utah, 1973. DA 34, p2001.

1280 Peck, Malcolm Cameron. "Saudi Arabia in United States Foreign Policy to 1958: A Study in the Sources and Determinants of American Policy." Fletcher School of Law and Diplomacy, 1970. X 1970, p286, ADD.

1281 Penrose, Stephen B. L. "From Suez to Lebanon: Soviet-American Interaction in the Middle East, 1956-1958." Fletcher School of Law and Diplomacy, 1973. Selim, 92.

1282 Peretz, Don. "Israel and the Arab Refugees." Columbia University, 1955. DA 16, p563.

1283 Perry, Glenn Earl. "United States Relations with Egypt, 1951-1963: Egyptian Neutralism and the American Alignment Policy." University of Virginia, 1964. DA 25, p3670.

1284 Pfau, Richard Anthony. "The United States and Iran, 1941-1947." University of Virginia, 1975. DA 36, p6245.

1285 Phillips, Clifton J. "Protestant America and the Pagan World: The First Half Century of the American Board of Commissioners for Foreign Missions, 1810-1860." Harvard University, 1954. W 1954, p239, DDAU.

1286 Phillips, Dennis Heath. "The American Presence in Morocco, 1880-1904." University of Wisconsin, 1972. DA 33, p3553.

1287 Platt, Alan R. "The Olympic Games and Their Political Aspects." Kent State University, 1976. DA 37, p53453.

1288 Pompa, Edward M. "Canadian Foreign Policy during the Suez Crisis, 1956." St. Johns University, 1969. DA 30, p3406.

1289 El-Quazzaz, Marwan H. "A Comparative Analysis of United States Policy in the 1956 Suez War and the

1967 Arab-Israeli War." Southern Illinois University, 1976. DA 37, p6037.

1290 Rahinsky, Herbert. "United States Foreign Policy and the Arab Refugees." New York University, 1971. DA 32, p2616.

1291 Raleigh, Edward A. "An Inquiry into the Influences of American Democracy on the Arab Middle East, 1819-1958." Pacific University, 1960. X 1960, p111, ADD.

1292 Reich, Bernard. "Israel's Foreign Policy: A Case Study of Small State Diplomacy." University of Virginia, 1964. DA 25, p3670.

1293 Richardson, Channing Bulfinch. "The United Nations and Arab Refugee Relief, 1948-1950: A Case Study in International Organization." Columbia University, 1951. DA 11, p1089.

1294 Ricks, Eldin. "United States Economic Assistance to Israel, 1949-1960." Dropsie University, 1970. X 1970, p73, ADD.

1295 Rifai, Abdul Halim. "The Eisenhower Administration and the Defense of the Arab Middle East." American University, 1966. DA 27, p3101.

1296 Rowden, Paul Dennis. "A Century of American Protestantism in the Middle East, 1820-1920." Dropsie University, 1959. X 1959, p152, ADD.

1297 Rowland, Howard Douglas. "The Arab-Israeli Conflict as Represented in Arabic Fictional Literature." University of Michigan, 1971. DA 32, p4021.

1298 al-Rubaiy, Abdul Amir. "Nationalism and Education: A Study of Nationalistic Tendencies in Iraq Education." Kent State University, 1972. DA 33, p5027.

1299 Al-Saadi, Mohammed Ali. "The Jordan River Dispute: A Case Study in International Conflict." University of Massachusetts, 1969. DA 30, p784.

1300 Al-Sabea, Taha Hussain. "Middle East Oil and

Nationalization: An Economic Analysis." University of Southern California, 1969. DA 30, p1717.

1301 Sabri, Marie Aziz. "Beirut College for Women and Ten of Its Distinguished Pioneering Alumnae." Columbia University, 1965. DA 26, p6454.

1302 Sachar, Howard M. "The United States and Turkey, 1914-1927: The Origins of Near Eastern Policy." Harvard University, 1953. W 1953, p236, DDAU.

1303 al-Saghieh, Khaled I. "Nationalism in Morocco, a Study of Recent Developments with Special Reference to the Moroccan Question in the United Nations." American University, 1955. DDAU 22, p229.

1304 Salameh, Joseph I. "Lebanon at the United Nations: A Case Study." Georgetown University, 1962. Index, 1961, p182, ADD.

1305 Saliba, Samir Nicholas. "The Jordan River Dispute." Tulane University, 1966. DA 27, p1423.

1306 Samii, Cyrus B. "The Arab-Asian Bloc in the United Nations." University of Kansas, 1955. 22, p234, DDAU.

1307 Sam'o, Elias. "The Arab States in the United Nations: A Study of Voting Behavior." American University, 1967. DA 28, p1489.

1308 Ali-Sankari, Farouk. "The United Nations Truce Supervision Organization in Palestine." Claremont Graduate School, 1968. DA 29, p4081.

1309 Savage, Marie M. "American Diplomacy in North Africa, 1776-1817." Georgetown University, 1949. 16, p134, DDAU.

1310 Savage, Ralph Lee. "Israeli and American Jewish Attitudes in 1971 on the Future of Israel's Conquered Territories: A Comparative Analysis." University of Southern Mississippi, 1972. Selim, 104.

1311 Shaheen, Ghaleb S. "The Foreign Policy of Lebanon." Syracuse University, 1959. DA 20, p2879.

1312 Shaker, Fatina Amin. "Modernization of the Developing Nations: The Case of Saudi Arabia." Purdue University, 1972. DA 34, p433.

1313 Sherwin, Ronald Graham. "Structural Balance and the International System: The Middle East Conflict, 1967." University of Southern California, 1972. DA 33, p1807.

1314 Shwadran, Benjamin. "The Middle East, Oil, and the Great Powers." Clark University, 1956.

1315 Sim'an, Emile S. "The Persian Gulf as a Subordinate System of World Politics." Indiana University, 1977. DA 38, p5035.

1316 Simpson, Dwight J. "British Palestine Policy, 1939-1949." Stanford University, 1950. 17, p180, DDAU.

1317 Skinner, Charles Wickham. "Production Management in United States Companies Manufacturing in Turkey." Harvard University, 1961.

1318 Snetsinger, John G. "Truman and the Creation of Israel." Stanford University, 1970. DA 31, p1742.

1319 Snider, Lewis W. "Middle East Maelstrom: The Impact of Global and Regional Influences on the Arab-Israeli Conflict, 1947-1973." University of Michigan, 1975. DA 36, p6940.

1320 Soffer, Ovadia M. "The United Nations' Peacemaking Role in the Arab-Israeli Conflict, 1967-1977." City University of New York, 1977. DA 38, p3040.

1321 Sowayyegh, Abdul Aziz Hussein. "Oil and the Arab-Israeli Conflict: A Study in Arab Oil Strategy Between 1948-1973." Claremont Graduate School, 1977. DA 37, p7302.

1322 Stackman, Ralph R. "Laurence A. Steinhardt: New Deal Diplomat, 1933-1945." Michigan State University, 1967. DA 28, p4106.

1323 Stevens, Richard Paul. "The Political and Diplomatic

Role of American Zionists as a Factor in the Creation of the State of Israel." Georgetown University, 1960. X 1960, p109, ADD.

1324 Stillman, Arthur McLean. "The United Nations and the Suez Canal." American University, 1965. DA 26, p1754.

1325 Stock, Ernest. "Israel on the Road to Sinai: A Small State in a Test of Power." Columbia University, 1963. DA 28, p1116.

1326 Suleiman, Fuad K. "The Arab Boycott of Israel." Fletcher School of Law and Diplomacy, 1966. Selim, 116

1327 Sutcliffe, Claud R. "Change in the Jordan Valley: The Impact and Implications of the East Ghor Canal Project, 1961-1966." Princeton University, 1970. DA 31, p4238.

1328 Tabari, Keyvan. "Iran's Policies Toward the United States during the Anglo-Russian Occupation, 1941-1946." Columbia University, 1967. DA 28, p1881.

1329 Tansky, Leo. "Comparative Impact of United States and USSR Economic Aid to Underdeveloped Countries with Special Reference to India, Turkey, and the United Arab Republic." American University, 1964. DA 26, p746.

1330 Tarr, David W. "American Power and Diplomacy in the Middle East." University of Chicago, 1961. X 1961, p160, ADD.

1331 Taylor, Alan R. "The American Protestant Mission and the Awakening of Modern Syria, 1820-1970." Georgetown University, 1958. X 1958, p91, ADD.

1332 Tennenboim, Mark. "Soviet-Egyptian Relations, Oct. 1964-Sep. 1970: Brezhnev and Abd al-Nasir." New York University, 1977. DA 38, p2283.

1333 Thorpe, James Arthur. "The Mission of Arthur C. Millspaugh to Iran, 1943-1945." University of Wisconsin, 1973. DA 35, p387.

1334 Trask, Roger Reed. "The Relations of the United

States and Turkey, 1927-1939." Pennsylvania State University, 1959. DA 20, p3720.

1335 Trice, Robert Holmes, Jr. "Domestic Political Interests and American Policy in the Middle East: Pro-Arab Corporate Non-Governmental Actors and the Making of American Foreign Policy, 1966-1971." University of Wisconsin, 1974. DA 35, p6790.

1336 Tunc, Gungor. "Market Potential for Turkish Tobacco in the United States." University of Wisconsin, 1969.

1337 Turner, Jack Justin. "Arab-Asian Positive Neutralism and United States Foreign Policy." University of Kentucky, 1969. DA 30, p3532.

1338 Turner, Michael Allan. "The International Politics of Narcotics: Turkey and the United States." Kent State University, 1975. DA 36, p6295.

1339 Wagner, Abraham R. "The Six Day War: A Study in Crisis, Decision-Making." University of Rochester, 1973. Selim, p121.

1340 Walt, Joseph W. "Saudi Arabia and the Americans, 1928-1951." Northwestern University, 1960. DA 21, p1548.

1341 Weems, Miner Lile. "The Propaganda Struggle in the Middle East, 1955-1958." Georgetown University, 1962. Index, 1961, p180, ADD.

1342 Weisband, Edward A. "Anticipating the Cold War: Turkish Foreign Relations, 1943-45." Johns Hopkins University, 1970. DA 34, p844.

1343 Wendzel, Robert Leroy. "United States National Interests and the Middle East, 1955-1958." University of Florida, 1965. DA 26, p4790.

1344 Wilmington, Martin W. "Economic Regionalism in the Middle East during World War II (the Middle East Supply Centre)." New York University, 1960. DA 22, p461.

1345 Windmueller, Steven Fred. "American Jewish Interest Groups: Their Roles in Shaping United States Foreign Policy in the Middle East. A Study of Two Time Periods: 1945-1948, 1955-1958." University of Pennsylvania, 1973. DA 34, p5288.

1346 Wolf, John Berchmans. "An Interpretation of the Eisenhower Doctrine: Lebanon, 1958." American University, 1968. DA 29, p949.

1347 Wolfowitz, Paul D. "Nuclear Proliferation in the Middle East: The Politics and Economics of Proposals for Nuclear Desalting." University of Chicago, 1972. 1971, p302, ADD.

1348 Wright, Lenoir Chambers. "United States Policy Toward Egypt, 1830-1914." Columbia University, 1953. DA 14, p179.

1349 el-Yacoubi, Hassan Hassan Sheikh. "The Evolution of Palestinian Consciousness." University of Colorado, 1973. DA 34, p7858.

1350 Yizhar, Michael. "The Eisenhower Doctrine: A Case Study of American Foreign Policy Formulation and Implementation." New School, 1969. DA 30, 5049.

1351 Younis, Adele Linda. "The Coming of the Arabic-Speaking People to the United States." Boston University, 1961. DA 22, p1151.

1352 Zakhem, Samir Hanna. "Lebanon between East and West: Big Power Politics in the Middle East." University of Colorado, 1970. DA 31, p3006.

1353 Zindani, Abdul Wahed Aziz. "Arab Politics in the United Nations." Notre Dame University, 1976. DA 37, p3891.

AUTHOR INDEX

(Many of these works are cited more than once in the bibliography; here, the reference is to the most significant location.)